GLOBAL JEWISH FOODWAYS

GLOBAL
JEWISH
FOODWAYS

A HISTORY

....

Edited and with an introduction by
Hasia R. Diner and Simone Cinotto
Foreword by Carlo Petrini

UNIVERSITY OF NEBRASKA PRESS
LINCOLN AND LONDON

Acknowledgments for the use of copyrighted
material appear on page 317, which constitutes
an extension of the copyright page.

Library of Congress
Cataloging-in-Publication Data
Names: Diner, Hasia R., editor.
| Cinotto, Simone, editor.
Title: Global Jewish foodways: a history
/ edited and with an introduction by
Hasia R. Diner and Simone Cinotto;
foreword by Carlo Petrini.
Description: Lincoln: University of Nebraska
Press, [2018] | Series: At Table | Includes
bibliographical references and index.
Identifiers: LCCN 2017026973 (print)
LCCN 2017027895 (ebook)
ISBN 9781496206091 (epub)
ISBN 9781496206107 (mobi)
ISBN 9781496206114 (pdf)
ISBN 9781496202284 (cloth: alk. paper)
Subjects: LCSH: Jews—Food—History.
Jewish cooking—History.
Classification: LCC TX724 (ebook)
LCC TX724 .G635 2018 (print)
DDC 641.5/676—dc23
LC record available at
https://lccn.loc.gov/2017026973

Set in Merope by Mikala R Kolander.
Designed by N. Putens.

CONTENTS

PART 4

The Food of the Diaspora: The Global Identity, Memory, and History of Jewish Food

ILLUSTRATIONS

FOREWORD

....

CARLO PETRINI

In any culture, in any civilization, in any historical or geographical context, food always serves as a source of identity, community, and sociability. Food mediates with the divine, functions as a bridge across or as a wall between social classes, and provides a way to structure economic transactions. Of course it makes for a celebration of joy and must be present at rites of passage in the life cycle. While true in all cases, some cultures and some peoples place greater emphasis, sanctity, and importance on food, because historical circumstances forced them to do so. In some historical and cultural contexts food emerged as central to their narratives of identity and spirituality. In this, perhaps, no other group can compare to the Jewish people. *Jewish Global Foodways: A History* makes this point in a compelling manner.

The product of rigorous research, this book also proves to be a pleasure to read, as it traces the relationship between Jews and food, and the functions and meanings food had during the major turning points in their history, as they faced many different diasporas and migrations, wars, and their search for new lands, including the formation of the Jewish state in Israel.

This book offers fascinating food stories as it engages such overarching themes as travel, movement, and exile in modern Jewish history. Because of the turbulent and complex historical circumstances and suffering that Jews confronted in so many places, these issues have constituted their common heritage and have helped them shape their "mobile" identities, loosened from any one land, giving them a wide and ever changing geopolitical context. Because of this, food has had a vital role in reinforcing feelings of identity and community and providing narratives of affiliation, solidarity, and uniqueness. Acknowledging all these common themes that transcend time and place does not, however, mean that one can overlook the differences that also affected, modified, and shaped Jewish identity and food culture.

Editors Hasia Diner and Simone Cinotto have produced here a highly valuable work, which offers much food for thought as it embraces different and interconnected dimensions of Jewish food history, such as culture, spirituality, rituality, and migration. However, the value of this book is not limited to the excavation of the past, although the past ought to be studied. Today more than ever it is vital to reflect on the value and meaning we assign to food. In our contemporary world, food has rapidly become a mere commodity, evaluated and measured exclusively in terms of price. The declining social value of food can be considered one of the chief defects of our food system, linked to the unprecedented degrees of environmental destruction, social injustice, and waste it promotes. The bulwarks of culture and tradition, which historically created and supported the deep value of food, have likewise been diminished in our own time.

But we cannot afford to dispose of the heritage of experience, tradition, conviviality, and commonality that the world's peoples have created, articulated, and conveyed through food. On the contrary, this legacy has to be preserved, rediscovered, and understood. The essays included in this collection are important exactly because they are very useful contributions to the decodification and interpretation of the history of the relationship between Jews and food. Enjoy the read.

ACKNOWLEDGMENTS

My first thanks go to Simone Cinotto, a world-class scholar of food and migration and a world-class colleague, whose enthusiasm, hard work, and dedication made this volume possible. The volume grew out of a conference, and his cheerful and diligent attention to detail enabled scholars to gather in a beautiful space in Pollenzo, Italy, to hear the papers, exchange ideas, talk with each other, and yes, eat well. The logistics of the conference and its ensuing book also needed the labor of the staff of the Department of Hebrew and Judaic Studies at New York University who handled the welter of logistics with grace and competence. Finally, Alex Goren and the Goldstein-Goren Foundation provided most of the funding for the conference, and without the funding, we would have had no chance to meet, learn, and then share with each other. We thank him deeply.

— HASIA DINER

It is indeed a distinct privilege to end up closely collaborating with someone you have admired for very long through the medium of her books and conference presentations! I thank Hasia Diner for the opportunity she granted me to help organize the joint conference on "The Global History on Jewish Food" held in Pollenzo, Italy, in 2014, during which the idea of this book first materialized. Together we were able to gather first-rate scholars and their essays on the topic. Working with Hasia to edit this volume has also been a valuable, delightful, and fun experience from day one to the end. For their enthusiastic support of the original conference, I thank the president, Carlo Petrini, along with my colleagues, the staff, and the students of the Università di Scienze Gastronomiche Pollenzo. Exploring Jewish foodways from different scholarly perspectives and in different times and places has been tremendously enriching for my research interests in the history of food, migration, and diasporas; the history of consumer culture and ethnicity; and the history of taste. For this, I want to thank all the contributors to this volume, who entrusted us with their essays and intellectual efforts. Finally, I have finished my share of the editorial work on this book, and I am writing these notes, while spending the winter holidays with my children Ferdinando and Cristina. With their wittiness, humor, and love they made my work even more gratifying and one more time gave real sense to what sociologists of the family sometimes call "quality time."

—SIMONE CINOTTO

Introduction

Jewish Foodways in Food History and
the Jewish Diasporic Experience

....

SIMONE CINOTTO AND HASIA R. DINER

Food studies, an academic field now counting legions of students and practitioners all over the world and institutionalized in departments at major international universities, received scant recognition even as recently as twenty years ago. Many historians, in particular, considered food ephemeral, quotidian, and too associated with women to be worthy of serious study. Feminist historians thought of it as too associated with women's traditional role in the kitchen to be worthy of research and analysis. This all changed at the end of the twentieth century with the emergence of discourses in postindustrial societies, stemming from an emerging disillusionment with modern agribusiness and the global politics of food, a critique that critically linked food to the formation of consumer identities, class and racial distinctions, and health, and identified the sustainable production and consumption of food as a crucial global environmental and political issue. The cultural turn in academia, which legitimized the dynamics of everyday life as a worthy object of research, emphasized how such categories as gender, race, nation, and class, all constructed, helped make food a vibrant scholarly concern.

Scholars of the Jewish past had paid equally little attention to food as a shaping force in the experiences, across time and place, of the women and men whom they studied. Their long and deep interest in the intellectual history of the Jews, the development of great ideas, the history of antisemitism, and the political history of Jewish rights, denied and acquired, interested them and seemed paramount. What went on in kitchens and around dinner tables seemed profoundly less important.

Jewish historians, like so many others before the latter decades of the twentieth century, expressed little interest in the work being done in other academic fields. They did not find themselves drawn to, for example, anthropology with its deep concern for everyday life, and its focus on culture in the sense of the ordinary and routine practices of people in a given place, and the meaning they attributed to those activities. Most Jewish studies scholars, especially the historians, turned to the archives and to canonical texts for their sources. Food, like so many other details of lived life, seemed to have paled in comparison to great breakthroughs in Jewish scholarship and the continuous history of suffering, the focus of Jewish historical research until just a few decades ago.

JEWISH FOODWAYS AND THE BIRTH OF FOOD STUDIES: FOUNDATIONAL EARLY ANTHROPOLOGY OF JEWISH FOOD

Scholarly avoidance of food as a key element in understanding Jewish history, around the globe and stretching across millennia, offers us a particular irony and a starting point for introducing this book, *Global Jewish Foodways*. The interdisciplinary study of food effectively originated in the scholarly examination of Jewish foodways. By the 1960s anthropologists started seriously tackling a series of vital questions, which took them, almost automatically, to the Jewish tradition and its experience. From a nutritional perspective, why do humans not eat everything and anything edible? Even if the item could provide the nutrition needed and was digestible to the body, why do people, each within their own group, behave so selectively in their decisions as to what to put in their mouths and ingest? Why have their choices about what to eat and not to eat, what foods can be combined and which must remain apart, and what cooking techniques they will and will not employ been so group specific? If food, its preparation and consumption, represents the fundamental and unifying condition of human survival, then why have different human groups developed food habits that emerged as the most distinctive trait differentiating one collectivity from another? These challenging questions led back almost inevitably to the Jews, their food systems, and the ways in which this group of people engaged with the world around them and their own bodies.

A number of key scholars, anthropologists mostly, first identified such questions as more than just important, but indeed as fundamental to understanding the inner workings of human culture, and in that process what Jews ate — and did not eat — served as a powerful example. French anthropologist Claude Lévi-Strauss (1908–2009) earlier connected dietary choices and disgusts to binary divergences deeply rooted in the underlying and unconscious cultural structures of traditional societies, the most basic of them being the opposition between the "raw," signifying nature, and the "cooked," signifying culture.[1]

His student Mary Douglas (1921–2007) brought the structuralist model to a new level by interrogating dietary taboos in literate societies and describing food choices and prohibitions as reflections of any single culture's cosmology and view of the world. Central to Douglas's theory is the cultural binary opposition between the "pure" and the "impure," according to which some foods are associated with and become symbolic of "polluted" and "dirt."[2] The British anthropologist came to her conclusions in her best-known book, *Purity and Danger: An Analysis of the Concepts of Pollution and Taboo*, by focusing on the Hebrew Bible, and especially on the rules about "Clean and Unclean Food." Leviticus 11 states that "You may eat any animal that has a divided hoof and that chews the cud. . . . The pig, though it has a divided hoof, does not chew the cud; it is unclean for you. . . . Of all the creatures living in the water of the seas and the streams you may eat any that have fins and scales. . . .

[Carnivore] birds you are to regard as unclean and not eat because they are unclean.... You must distinguish between the unclean and the clean, between living creatures that may be eaten and those that may not be eaten." Such a neat systematization of land, water, and sky animals that can and cannot be eaten encodes, for Douglas, a notion of holiness or purity that reflects Israelite self-identification as a holy people and a distinct vision of the world. In other words, biblical dietary laws are the most advanced codification of the indissoluble interconnection between the culture, morality, and notions of distinction of a given society and its foodways.[3] From her analysis of Leviticus, Douglas concluded that food has first to be "good to think" to be deemed "good to eat," and that the cultural acceptability and desirability of food, combination of ingredients, and meal patterns vary according to the nuanced variations of cultures, rooted in the deep mental structures characteristic of any single human group. Economic and technological considerations involved in the production, distribution, and consumption of food influence food choices to a certain extent, but they always take second place to culture in shaping those choices.

The next addition to this emerging intellectual paradigm, which put food and the Jews squarely into the center of cultural analysis, came from the United States. With his book *Good to Eat: Riddles of Food and Culture*, American materialist anthropologist Marvin Harris (1927–2001) vocally reacted to Douglas's theory, sparking the first and perhaps most illustrious diatribe in food studies. Harris bluntly inverted the terms in the hierarchies of food choices and taboos as delineated by Douglas: food has to be first "good to eat"; that is, the investment in its production and marketing must make economic and political sense, before culture intervenes to sanction its edibility, or, to say it with Douglas, "purity." Harris most famously took stock of the "Abominable Pig" of the Jewish tradition, placing it in its original environment, the Middle East (the westernmost angle of the Fertile Crescent, where agriculture, urbanization, and the stratification of society into classes first began in the Neolithic age). According to Harris, archaeological evidence suggests

that when, in prebiblical times, Israel was covered with shady forests—
the ideal environment for pigs, which do not sweat and cannot stand
the heat—local people farmed and ate them. It was only when environmental change and overpopulation exhausted the forests, pig farming
became uneconomical, and the consumption of its by-then expensive
meat turned into a potential source of social conflict that cultural norms
proscribing pork were interiorized as taboo and eventually translated
into religious rule. Expanding on this analysis, and from an examination of other case studies that ranged from the Hindu sacred cow to
the categorization of the dog as pet in Western societies, Harris saw
the cultural explanation for food preferences and anathemas as a mere
superstructure to the material reasons that actually shape the foodways
of different human groups.[4]

These seemingly opposite and irreconcilable views provided early
and persuasive general theories on the origins of foodways and lead to
the creation of food studies as a scholarly field. While placing Jewish
dietary rules at the very foundation of the study of culture, although
differently, they share with each other some significant shortcomings
that this book aims to overcome. First, following the Western philosophical tradition originating with Plato that separates the spirit and
the body, both Douglas and Harris, albeit on opposite terms, sharply
distinguish between the material and symbolic nature of food, which, as
the essays in *Global Jewish Foodways* insist, are instead intertwined and
inseparable. Second, neither theory takes into account historical change
and the constant and ubiquitous exchanges between cultures; instead
they take foodways, in particular Jewish foodways, as impermeable and
immutable, generating deep cultural structures for Douglas and physiological and environmental ones for Harris. Only in his final chapter
on meat consumption in twentieth-century, capitalist United States
does Harris pay attention to the changing dynamics of food systems.
Finally, with their insistence on solving the riddles of food taboos, both
Douglas and Harris accept religious norms as evidence of the developing construction of distinctive foodways in a given premodern society

rather than for what they constituted in the first place, manifestations of religious expression and the relation of believers with God, which shape relations within the community of believers and between it and outsiders.

FOOD AND RELIGION: SACREDNESS AND RITUALITY OF JEWISH FOOD

A more recent intervention on this matter has called for an historically and analytically broader perspective that we hope *Global Jewish Foodways* will help fulfill. Religious studies scholar Corrie E. Norman, the author of the entry on "Food and Religion" in *The Oxford Handbook of Food History*, decries historians' predominant focus on taboos and fasting at the expense of a more comprehensive vision of the relationship between eating and faith. In her call she also, like the scholars who preceded her, draws attention to Jewish history. As Norman observes, food is central to the theology, liturgy, and myths of creation of nearly all known religions. From Adam and Eve's apple to the Hindu creator god Brahma hatching from the cosmic egg Hiranyagarbha, to the Popol Vuh creation of man from maize, food is the founding substance and metaphor of many traditions and is ubiquitous in religious ceremonials: Hindus feed their deity; offering food is one of the most common rituals in Buddhism; and the body of Christ is shared in bread and wine in the Holy Communion rites of Christianity. However, Norman notes that "more thought has been given to the origins of the ancient Hebrew dietary laws than any other religion-related food topic" and that students of food and religion have paid more attention to Jewish foodways than to those of any other creed in ways that transcend the subject of prohibitions to include ritual food consumption, the spiritual bases of the humane treatment of slaughtered animals, the prescribed feeding of the poor, and so on.[5] Theology scholar Nathan MacDonald explored food and its symbolism in the Old Testament and the world of ancient Israel, mixing the examination of biblical descriptions of the

Israelite diet with an archeological approach.[6] Analyzing rabbinic texts written in third-century Palestine, Jewish studies scholar Jordan D. Rosenblum argued that in early Judaism, dietary regulations, cooking practices, and conviviality shaped eating into a form of communication with the divine as well as representing a fundamental source of distinct identity invested with religious significance.[7]

The historical debate on Jewish foodways, however, has recently expanded beyond biblical texts and ancient times as it now is asking how kashrut actually functioned in different places, different times, and under different circumstances. The newer scholarship that this volume illuminates examines the historical specificities of the lived Jewish experience, in both religious and communal contexts, and explores the multiple ways food served, and continues to serve, as an organizing principle.

More recent scholarship has situated Jewish life and the centrality of food mostly in their diasporas, in the vast expanses of the world where they lived for millennia, acknowledging that they made their homes on every continent, in basically every land. So, too, scholars and historians have looked far beyond the ancient world and charted the intense involvement of Jews with food well into the twenty-first century. David Kraemer's book *Jewish Eating and Identity Through the Ages* claims "to interpret Jewish eating practices in these many ages as keys to understanding current Jewish identities."[8] Kraemer insists on cooking and eating practices as symbolic producers of difference, as in the case of the separation of milk and meat that separated "pious" from "common" Jews in sixteenth-century Poland, just as it separates "orthodox" from "nonobservant" Jews in contemporary North America. His work focuses in particular on rituals, which originated in the early rabbinic period but developed into "culturally specific strategies for . . . creating a qualitative distinction between the 'sacred' and the 'profane'" that made Jewish meals Jewish and tapped the rhythm of the Jewish calendar and cycle of life in different, multiple historical and geographical contexts.[9]

FOOD AND DIASPORA: MIGRANT JEWISH FOODWAYS

The focus on practices, rituals, and meals has been common in most of the recent literature, offering a fruitful trajectory for understanding the significance of food in the Jewish diasporic experience, which is the primary subject of *Global Jewish Foodways* as well as a decisive contribution to the historical study of food, migration, and mobility.

The Jewish diaspora, as both noun and verb, has involved an ongoing and global process of movement and settlement since pre-Roman times, beginning with the Assyrian exile from Israel of 733 BCE. The unsettling results of the uprisings against the Romans and the destruction of the second temple in 70 and 135 CE sent out Jews to every corner of the Old World, including Ethiopia, Yemen, Persia, India, and China. Since the Middle Ages, the establishment of permanent residency in communities small and large, such as the Pale of Settlement in Imperial Russia (1791–1917), intertwined with persecutions and removals, such as the expulsion from England in 1290 and the expulsion from Spain in 1492. The great migration of the late nineteenth and early twentieth century propelled Jews virtually everywhere in the world. The post–World War II return to Israel and the construction of the modern Jewish state overlapped, from 1948 to the early 1970s, with the expulsion of Jews from the Arab and Muslim countries of the Mediterranean and the Middle East.

Within this metahistorical experience of impermanence and mobility, everyday meals and eating rituals became vital, distinctive markers of identity for Jews in the different places they dispersed and resettled to. Meals and rituals speak of the specific supply and market conditions Jews encountered and created; of the social, gender, and religious articulation of each Jewish community; and of the negotiations and representations stemming from the encounters between Jews and non-Jews, which were shaped by a range of specific cultural, legal, political, and economic circumstances.

At least one major divide differentiated early on the foodways of the Sephardi Jews of the Mediterranean basin from those of the Ashkenazi Jews of Northern and Eastern Europe, as well as those who lived in the

Arab lands of North Africa and southwest Asia, as they lived in very diverse ecological, human, and cultural environments and observed different subsets of Jewish religious practices. And yet, even these two culinary universes achieved consistency by kashrut rules (excepting those cases where Jews willingly or unwillingly disregarded them), thus constituting a common, shared, and distinctive dietary idiom, even as Jews literally found themselves on the move.

As such, the Jewish case has appeared to scholars of food and migration as the most illuminating example of the centrality of food in the everyday life and identity of mobile people, as they created community and nation in motion, and of the vital importance of mobile people in promoting food exchange. For Jews, in every one of their many diasporas, providing for their communal food system created a disproportionate share of their entrepreneurs, workers, and merchants. The Jewish diaspora did nothing less than reshape markets and taste, connect distant places through food trade routes, and enrich the foodscapes of their newly chosen cities, regions, and nations with diversity and choice.[10]

The essays in *Global Jewish Foodways* especially address the amazing diversity of political, economic, and cultural changes implicating "Jewish food" across the varied settings to which Jews migrated and then lived as part of their diaspora. Similarly, as with the foodways of other groups that formed large diasporas in the modern age — Africans, Italians, Chinese, Indians, and Mexicans — the historical study of Jewish foodways and mobility has concentrated especially on the United States, and on a moment, the turn of the twentieth century, when massive immigration from Eastern Europe and elsewhere intertwined with the racial, cultural, and political redefinition of the American nation, the industrialization of food and the emergence of mass consumerism, and the deployment of U.S. empire, which, among other things, exported on a global scale narratives of cultural difference often commodified into "ethnic food." Within this literature, Hasia Diner's *Hungering for America: Italian, Irish, and Jewish Foodways in the Age of Migration* has been particularly valuable for its comparative approach. By relating the trajectory of Jewish foodways from the Old World to America to those of the other two largest contemporary European migrant groups, Diner made the specificities of Jewish food as a medium of identity and difference in the diaspora emerge with clarity. Diner argues that Irish, Italians, and Eastern European Jews all experienced hunger in their countries of origin and looked at America as a place where food was abundant and democratically available even to working people. For all these mobile people, the encounter with and participation in the U.S. marketplace made possible the realization of elaborate family and community eating rituals and thus played an important role in the parallel processes of ethnicization.

Yet the three migrant groups articulated quite different relations with food in the course of fashioning their diasporic communities. Those were rooted in their histories prior to emigration. On their island, the Irish had seen the formation of a national food culture crippled by British colonialism: memories of famine, exploitation, and a monotonous diet in the homeland caused Irish Americans not to consider food as a significant component in the shaping of their identity. Italian immigrants, conversely, had associated good and abundant food with the condition of full humanity only the rich in their native rural villages could enjoy. Once in the United States, Italians enthusiastically endorsed cooking, eating, and involvement in the food business as pivotal elements in the formation of their diasporic identity, which accordingly emphasized the private values of domesticity, intimacy, and conviviality. Just like their Italian counterparts, poor Eastern European Jews in their villages, towns, and urban ghettos had contrasted their scarce everyday diets with those of the affluent.

However, religious practices and beliefs interacted much more decidedly with class in determining what and how much people ate. "The masses of East European Jews . . . believed that God intended them to eat well because their own sacred texts told them so."[11] Jews in Eastern Europe "knew hunger" but were also familiar with a system of intra- and cross-class solidarity based on food gifts and sharing. Public banquets and Sabbath food distribution were common in the shtetl. In the United States, immigrants and their children not only expanded their levels of food consumption like the Italians did, but also embraced culinary experimentation, developing a taste for mass-produced branded products and curiosity for other minorities' food. (An example of the eagerness of Jewish immigrants and their children to cross the boundaries of taste in the multiethnic American city—their penchant for Chinese restaurants as preferred locations for eating out—is explored in an article by independent culinary historian Hanna Miller).[12] Therefore, while eating and preparation patterns continued to be central to the definition of Jewish American identities, the observance of religious dietary directives was a conflicting terrain, especially along generational lines.[13]

The focus on food and identity negotiation at the borders and within the Jewish community that Diner introduced in her analysis of migrant Jewish foodways has been reprised by a number of other works about the mobile Jewish culinary experience in America and elsewhere, from Italy to England, France, French Algeria, and Mexico.[14] A particular strain of the Jewish experience with food and mobility that has attracted—not surprisingly—much attention from historians is the participation of diasporic Jews in the construction of a food system and a national food culture in Israel, as part of the formation of the Jewish state in the Middle East. Immigration into the diasporic home, encouraged by the World Zionist Organization, began in the prestate period before World War II, involving for the most part Jews from Eastern Europe. After the war, the Nazi genocide in Europe, and the growing hostility against Jews living in Arab countries, migration became at the same time very large (between 1948 and 1951, as many as seven hundred thousand people immigrated to Israel, doubling the Jewish population of the country) and diverse, as Ashkenazim from Europe and Middle Eastern Jews were almost equally represented among immigrants. Settlement, agriculture, and the formation of a national food system emerged as priorities of the Zionist state and, as such, politically and symbolically vital to the process of state-building.

These priorities immediately became pivotal political and cultural issues in the emerging conflict with Arab Palestinians. As a result, food emerged as, and remained, a highly contested terrain for the negotiation of Israeli identity between the politically dominant European Jews and Middle Eastern Jews and between Jews and the Palestinians in Israel. At the culinary and gustatory level, the advancing Middle Easternization of Israeli national cuisine was therefore an uneven process that reflected multiple political tensions, based in different, divergent histories of mobility, uprootedness, diaspora, and resettlement—of people as well as foods and culinary cultures.[15] The case of falafel—the deep-fried balls of grounded dry chickpeas and spices ubiquitous in Israel today but lacking a history as part of Jewish cuisines—is illuminating: what for one group is the icon of modern Israeli gastronomy and multiethnic identity is for the other the symbol of wrongful cultural appropriation.[16]

FOOD MORALITIES AND CONFLICTS:
EVERYDAY POLITICS OF JEWISH FOOD

The articulation of the Israeli-Palestinian conflict in the material and symbolic idiom of food introduces us to other etymologically related dimensions of food and mobility that have found in the history of Jewish foodways an illuminating case study—those of the mobs, political mobilization, and social movements. Historians such as E. P. Thompson and Eric Hobsbawm related the widespread emergence of food riots in early industrial capitalist society to the breakage of ancient regime expectations from the rural and urban poor that the elite would provide them with the minimal means of survival in times of famine. The demise of the old systems of assistance based on the moral obligation of those in power toward the destitute added to the inability of states and cities, in an age when the modern welfare state was still to come or nascent, to cope with population growth and mass urbanization and efficiently distribute the food that industrialization and global trade had made more plentiful.

Paradoxically, food riots multiplied in the nineteenth century, when food supply had, overall, become more dependable than ever before.[17] Jewish political consciousness and involvement, in particular among the Socialist ranks, made them into initiators and participants of some landmark food revolts. Jewish women played a critical role in the bread riot that erupted in Petrograd on March 8, 1917, International Woman's Day, in response to the rationing of bread and flour enforced by the czarist government, which represented the first mass uprising of the February Revolution that lead to the czar's abdication.[18] For historian Paula Hyman, the boycott of kosher meat conducted by Jewish women on the Lower East Side of Manhattan and in Williamsburg, Brooklyn, in 1902 had an underlying political significance, beneath the appearance of the outburst of uncontrollable rage of a premodern mob: it was strategic for Jewish women to mobilize in an area—securing food for their families—that was legitimately open to them in the eyes of the community to achieve the broader ultimate goal of reclaiming space for women's active political participation.[19]

A most extreme example of the anthropological experience of solidarity and resistance to induced starvation is the history of foodways in Nazi concentration camps during the Shoah. As Primo Levi noted in *Survival in Auschwitz (If This Is a Man)*, the collective experience of being methodically deprived of the most basic necessities of life, such as food— being forced to scrape the dirt for putrid potato peels or pilfering food from a dead body in order to survive for another day—resulted in the surfacing of the most rudimentary, essential, and naked structures of humanity, stripped of any trace of culture, the depository in which Mary Douglas has seen the source of the food choices, tastes, and memories that make social life meaningful.[20] Other accounts, however, emphasize resistance to the dehumanizing effects of starvation, the blossoming of interpersonal support networks, the implementation of social systems of food appropriation, and examples of food sharing, which in turn counteracted severe malnutrition and enhanced the chances of survival of Jewish prisoners.[21] Cultural survival was enacted among women through "virtual cookbooks," food talks, and memories, which, in the practical absence of food, nurtured friendship and community, subverting the isolation stemming from the disintegration of families.[22]

FOOD AND SOCIAL MOBILITY: JEWISH FOOD BUSINESS, MARKETS, AND TASTE

A further dimension of mobility in which the global Jewish experience played an absolutely central role in the world history of food can be seen in the matter of social mobility. Partly because of the long-established and widely enforced exclusion from property owning and farming, Jews have been internationally overrepresented in food trade and food industry, with two critical consequences. On the one hand, they have been critical actors and promoters of food exchange and food change in different parts of the world and among different populations; on the other, food-related occupations have always been important in the economic life of Jewish communities. In eighteenth- and nineteenth-century Europe, peddling food, which involved moving across long distances and interacting with many non-Jewish customers, was one of the most popular ways for Jews to enter self-employment with a very limited starting capital. At the turn of the twentieth century, the Jewish peddler of New York City became an icon of the great migration to America, transforming urban street vending and the food marketplace, and introducing to the American palate, in tandem with the Jewish delicatessen store, a variety of now quintessential New York foods, from the bagel to cream cheese, lox, pastrami, knishes, blintzes, bialys, kugels, latkes, challahs, babkas, and rugelach.[23] At least one of these foods, the bagel, has long since transcended the local dimension of the city to become one of the handful of truly global foods, a course of mobility that included its novel "return" to Israel.[24] In places like New York, London, and other large cities, the effort to maintain the culinary structures of material, religious, and cultural self-sufficiency helped create an ethnic economy providing opportunities for upward social mobility to immigrant capitalists and jobs to workers in the community.

Petty and bigger food entrepreneurs especially counted on cultural capital—particularly their exclusive capacity to understand and cater to the special preferences and needs of Jewish customers—and social capital—the exclusive advantages they enjoyed from being embedded in distinctive networks of relations, from access to credit to community support—which they owned as Jews to thrive in their business.[25]

Industrial food production and its complexity, in fact, have made the sets of regulations and processes that make food kosher, suitable for a Jewish religious diet, look like an effective response to the fears, anxieties, and increasing unawareness of Jewish and non-Jewish consumers alike about the origins of the food that comes to their table. Jewish dietary laws, and the standardized systems of certification that control processors' observance of those rules, suit especially well contemporary food culture and eaters concerned with food's origins, traceability, labeling, authenticity, safety, and nutrition value. In the United States and elsewhere, corporate food producers have noticed the marketing potential of kosher-certified food so much that kosher food products— ranging from canned vegetables and fruit to sugar, flour, eggs, dairy, and sodas—now occupy a robust share of the market, extending well beyond observant religious consumers.[26] The kosherization of America and the world, as some critics have called the process, again presents central questions of food, people, ideas, and capital mobility. These questions focus attention on matters of cultural identity and difference, unequal relations of power, discrimination, and fascination with the other that the historical study of food demands, and which this book in particular seeks to present, if in an episodic fashion.

APPROACHES TO UNDERSTANDING GLOBAL JEWISH FOODWAYS

The chapters in this volume address all of these pivotal issues in the history of global Jewish foodways, Jewish cooks, and Jewish eaters, covering a time span of five centuries and the spatial canvas of the five continents. To be sure, the book makes no claim to being exhaustive or to covering the subject in its totality. It recognizes the impossibility of doing so, but rather hints through a number of specific situations and settings how many more stories await to be told.

The chapters in part 1 of Global Jewish Foodways, "Crossing and Bridging Culinary Boundaries: Resistance, Resilience, and Adaptations of Jewish Food in the Encounter with the Non-Jewish Other," look at foodways as means of negotiation and reaffirmation of Jewish minority identities in different conditions of interaction with gentiles. In the opening chapter, Flora Cassen approaches food as part of the intercultural exchange, trust, and suspicion between Christians and Jews in early modern Italy. Renaissance Jews and Christians in fact shared many culinary habits, Cassen argues, and most of what is known today as Jewish food in Italy, like goose salami and deep-fried artichokes, has deep roots in local cuisines of the time. The frequent sharing of the same table among Jews and Christians, though, coexisted with destructive ideas about Jewish food and its impact on individual Christians' religion and imagined scenarios in which Jews consumed Christian blood.

In the following chapter, Hasia Diner analyzes a particular group of Jews on the move, late nineteenth-century peddlers in the "New World," and the traveling of their religiously prescribed dietary laws with them. Moving over long distances from their home communities and across regional, national, and cultural boundaries, in Europe and in other "new worlds," peddlers mostly interacted with and sojourned with non-Jews, performing and negotiating their Jewish identity through their distinctive foodways, while being "forced to decide on their own what to eat, and what not to eat." The mobility inherent to an itinerant trade resulted, therefore, in the mobility and exchange of food, taste, and ideas about identity and diet, at the same time as food reinforced its significance for migrant Jewish peddlers.

The third chapter of the section, Nancy Berg's "Jews among Muslims: Culinary Contexts," looks at Jewish cuisines of Egypt and Iraq, as revealed in cookbooks, websites, memoirs, and novels written in the wake of the mass departure of Egyptian and Iraqi Jewry, which function as collective biographies articulating the histories and memories of these communities' respective pasts. While the observation of kashrut rules and the prohibition on cooking on the Sabbath clearly differentiated Jews from the rest of the population, similarly to what happened in early modern Italy, these practices also brought them closer to their Muslim neighbors because of similarities in food prohibitions for Jews and Muslims, and the local ingredients were more abundant than in Central and Eastern Europe, for example. As a result, Berg uncovers "greater distinctions between national [Egyptian and Iraqi] diets, than between those of Jews and Arabs." In Iraq, where Jews had been part of the population since Babylonian times, Mizraḥi Jewish cuisine proved deeply integral to the national food landscape, and included iconic dishes such as *t'beet*, the stuffed skin of chicken stewed in rice.

The chapters included in part 2 of the book, "The Politics of Jewish Food: Culinary Articulations of Power, Identity, and State," illustrate the ways in which food has been a political factor in the participation of Jews in nation-building processes and the formation of states, beginning with modern Israel. Ari Ariel looks at how the melting pot ideology promoted by Ashkenazi Israeli political leaders in the 1950s and 1960s was designed to forcefully integrate Middle Eastern Jewish culture, including Mizraḥi foodways, thought to be inferior and suspect. Ashkenazi hegemonic politics of food included pressuring Middle Eastern Jewish immigrants to Israel to adopt Western foodways and administrating permissions for Middle Eastern food producers to use kosher certification selectively.

In his essay "Soviet Jewish Foodways: Transformation Through Detabooization," Gennady Estraikh creates a neologism—detabooization—as he discusses similar conflicts in the history of Jewish food in the Soviet Union. The degree of acceptance, recognition, and endorsement of Jewish foodways in the Socialist state ranged, according to the oscillations of the political climate and ideology, from the valorization of dishes and recipes—like the gefilte fish, tzimmes, and forshmak popular in the Jewish Autonomous Region, established in 1934 in the Russian Far East, as specialty foods enriching the cultural palette of the multiethnic

USSR—to the overall condemnation of the cuisine inspired by religion as counterrevolutionary.

Concluding the section, Joëlle Bahloul also looks at a process of negotiation; in this case, the integration of the foodways Sephardi Jews brought with them, as they emigrated from colonial North Africa to France in the mid-twentieth century, with the core precepts of French Republican ideology and their full participation in French society and culture. On the gastronomic level, such negotiation mostly resulted in the articulation of Frenchified weekday menus and kosher festive meals, thereby reflecting the developing separation between public Frenchness and private Jewishness, while trying to comply with the fundamentals of observing dietary law.

Following up on the examination of the conundrum between affiliation and integration, the three chapters in part 3 of this book, "The Kosherization of Jewish Food: Playing Out Religion, Taste, and Health in the Marketplace and Popular Culture," illustrate the diversity of discourses—articulated into modern nutritional science, cookbooks, and art, respectively—that formed the definition of "Jewish food," and its palatability, under different political, cultural, and marketplace conditions. In the section's opening chapter, Rakefet Zalashik argues that in the 1920s and 1930s Eastern European Jewish elites co-opted kashrut rules into positivist scientific discourses about healthy nutrition and hygiene with which to reform and shape poor and uneducated Jews into modern Jewish consumers, as they were encountering an unprecedented quantity and variety of foods and other products made available by mass production.

Similarly, as Adriana Brodsky suggests in her chapter, "The Battle against Guefilte Fish: Asserting Sephardi Culinary Repertoires among Argentine Jews in the Second Half of the Twentieth Century," kosher cookbooks played a dramatically important role in the construction of a respectable middle-class identity for Sephardi immigrants to post–World War II Argentina. The images of table manners, taste, and modernity conveyed by cookbooks helped Argentinian Sephardim to use their exotic Syrian, Turkish, and Moroccan dishes and flavors to relate to, and distinguish themselves from, the majority Ashkenazi Jews, as well as find a meaningful place in the Argentine nation.

The chapter closing the section, Yael Raviv's "Still Life: Performing National Identity in Israel and Palestine at the Intersection of Food and Art," explores the changing role of food in art in relation to the articulation and performance of Jewish national identity in Israel in comparison to Palestinian artwork. Focusing on rural images and iconic food products as symbols of national identity and unity in the formative years of Israel—many of them, such as the olive, the orange, and the prickly pear, signifying rootedness in the land in both Israeli and Palestinian cultures—the chapter concludes with the shift, in more recent artwork, to the use of food as a tool for political commentary and for exploring ethnic affiliation in a post-Zionist and global era.

The fourth and final section of the book interrogates the meaning of Jewish foodways in the diaspora at the intersection of history and memory. Marion Kaplan's chapter, "From the Comfort of Home to Exile: German Jews and their Foodways," traces how German Jews adapted to German cuisine from the Imperial era (1871–1918) through the Nazi period (1933–1945) and, later, to food cultures in Portugal, as sojourners en route to safety, and in the different environments of two of their lands of refuge, a small community in the Dominican Republic and the United States. The material and cultural contextuality of the culinary adaptability and maintenance of certain Jewish food customs, especially family meals at holidays, reveals itself in the adoption of dried cod, tomato, and olive oil in exchange for the introduction of German cakes and donuts in Portuguese cuisine in Portugal; the assimilation into the Jewish immigrant diet of previously unknown tropical fruits in the Dominican Republic; and the combination of a mostly Eastern European Jewish culinary repertoire with mass-produced American food, which sometimes included the forbidden bacon, while retaining some aspects of their German Jewish eating identities, in the United States.

Annie Polland closely examines a popular Yiddish cookbook—Hinde

Amchanitski's *Lehr-bukh vi azoy tsu kukhen und bakhen*—published in 1901, in the largest Jewish community of the Western Hemisphere, the Lower East Side of Manhattan, to describe the foodscape created by Eastern European Jewish immigrant families as they filled the tenements of New York. As immigrant mothers and wives assumed the responsibility of managing the household, which included shopping, cooking, cleaning and managing the household economy, Polland concludes, they became essential agents of Americanization.

Finally, Marcie Cohen Ferris, in "Dining in the Dixie Diaspora: Jewish Foodways in the American South," points to the fact that Jewish food vendors, cooks, and eaters in the pre–World War II American South had to doubly adjust to a largely Christian milieu and a biracial, segregated, racist society. Eating between these two worlds required a fine-tuning negotiation of identity that was reflected in the religious and culinary evolution of Southern Jewish life from the first colonial settlers to contemporary Jewish Southerners. Subregional differences in markets and racial balances, from Atlanta to Savannah, to Charleston, to the Mississippi Delta region resulted in the "integrated outsiders," whom she refers to as "Dixie Jews," producing as many kosher cuisines as the circumstances they had to navigate. The case presented by Ferris, covering more than a century, and shifting from history to memory and back, conveniently and beautifully encapsulates the tension between adaptation and resistance to acculturation within very different economic, political, religious, and social situations that characterizes the fascinating and instructing story of Jews and their food in the diaspora.

Readers can know that we admit that these stories of Jewish migration and Jewish food, of Jewish history and the impact of change on foodways, represent a mere sliver of the possible. The myriad other histories not included have been left out not because we deemed them unimportant or lacking in analytic significance but rather because not enough scholarly energy has been expended on studying them. For example, we have no real history of the foods of the Jews of Ethiopia, whether in their homeland or upon their migration to Israel in the 1990s.

No historian of food or of the Jews has tried her hand at the foods of the Africans who lived in the Caribbean, enslaved by Jewish planters. Would that we had real scholarship on the food history of the Lithuanian Jews who settled in South Africa or the Balkan Jews who settled in the Amazon River basin. All of these represent not only experiences that would enrich Jewish history but food history as well, and we can hope that scholars reading this book will be inspired to think of these projects and so many, many more.

All in all these essays, each focusing in its own way on a particular moment in Jewish history, make it clear that food matters. The history of the Jews, their migrations, their settlement patterns, and the contours of their communal lives cannot be told without food. While food alone did not make their histories, food, always present, cannot be removed. These essays also show dramatically that Jews are good to think with and about. Whether concerned with physical, social, or cultural movement, historians would do well to think about the history of the Jews, a drama played out on every continent over thousands of years. In every place they went they not only brought their normative texts, their experiences forged elsewhere, and their internal divisions, but they navigated the political and economic challenges of the new. How they did so differed dramatically from one situation to the next, but in doing so they offer a template that historians can draw upon as they contemplate other people, at other times, in other settings. These essays, eclectic in subject matter, drawn from a multitude of places and times, some very specific, others broader, should—and here, please excuse a trite phrase that food historians abhor—whet our appetites to know more and add to this already rich trove.

NOTES

1. Claude Lévi-Strauss, *The Raw and the Cooked: Mythologiques, Volume 1* (Chicago: University of Chicago Press, 1969).
2. Mary Douglas, *Purity and Danger: An Analysis of the Concepts of Pollution and Taboo* (London: Routledge and Kegan Paul, 1966).

3. Douglas, *Purity and Danger*, 41–57.

4. Marvin Harris, *Good to Eat: Riddles of Food and Culture* (New York: Simon and Schuster, 1985).

5. Corrie E. Norman, "Food and Religion," in *The Oxford Handbook of Food History*, ed. Jeffrey M. Pilcher (New York: Oxford University Press, 2012), 417.

6. Nathan MacDonald, *Not Bread Alone: The Uses of Food in the Old Testament* (Oxford UK: Oxford University Press, 2008); Nathan MacDonald, *What Did the Ancient Israelites Eat?: Diet in Biblical Times* (Grand Rapids, MI: William B. Eerdmans, 2008).

7. Jordan D. Rosenblum, *Food and Identity in Early Rabbinic Judaism* (New York: Cambridge University Press, 2010).

8. David Kraemer, *Jewish Eating and Identity Through the Ages* (New York: Routledge, 2007), 4.

9. Kraemer, *Jewish Eating and Identity Through the Ages*, 74. For an example of articulation of the sacred through food preparation and consumption, see Susan Starr Sered, "Food and Holiness: Cooking as a Sacred Act among Middle-Eastern Jewish Women," *Anthropological Quarterly* 61, no. 3 (July 1988): 129–39.

10. Donna R. Gabaccia, "Food, Mobility, and World History," in *The Oxford Handbook of Food History*, ed. Jeffrey M. Pilcher (New York: Oxford University Press, 2012), 305–23.

11. Hasia R. Diner, *Hungering for America: Italian, Irish, and Jewish Foodways in the Age of Migration* (Cambridge MA: Harvard University Press, 2001), 175. On Italian immigrant food habits in the United States, see also Simone Cinotto, *The Italian American Table: Food, Family, and Community in New York City* (Urbana: University of Illinois Press, 2013).

12. Hanna Miller, "Identity Takeout: How American Jews Made Chinese Food Their Ethnic Cuisine," *Journal of Popular Culture* 39, no. 3 (2006): 430–65.

13. Diner, *Hungering for America*.

14. Lara Rabinovitch, "A Peek into Their Kitchens: Postwar Jewish Community Cookbooks in the United States," *Food, Culture and Society* 14, no. 1 (2011): 91–116; Rachel Gross, "Draydel Salad: The Serious Business of Jewish Food and Fun in the 1950s," in *Religion, Food, and Eating in North America*, ed. Benjamin E. Zeller, Marie W. Dallam, Reid L. Neilson, and Nora L. Rubel (New York: Oxford University Press, 2014), 91–113; Samira K. Mehta, "'I Chose Judaism but Christmas Cookies Chose Me': Food, Identity, and Familial Religious Practice in Christian/Jewish Blended Families," in *Religion, Food, and Eating*, ed. Zeller et al., 154–74; Nora L. Rubel, "The Feast at the End of the Fast: The

Evolution of an American Jewish Ritual," in *Religion, Food, and Eating*, ed. Zeller et al., 234–52; Steve Siporin, "From Kashrut to *Cucina Ebraica*: The Recasting of Italian Jewish Foodways," *Journal of American Folklore* 107, no. 424 (1994): 268–81; Maria Diemling and Larry Ray, "'Where Do You Draw the Line?': Negotiating Kashrut and Jewish Identity in a Small British Reform Community," *Food, Culture and Society* 17, no. 1 (2014): 125–142; Joëlle Bahloul, "Food Practices among Sephardic Immigrants in Contemporary France: Dietary Laws in Urban Society," *Journal of the American Academy of Religion* 63, no. 3 (1995): 485–96; Willy Jansen, "French Bread and Algerian Wine: Conflicting Identities in French Algeria," in *Food, Drink and Identity: Cooking, Eating, and Drinking in Europe since the Middle Ages*, ed. Peter Scholliers (New York: Berg, 2001), 195–218; Paulette Kershenovich Schuster, "Jewish Food in Mexico: Reflections of a Community's History, Culture, and Values," REVER: *Revista de Estudos da Religião* 15, no. 1 (2015): 58–79.

15. Orit Rozin, "Food, Identity, and Nation-Building in Israel's Formative Years," *Israel Studies Forum* 21, no. 1 (2006): 52–80; Yael Raviv, "The Hebrew Banana: Local Food and the Performance of Israeli National Identity," *Food, Culture and Society* 5, no. 1 (2001): 30–35; Ronald Rantaa, "Re-Arabizing Israeli Food Culture," *Food, Culture and Society* 18, no. 4 (2015): 611–27; Deborah Golden, "Nourishing the Nation: The Uses of Food in an Israeli Kindergarten," *Food and Foodways* 13, no. 3 (2005): 181–99.

16. Yael Raviv, "Falafel: A National Icon," *Gastronomica* 3, no. 3 (2003): 20–25; Liora Gvion, *Beyond Hummus and Falafel: Social and Political Aspects of Palestinian Food in Israel*, trans. David Wesley and Elana Wesley (Berkeley: University of California Press, 2012).

17. E. P. Thompson, "The Moral Economy of the English Crowd in the Eighteenth Century," *Past and Present* 50, no. 1 (1971): 76–136; Eric Hobsbawm, *Social Bandits and Primitive Rebels* (New York: Free Press, 1960).

18. Barbara Alpern Engel, "Not by Bread Alone: Subsistence Riots in Russia during World War I," *Journal of Modern History* 69, no. 4 (1997): 696–721.

19. Paula E. Hyman, "Immigrant Women and Consumer Protest: The New York City Kosher Meat Boycott of 1902," *American Jewish History* 70, no. 1 (1980): 91–105.

20. Primo Levi, *Survival in Auschwitz: The Nazi Assault on Humanity* (New York: Simon and Schuster, 1993).

21. Shamai Davidson, "Human Reciprocity among the Jewish Prisoners in the Nazi Concentration Camps," in *The Nazi Concentration Camps: Structure and*

Aims, the Image of the Prisoner, the Jews in the Camps, ed. Yisrael Gutman and Avital Saf (Jerusalem: Yad Vashem, 1984), 568–96; Joel E. Dimsdale, "The Coping Behavior of Nazi Concentration Camp Survivors," *American Journal of Psychiatry* 131, no. 7 (1974): 792–97.

22. June Feiss Hersh, *Recipes Remembered* (New York: Museum of Jewish Heritage, 2013); Cara De Silva, ed., *In Memory's Kitchen: A Legacy from the Women of Terezin* (Northvale NJ: J. Aronson, 1996).

23. Joan Nathan, *Jewish Cooking in America* (New York: Knopf, 1994); Jennifer Berg, "From the Big Bagel to the Big Roti? The Evolution of New York City's Jewish Food Icons," in *Gastropolis: Food and New York City,* ed. Annie Hauck-Lawson and Jonathan Deutsch (New York: Columbia University Press, 2008), 252–73.

24. Maria Balinska, *The Bagel: The Surprising History of a Modest Bread* (New Haven CT: Yale University Press 2009).

25. Alan M. Kraut, "The Butcher, the Baker, the Pushcart Peddler: Jewish Foodways and Entrepreneurial Opportunity in the East European Immigrant Community, 1880–1940," *Journal of American Culture* 6, no. 4 (1983): 71–83; Andrew Godley, *Jewish Immigrant Entrepreneurship in New York and London 1880–1914: Enterprise and Culture* (New York: Palgrave, 2001).

26. Timothy D. Lytton, *Kosher: Private Regulation in the Age of Industrial Food* (Cambridge MA: Harvard University Press, 2013); Roger Horowitz, *Kosher USA: How Coke Became Kosher and Other Tales of Modern Food* (New York: Columbia University Press, 2016).

PART 1

Crossing and Bridging Culinary Boundaries

Resistance, Resilience, and Adaptations of Jewish Food in the Encounter with the Non-Jewish Other

1

The Sausage in the Jews' Pantry

Food and Jewish-Christian Relations in Renaissance Italy

....

FLORA CASSEN

When friends choose a restaurant in the contemporary Western world, they face a range of choices—French, Ethiopian, Middle Eastern, or Asian, to name just a few—that cross national and even continental boundaries. Excitement for global cuisines is often seen as a mark of cultural openness and cosmopolitanism. Such enthusiasm raises eating from a humble activity necessary for survival to a cultural experience that, we believe, enriches our palate and teaches us to appreciate the world's diversity. Indeed, eating represents an intimate experience of foreign cultures in which we quite literally ingest their flavors, tastes, and textures to nourish our bodies. In today's popular culture where famous chefs can become television network stars and the "fusion" of different cuisines is celebrated, strange or unusual foods are more likely to arouse a diner's curiosity than suspicion. But while we eat the food of the "other" without fear, people in the early modern era tended to be more wary of foreign foodways.

Recent scholarship on both the European and Ottoman worlds during early modern times has highlighted the role of food not only as a sign of identity, but also as a strong marker of difference.[1] In his work on food in Ottoman travel narratives, Eric Dursteler suggests that travelers sometimes so closely connected diet to a person's ethnic identity that they thought that eating too much of a certain food could alter their own identity.[2] Food was of particular concern to early modern travelers for whom "those who eat similar foods are trustworthy and safe, while those whose foods differ are viewed with suspicion and even revulsion."[3]

Equating food with trust also carried particular weight for early modern Italian Jews, a group one could perhaps characterize as "local others." On the one hand, Jews had been a presence, albeit a small one, on the Italian Peninsula since at least Roman times, spoke Italian, and participated in Italy's economy and culture. On the other hand, their beliefs, traditions, and dietary laws set them apart from the Christian majority. For the latter, Jewish dietary laws and culinary habits were a source of curiosity, but also of intense fear.[4] Nothing less than purity and holiness were at stake. In Christian doctrine and theology, where Jews were sometimes seen as the "polar opposites" of Christians, Jewish food was conceived of as impure.[5] Jews, on the other hand, conceived of their own dietary laws, and the fact that God had asked them to eat differently than gentiles as proof of their holiness: it was precisely because they were pure, and to preserve their purity, that they had to abstain from certain foods and from sharing meals with non-Jews.[6]

Despite the mutual prohibitions against sharing meals, there are numerous examples of early modern Italian Jews and Christians eating together and trying each other's foods.[7] This was true in the larger cities where Jews often lived in ghettos and where institutions of communal life were established, but it was also the case in small towns where Italian Jews lived in relative isolation from other Jews. In fact, if one were to map and count the Jewish settlements across the north and center of the Italian Peninsula, it would become apparent that the Jewish population was (as it had been since the late Middle Ages) "distinguished by the breadth of its dispersal; settlements, often limited to single families, were spread over a considerable number of city-states, walled towns, and villages, linked by poor or inconvenient communications."[8] While the structure and lifestyles of the larger, often-ghettoized Jewish communities have been amply studied, the specificities of Jewish life in small towns are not as well known.[9]

The first part of this essay begins to address this lacuna by focusing on the living and eating habits of the Nantua family, the only Jewish family in the small town of Gavi in the Ligurian Alps. Since eating and living habits were (and are) an integral and intimate part of people's daily lives, examining these questions with regards to the Nantua family sheds new light on Jewish life and Jewish identity in small towns in early modern Italy. The second part of the essay contrasts this information on the Jews' actual eating habits with imagined ideas about Jews and their food among the majority population. For, indeed, while in reality Jewish and Christian eating habits had much in common, in the imagined realm, they were often portrayed as antithetical. Thus, I argue that in addition to nourishing the physical bodies of early modern Italians of all faiths, food both nurtured relations and generated conflicts among Jews and between Jews and Christians.

ITALIAN JEWISH FOOD, THEN AND NOW

Before we can address the question of Jewish identity and Jewish-Christian relations with regard to food, it is useful to explore what was or is "Italian Jewish food." Today, tourists who would like to sample Italian Jewish food are usually sent to the Roman ghetto, a small neighborhood that starts at the southern edge of the Campo di Fiori. This neighborhood includes the popular Via Portico d'Ottavia, known for its festive atmosphere and good restaurants. However, a quick overview of the food offered in the restaurants of this Roman ghetto illustrates how complicated the concept of Jewish food is. Piperno, the oldest restaurant in the ghetto, sells a number of dishes that it claims have a Jewish origin: *carciofi alla giudia* (artichokes Jewish style), *carne secca* (salted and dried beef), pasta with chickpeas, stuffed zucchini, fried cod, and fried mozzarella.[10] The carciofi, or artichokes, are the most famous Jewish-Italian dish.[11] The carciofi have been associated with Jews and prepared in a similar way since at least the sixteenth century.[12] The carne secca was a meat preparation based on Jewish dietary regulations that required salting the meat to remove the blood. But the other specialties—fried cod, mozzarella, stuffed zucchini—were traditional Roman fare, also adopted by Jews. Complicating the situation, Piperno also serves numerous dishes with prosciutto and shellfish—foods that Jewish religion absolutely forbids. Another Jewish restaurant in the ghetto, Mama Kosher Food, does follow Jewish dietary laws but specializes in roast beef sandwiches and burgers—typical American cuisine.[13] A third kosher restaurant, BaGhetto, sells falafel, hummus, and other Israeli and Middle Eastern fare.[14] Thus today in the Roman ghetto, Jewish food can be "authentic" Roman food that is not kosher, or kosher food that is often more typical of the cuisine of the United States or the Middle East than of Italy. If the concept of modern Italian Jewish food is complicated, can one find more clarity in the early modern world?

In his book *Mangiare alla giudia: Jewish Food from the Renaissance to Today*, Ariel Toaff pointed out that, in Italy, eating kosher and "eating Jewish" (*alla giudia*) were two different, though often overlapping ways of eating. Kosher designated compliance with the dietary regulations of the Hebrew Bible. Jewish-style food, on the other hand, was a cuisine heavily reliant on local eating habits and ingredients, combined with influences or ingredients that originated in the places where the Jews had come from.[15] By the fifteenth and sixteenth centuries, Italian Jewry had become a true melting pot. The *italiani* were the Italian Jews, who claimed to have been there since Roman times. In the thirteenth and fourteenth centuries, Jews expelled from France and Germany crossed the Alps and settled in the peninsula. Likewise, after the expulsion from Spain in 1492, Spanish and Sicilian Jews immigrated to Italy. Later Levantine Jews (usually from the Ottoman Empire) moved in to establish trading posts and some of them stayed.[16] These different groups intermingled but kept some of their cultural, historical, and culinary traditions. Carciofi alla giudia, for example, is believed to have been a recipe from Spain or the Levant brought in by Sicilian Jews, which then slowly spread to other Italian Jewish communities and became the icon of Italian Jewish cuisine.[17]

Among the sources used by Toaff is a Hebrew-Italian dictionary published in Venice in 1579 that contained a detailed list of foods that the Jews ate. It included turnip, chard, dill, lettuce, endive, pumpkins, watermelons, cucumbers, roots, onions, leeks, garlic, dried fruits, apples, pears, olives, dates, almonds, chestnuts, pasta, eggs, meats, bread, and wine. Surprisingly some of the vegetables most closely associated with Jewish Italian cuisine today, such as artichokes or zucchini, were not on the list. This suggests that, by and large, Jews ate a diet very similar to that of their non-Jewish neighbors.[18]

Perhaps, then, we need to turn to the rules of kashrut, the dietary regulations of the Hebrew Bible, to explore differences between the Jews' diet and that of the rest of the Italian population. Leon Modena, a Venetian rabbi from the seventeenth century, wrote a compilation of Jewish rituals for a Christian audience: *Historia de Riti Hebraici*—the History of Jewish Rituals, first published in 1638. Part 2, chapter 7—"Of the foods that are always forbidden and how we eat meat"—presents an overview of the kashrut rules related to meat. The allowed meats—which excludes pork, horse, and rabbit—could only be eaten if the animals had been slaughtered properly, which meant that their trachea and esophagus had been slashed with a very sharp knife so as to drain the blood and the animal was found to be healthy upon careful inspection after the slaughter. Then many parts, such as fat and sinews, had to be discarded. It is for this reason, writes Modena, "that in many parts of Italy, and especially in Germany, we do not eat the hindquarter of the animal for there are nerves and a lot of fat there."[19]

The rules regarding kosher meat were prohibitive. To eat kosher meat, Jews had to have their own butcher and a larger supply of animals than did the Christians—because a significant amount of the animal had to be discarded. Jewish butchers sometimes received permission to sell the discarded parts to Christians, but not always, as this was a source of tension and suspicion. For Angelo di Castro, a prominent fifteenth-century professor of law at Padua, consuming meat slaughtered by Jews was a mortal sin: "If a Jew purchases an entire lamb or calf, slaughters it and prepares it in other ways in accordance with his rites . . . but then sells, gives or otherwise yields the hindquarters . . . it is clear that the Christian who accepts and consumes this meat has committed a mortal sin." The reason, di Castro explained, was that eating this meat was contrary to Christian law, which prohibited Christians from using or consuming "Jewish food," defined as food purchased and prepared by Jews.[20] John Capistran, a powerful fifteenth-century Franciscan friar, went further, arguing that all food merely handled by Jews was impure: "How can it be fitting for Christians to eat the meat which the criminal and putrid hands of the unbelieving, faithless Jews treat as refuse?"[21] Given this rhetoric, the sale of meat to Christians was potentially fraught with danger. But if Jews could not sell the parts of the animal that they didn't eat to Christians, the cost of a pound of kosher meat increased in price significantly.

In larger Jewish communities, and especially in the ghettos that were introduced at the beginning of the sixteenth century in Venice and then spread rapidly to the rest of Italy, the Jews could and did establish the structures necessary to provide kosher food to their populations.[22] However, as indicated earlier, a large fraction of Italian Jews lived outside of the large communities and ghettos.[23] Observing this situation in Tuscany prior to the establishment of the ghetto of Florence in 1571, Stefanie Siegmund goes as far as rejecting the term *community*: "Rather than referring to the Jews of pre-ghetto Florence . . . as a community, we might call them a constellation."[24] Moreover, Siegmund argues that it was the creation of the ghetto that led to the establishment of Jewish institutions, which had been absent in Tuscany in the pre-ghetto days.[25] For indeed, Jewish dietary regulation not only impacted a person's diet, it also contributed to the cohesiveness of communities by promoting the necessary social, commercial, and communal infrastructure needed to abide by Jewish law. In places where a few individual Jews lived and

such infrastructure was absent, we have comparatively little information about the Jews' diet and lifestyle, and perhaps more importantly,
on what even made their lifestyle "Jewish."[26]

The story of the Nantua brothers—the Jews who, as in the title of this
essay, had sausage in their pantry—allows us to explore this question.
Their situation cannot, as a matter of course, be generalized to all Italian Jews in similar living situations; however the Nantuas' lives are the
object of an unusually large amount of documentation in the Genoese
archives, due to their business activities and related litigations. Even
though it is specific to them, this documentation also opens a window
onto their daily lives; and to the extent that activities such as eating
or sleeping are universal, perhaps the Nantuas' situation can serve as
a starting point for investigations of other Jews. The Nantua brothers
did not leave us with personal writings describing their lives, though
the absence of personal sources should not lead us to underestimate
the complexity of their lives, which, as we will see, required them to
balance the demands of integration into rural Italian society with being
members of a minority group.

IN THE HOUSE OF THE NANTUA FAMILY

The brothers Lazaro and Angelino Nantua ran a pawnshop together
and lived with their families in the same house in Gavi. There were no
other Jews in Gavi, so their house was the only Jewish house in town.
In 1567 the Republic of Genoa ordered the expulsion of all the Jews, but
the people of Gavi intervened on their behalf and they were allowed to
stay.[27] When the doge of the republic asked the *podestà* (local captain)
of Gavi to send him a report on the Jewish population of his town, ten
years later, we learn that Angelo and Lazaro still resided there. Like
their father and uncle, the brothers and their families lived together
in a house and ran a pawnshop (inherited from their father), through
which they earned two thousand scudi a year. They charged six dinars
per lira each month and less for the people of Gavi.[28] The advantageous
credit rates that the people of Gavi enjoyed was one of the reasons that

the people of Gavi had protected the family and argued against their expulsion back in 1567.

The next decade went by without incident, but in 1592 the situation of Angelino and Lazaro changed.[29] In February Angelino had a run-in with the chancellor of the town, Gio Battista Mayda, whom Angelino reportedly insulted and then hit in the face, causing him to bleed and suffer a swollen eye.[30] In his two-page letter to the doge and the *governatori*, Mayda described his fight with Angelino on the first page, followed by a description of Angelino and Lazaro's outrageous behavior, in particular their refusal to wear the Jewish badge as prescribed. Instead, they wore a bit of yellow rope hidden under their arms.[31] The doge, taking direct interest in the matter, asked that Angelino be imprisoned and sent to Genoa, and that their clothes and books be confiscated.[32] Thus a detailed inventory was taken of everything in the Nantua brothers' house, which revealed a fascinating accumulation of things.[33]

They had chests and chests of clothes (many of which had been pawned), jewelry, furniture, and an impressive cache of weapons (which Jews, in principle, weren't allowed to have). The only Jewish ritual object that they had was "a chest with the five books of Moses" and a "jar for circumcision."[34] With so few ritual objects and the lack of a local community, it is hard to imagine what their Jewish religious life felt or looked like. Nevertheless, a closer look at their furniture, their eating utensils, and their cookware opens a window into core aspects of their daily lives.

Using the inventory preserved in the archives of Genoa, I will describe the house and list the objects relevant to food preparation and consumption, which represent only a portion of all the objects listed in the inventory. Their house was large and had two floors and a cellar. The officials who drew up the inventory proceeded room by room, thereby giving us a layout of the house. They started on the first floor, which had an entry hall followed by two rooms (the second room belonged to "the mother of Lazarino"), a kitchen and a dining hall. In the room of Lazarino's mother, there were at least two dozen table cloths and fifty-four napkins, some of flax and some of linen. In the kitchen, they found nineteen flat plates and twenty-six deep round plates. To prepare and cook the food, there were two copper carving knives, four copper cake pans, two copper washbasins, one copper colander, nine copper pot lids, and seven ceramic candleholders. In the dining hall, they had "a table with its rug; six chairs for men; eight chairs for women."[35] *Da donna* chairs were a type of chair with a rush bottom; they were more comfortable than the ones with bare wood bottoms at a time when upholstery was still rare.[36]

While most early modern Italians would have sat on a bench and eaten on a table board on trestles rather than at a real table, the Nantuas could hold elaborate banquets at a large table on a rug, with fourteen chairs. The Nantuas also had many plates — large, small, flat, and deep — whereas it was customary at the time to put the food right on a tablecloth (which is why families had so many of them) or on a thick piece of bread shared between two people.[37] The Nantuas probably did not hold banquets on a regular basis, though, and each bedroom also contained a table or table board and minimal cooking and eating utensils, suggesting that individual family members or smaller parts of the family would have gathered together for meals in their separate living quarters. The lack of functional separation between sleeping and eating spaces was customary for the time, as the concept of a separate dining room was only starting to emerge and only the wealthiest families would have had enough space for it.[38] That the Nantua house had a large separate dining room is remarkable and suggests, along with the layout of the house and its furniture, that the Nantuas' lives resembled those of wealthy Christian families.

As for their Jewish identity, there were not, on the first floor, objects that would indicate Jewish religious practice. The chest with the five books of Moses and the jar for circumcisions were both on the second floor.[39] Whether this was driven by a conscious notion that their Jewishness was a private matter that ought to be displayed on the more secluded second floor rather than on the public first floor is not clear.

As the podestà and his men continued upstairs, the family's lifestyle came into clearer focus. The first room, which faced "the public street," contained mostly clothes. The "middle room" contained clothes as well, but, in addition, it functioned as the house's pantry. This configuration is unusual by today's standard but was quite common at the time as drier air upstairs would have aided the preservation of food.[40] The presence of kosher food in the pantry would constitute evidence of Jewish practice and perhaps identity. But would a lonely Jewish family in the Ligurian Mountains take the trouble to eat kosher meat and, in effect, significantly limit their diet? Or would they, as Toaff wrote about the Jews of Umbria, "compromise in order to survive," noting that "butchery was an area requiring just such flexibility."[41] For the Nantuas, not only survival, but also their status in town may have been at stake. Meat was such a staple of the early modern diet that Braudel called early modern Europe "carnivorous" and estimated that a German ate about 220 pounds of meat per year, while in Tuscany a person would have consumed about 88 pounds per year.[42] By 1550, even though meat consumption in Italy was on the decline, eating meat remained a status symbol, signaling wealth, good life, and health.[43] Taking into account the rules of kashrut, according to which certain parts of the animal had to be discarded, the Nantua family would need even more meat if they had wanted to keep up with their neighbors.

In their pantry, the Nantuas had "four *rub* of piazentino cheese, a *staio* of nectar in a saddlebag, a *rub* and a half of sausage, two *rub* of salted beef, a *staio* of wheat in a bag, and another bag with half a *staio* of wheat."[44] They stocked mostly dried food, which is to be expected given the challenges involved in preserving fresh food. Even if they had had some fresh food, there would be no point in recording it in an inventory drawn up for judiciary purposes, for the food would have perished by the time the document reached the doge. Piazentino cheese came from Sicily, so their diet was not limited to locally produced foods. The salted beef, called carne secca today, is still known as a typical Italian Jewish dish. It was beef that had been salted to remove the blood and then dried for preservation. Modena described the process in his Historia de Riti Hebraici: "Because of the above-mentioned prohibition against blood, we put the meat in salt and leave it there for an hour."[45] But what about the sausage? Was it bought from the neighborhood butchery? Did it contain pork?

In *Mangiare alla giudia*, Toaff devotes an entire chapter to goose meat, which he calls "the Jews' pig." He provides ample evidence that in the fifteenth and sixteenth centuries, the Jews of Lombardy and Piedmont specialized in breeding geese and in the large-scale commercialization of foie gras, sausages, salamis, and dried meat—all made from geese.[46] For example, in 1501, Abraham Sacerdoti from Alessandria, a small town in the Duchy of Milan at the time, was exempted from paying any kind of duties when going from town to town to sell dried or fresh goose meat. By the beginning of the seventeenth century, the ghetto of Carmagnola in Piedmont had become the largest producer of goose salami and sausage in the region.[47] Since Gavi was located in the center of that market, Lazaro and Angelino would have had an easy time procuring goose sausage, if they wanted. Absent the possibility of conducting an analysis of the piece of sausage in question, we cannot know for sure what it was made of. Still, while there is no reason to assume that it was made from pork, there is sufficient circumstantial evidence to suggest that it was not.

Lazaro's and Angelino's identification with Judaism was well established. Not only did they self-identify as Jews, the podestà and other townspeople likewise recognized them as such. Although these isolated Jewish settlements cannot be called communities, the Jews who lived in them shared a sense of sameness and belonging with Jews in other small settlements or ghettos.[48] This sense of sameness probably was strengthened and maintained through active networks by which they acquired kosher meat, sustained business or family contacts, arranged marriages and perhaps even organized gatherings for Jewish celebrations or festivals. If so, food naturally played a central role in the maintenance of these networks.

At the same time, evidence from their wine cellar suggests that the Nantuas were also well integrated into their local surroundings. Moving on to the cellar of the house, the examiners found a well-stocked wine reserve, which included wine that the Nantua brothers stored for Christian acquaintances: "two barrels with a capacity of twenty-eight bar with four metal hoops around each barrel; next another one of the same capacity almost full of wine inside; next two barrels of 25 bar in which there are ten bar of wine; next seven barrels of eighteen bar approximately two of these are full of wine and one of these belong to the captain [unnamed] and the other to signor Filippino, all of which is closed with four metal hoops, except for one of wood, for each barrel."[49] With large quantities of non-kosher wine, their house was not a strictly kosher house, although Leon Modena explained that Italian Jews took exception to the strict rules regarding kosher wine."[50] In chapter 8 of his *Riti*, "On Drinking," he wrote:

> There are those that, by the orders of the ancient rabbis, argue that it is forbidden for Jews to drink wine made or touched by a non-Jew, and this is a rule observed by Jews in the Levant and in Germany. But in Italy we do not comply with this rule, for we argue that it was ordered by rabbis who lived among idolaters to forbid trade with them, not for the nations amongst whom we live today.[51]

By arguing that kosher wine was a historical necessity when Jews lived among pagans, but that it had lost its usefulness now that they lived in Christian lands, Modena implied that it was a measure of protection against idolatry, rather than a means of separating Jews from Christians. In Italy, therefore, Jews and Christians drank the same wine, even though they often ate different meat. Storing wine for neighbors and acquaintances, and perhaps drinking with them on occasion as well, can be seen as a sign of trust and friendship. Wine functioned as a bridge between Jews and Christians while meat connected Jews living in small, isolated settlements.

FOOD AND JEWISH-CHRISTIAN RELATIONS

Interfaith relations, such as the ones forged between the Nantuas and their Christian neighbors, were not unique or limited to Jews in small towns. Even in ghettos, where there was a physical separation between Jews and Christians, the boundaries between the two groups were quite porous. Christians were curious about what the Jews did and ate in the ghetto. In his book on the Inquisition of Venice, Brian Pullan cites numerous examples of Christians visiting the ghetto and conversing with Jews.[52] The inquisition recorded the cases and issued warnings, but rarely condemned these people to heresy. However, if a Christian slept and/or ate in the ghetto, condemnation was usual. For instance, a Christian woman, Valeria Brugnaleschi, admitted to the inquisition in 1587 to having lived in the ghetto for two years during which she taught Jewish girls to read from the Old Testament. She ate and drank food and wine that the Jews supplied her. The food, she said, "was fish and matzoth, but never meat."[53] This remark about meat made to the inquisition in her defense reveals that eating with Jews and sharing their food was a social infraction, but that eating Jewish meat represented yet an additional and worse line that Valeria could have crossed but did not.[54]

One of the most remarkable events cited by Pullan is an annual ritual that took place at the end of Passover during which Christian bakers entered the ghetto with baskets of bread, while Jewish youngsters yelled "Pan! Pan! — Bread! Bread!" and threw mud and dirt at them.[55] When questioned by the inquisition, one of the Christian participants, the journeyman Leonardo Ceteli, said that "he did not know whether this was a rite carried out in disrespect of Christians."[56] Jewish historians are more familiar with a different scenario: that of Jews forced to barricade themselves in their houses during Holy Week, while processions of Christians threw stones at their homes. Holy Week violence was common in Renaissance Italy as the numerous *gride* (legal proclamations) requiring Jews to stay indoors during that week attest.[57] David Nirenberg has studied Holy Week riots in Spain in the fourteenth century and argued that such violence was "ritual" and that "these attacks lacked the face-to-face brutality we tend to associate with pogroms."[58] For Nirenberg, ritualized violence was different from cataclysmic violence and could be seen as having an integrative function. By reminding the population that the Jews were being punished for the crime of deicide year after year, it helped avert cataclysmic violence. For when violence was ritualized and confined to a yearly event, it was less likely to erupt in uncontrolled attacks on the Jews.[59]

In Renaissance Italy, too, usually during carnival celebrations, ritualized violence became a way to regulate relations between Jews and Christians. While in many carnival celebrations around the world, the social order was inverted for a day, in the Italian festivities, the social order was also simultaneously reaffirmed through mockery and abuse of the weaker groups in society. In Rome, Jews were forced to run naked in the streets and were stoned by onlookers. Often, at the end of the day, a Jewish convict was ritually put to death. (In Venice, pigs were chased through the street and stoned.)[60] Dana Katz attributes a similar function to art in Renaissance Italy: by "picturing violence," art often helped deflect real, physical attacks on Jews.[61] While condoning anti-Jewish violence within certain limits — on a painted canvas or during a carnival celebration — certainly gave expression to harsh anti-Jewish sentiments, the anti-Jewish violence that erupted unchecked outside of these frameworks was often far worse.

Yet, in the records that Pullan discovered, the opposite happened. The Jews' return from matzo (or unleavened bread) to bread was the occasion for a true role reversal in which Christian bakers were the victims of ritualized violence by Jewish youngsters throwing mud and dirt at them. This end of Passover celebration, in which food played a central role, may have had an integrative rather than divisive function, too. By inviting Christian bakers at their return to bread celebration, the Jews signified that they were part of Christian society; by throwing mud and dirt at them, they simultaneously, for a brief moment, reversed the power differential between Jews and Christians. Although declarations made to an inquisitorial tribunal need to be assessed with care, it is still significant that, when interrogated, one of the participants said that he did not know whether the celebration disrespected Christians. Perhaps this helped to temporarily (and safely) relieve the confinement of ghetto life and the Jews' marginalized status. At the end of the celebration, things returned to normal: the Jews remained in the ghetto while the Christians left.

But despite the similarities, the sharing, and the participating in each other's rituals, the Jews' diet continued to generate strong suspicion. At one level, this reflected the general phenomenon, observed by Dursteler, that in the early modern world, eating the same was a sign of trust, while eating differently was a source of suspicion.[62] Since Jews and Christians shared many culinary habits, this should have generated trust between the two groups, and indeed it did. Evidence such as lists of fines that Jews paid for "mixing, conversing, and eating" with Christians suggests that Jews and Christians probably shared meals on a regular basis.[63] Therefore, I suggest that this suspicion probably had its roots not in the Jews' actual diet, but in certain ideas about Jewish food, the purity of Christian society, and paradoxical beliefs about Jews and blood.[64]

The liquids one ingested and the liquids one's body was made of were key concepts informing medieval and early modern ideas of self and other. Medieval and early modern concepts of a healthful diet were largely based on theories from antiquity, especially the idea that the body's four humors, or liquids—blood, phlegm, yellow bile, and black bile—must be balanced through nutrition. All foods were classified according to the humor they were thought to affect, and the diet was adjusted according to what fluid was thought to be lacking (or overabundant).[65] Marsilio Ficino, a fifteenth-century humanist and translator of Plato's works, even argued that the cure for old age was to drink young blood: "Why shouldn't our old people, namely those who have no recourse, likewise suck the blood of youth?" He added that if a person had difficulties digesting raw blood, he or she could add sugar to sweeten it, and derive the same benefits.[66] At the same time, there existed a pervasive idea that Jews consumed Christian blood, not to benefit their health or hasten their conversion, but to harm Christianity.

Problematic ideas about Jews and blood reached their apex in blood libel or ritual murder accusations against Jews that first appeared in England in the thirteenth century and subsequently spread to other areas of Europe.[67] In Italy, the most prominent case was that of Simon of Trent in 1475, which led to the execution of sixteen Jews, and whose story was propagated through art and woodcuts across the peninsula.[68] Simon of Trent's was the most famous but not the only ritual murder case on the peninsula: in the Duchy of Milan alone, for example, accusations were made in 1453, 1458, 1476, 1477, 1481, and 1490. In those accusations, Jews allegedly murdered a Christian boy in order to reenact Christ's suffering and to use the boy's blood to bake Passover matzo. It was a powerful symbolic inversion of the Gospel story. During the last supper, Jesus had offered his body and his blood to his disciples. By literally taking him in, they professed their faith and ensured the survival of his message. However, in ritual murder accusations, Jesus's blood was represented by the boy's body as Jews allegedly tortured him in the same manner as their forefathers tortured Christ. After that, the boy's/Jesus's blood was not drunk but baked in the matzo and ingested by the Jews.

Thus, through torture, murder, and heat, the Jews symbolically destroyed the nourishment that the apostles had received and that had given life to a new religion. Then they ate the fruit of that destruction. In blood libel accusations, the food that the Jews ate was not simply different, strange, or exotic, it was the result of lethal criminal and ungodly activity. And the Jews, who, in reality, went to great lengths to remove all blood from their food, were portrayed not just as bloodthirsty but also as "blood-hungry" killers. Insofar as blood libel accusations turned Jewish food, especially the matzo, into innocent Christian blood, such ideas and beliefs about Jews and blood turned food into a strong barrier between Jews and Christians.

We conclude, then, that what the Jews actually ate—whether it was *mangiare alla giudia* or eating kosher—differed significantly from some Christian beliefs about Jewish food. To a large extent, Renaissance Jews and Christians shared the same food, and most of what is known today as Jewish food has deep roots in local Italian cuisines of the time. They drank the same wine and enjoyed breaking bread together, even if it meant braving the orders of the church. At times, they even participated in each other's rituals. But this reality coexisted with peculiar ideas about Jewish food and its impact on individual Christians' religion and imagined scenarios in which Jews consumed Christian blood. Therefore, food, real and imaginary, acted as both a bridge and a barrier between Jews and Christians.

I would like to thank Hasia Diner and Simone Cinotto for organizing the symposium where this paper was first presented, and for encouraging me to revise it for this volume. I thank Marcie Ferris for reading an early version and the anonymous readers for their helpful comments. I am grateful to the presenters and participants for discussing all manners of Jewish foodways with me, and to Laura Gianetti for pointing me to important new and old sources.

NOTES

1. Peter Scholliers, "Meals, Food Narratives, and Sentiments of Belonging in Past and Present," in *Food, Drink, and Identity: Cooking, Eating, and Drinking in Europe since the Middle Ages*, ed. Peter Scholliers (New York: Berg, 2001), 7–10; Anna Suranyi, "Seventeenth-Century English Travel Literature and the Significance of Foreign Foodways," *Food and Foodways* 14, no. 3–4 (2006): 123–49; Eric Dursteler, "Bad Bread and the Outrageous Drunkenness of the Turks," *Journal of World History* 25, no. 2–3 (2014): 203–28; Eric Dursteler, "Infidel Foods: Food and Identity in Early Modern Ottoman Travel Literature," *Journal of Ottoman Studies* 30 (2012): 143–60.

2. Dursteler, "Bad Bread," 207–8. In particular, it was the classical equation between certain foods as markers of civility and other foods as markers of barbarity that concerned European travelers visiting Ottoman countries.

3. Dursteler, "Bad Bread," 205; Dursteler, "Infidel Foods," 144.

4. Roberto Bonfil, *Jewish Life in Renaissance Italy* (Berkeley: University of California Press, 1994), 243–47; David Freidenreich, *Foreigners and Their Food: Constructing Otherness in Jewish, Christian and Islamic Law* (Berkeley: University of California Press, 2011), 110–28.

5. Freidenreich, *Foreigners and Their Food*, 123–26.

6. Freidenreich, *Foreigners and Their Food*, 21–26.

7. See, for example, the situation in early modern Venice where in spite of the ghetto and an active inquisition, Christians and Jews ate together and Christians even went into the ghetto to sample the food of the Jews. Brian Pullan, *The Jews of Europe and the Inquisition of Venice* (New York: I.B. Tauris, 1997), 147, 162, 164–65.

8. Ariel Toaff, *Love, Work, and Death: Jewish Life in Medieval Umbria* (Oxford: Littman Library of Jewish Civilization, 1996), 5.

9. Bonfil, *Jewish Life in Renaissance Italy*, 71–72, illustrates the swift and wide spread of ghettos with dates: "Venice 1516; Rome 1555; Florence 1572; Siena 1571; Mirandola 1602; Verona 1602; Padua 1603; Mantua 1612; Rovigo 1613; Ferrara 1624; Modena 1638; Urbino, Pesaro, Senigallia 1634; Este 1666; Reggio Emilia 1670; Conegliano Veneto 1675; Turin 1679; Casale Monferrato 1724; Vercelli 1725; Acqui 1713; Moncalvo 1732; Finale 1736; Correggio 1779." For additional scholarship on the ghettos, see Kenneth Stow, "The Consciousness of Closure: Roman Jewry and Its Ghet," in *Essential Papers on Jewish Culture in Renaissance and Baroque Italy*, ed. David Ruderman (New York: New York University Press, 1992), 386–99; Roni Weinstein, "The Jewish Ghetto in Relation to Urban Quarters in Italian Cities during the Early Modern Time—Similarities and Differences," *Zemanim* no. 67 (1999): 12–21; Kenneth R. Stow, *Theater of Acculturation: The Roman Ghetto in the Sixteenth Century* (Seattle: University of Washington Press, 2001); Stefanie B. Siegmund, *The Medici State and the Ghetto of Florence: The Construction of an Early Modern Jewish Community* (Stanford CA: Stanford University Press, 2006); Benjamin Ravid, *Studies on the Jews of Venice, 1392–1797* (Aldershot UK: Ashgate, 2003); Benjamin Ravid, "From Geographical Realia to Historiographical Symbol: The Odyssey of the Word Ghetto," in *Essential Papers on Jewish Culture*, ed. David Ruderman (New York: New York University Press, 1992), 373–85.

10. http://www.ristorantepiperno.it/index.htm.

11. The *New York Times* regularly runs articles on how to prepare the carciofi or where to eat them in Rome. See, for example, http://intransit.blogs.nytimes

.com/2010/03/05/in-season-and-delicious-artichokes-in-rome/ or http://www.nytimes.com/2014/04/09/dining/for-passover-fried-artichokes.html.

12. See the recipe written in the margin of Yoseph Sermonetta's book on Jewish festivals, cited by Ariel Toaff, *Mangiare alla giudia: La cucina ebraica in Italia dal rinascimento all'età moderna* (Bologna, Italy: Il Mulino, 2000), 34: "Artichokes are good when picked during their season, which begins in Rome in the middle of February and lasts throughout June. To make them 'alla giudia' they should be washed and then the tops of the hard leaves should be cut in the shape of a spiral so that the most tender and white parts are left. And then they should be fried in boiling oil in a skillet."

13. http://www.nytimes.com/2011/12/18/travel/its-kosher-in-romes-ghetto.html.

14. http://www.baghetto.com/.

15. Toaff, *Mangiare alla giudia*, 7–21.

16. Bonfil, *Jewish Life in Renaissance Italy*, 1–19. Sometimes the different Jewish communities had conflicting relations. For a discussion and overview on the debates on this, see Bernard D. Cooperman, "Ethnicity and Institution Building among Jews in Early Modern Rome," *AJS Review* 30, no. 1 (2006): 119–45.

17. Gillian Riley, *The Oxford Companion to Italian Food* (New York: Oxford University Press, 2007), 264–65.

18. Toaff, *Mangiare alla giudia*, 26–31. See also Elliott Horowitz, "Remembering the Fish and Making a Tsimmes: Jewish Food, Jewish Identity, and Jewish Memory," *Jewish Quarterly Review* 104, no. 1 (2014): 57–79; Michela Andreatta, "The Taste of Conviviality: A Poem on Food by Leon Modena," *Jewish Quarterly Review* 105, no. 4 (2015): 456–81.

19. Leone Modena, *Historia de gli riti hebraici dove si ha breve, e total relatione di tutta la vita, costumi, riti, et osservanze de gl'hebrei di questi tempi* (Paris, 1637), 48.

20. Cited in Freidenreich, *Foreigners and Their Food*, 191–192.

21. Freidenreich, *Foreigners and Their Food*, 193.

22. Stow writes of kosher butchers and kosher caterers in the ghetto of Rome who provided food not only for individuals and their families, but also for larger receptions. Kenneth Stow, *Theater of Acculturation: The Roman Ghetto in the Sixteenth Century* (Seattle: University of Washington Press, 2001), 11. In the case of Tuscany, see Siegmund, *The Medici State and the Ghetto of Florence*, 161–62, 396–400. Siegmund also argues that it was in fact the ghetto that promoted the creation of communal institutions for the provision and production of food.

23. Bonfil, *Jewish Life in Renaissance Italy*, 71–72, lists the ghettos with their creation dates. See note 9 of this chapter. But this still left much of the peninsula's

smaller cities and towns without ghettos. For scholarly work on the ghettos, see Stow, "The Consciousness of Closure," 386–99; Weinstein, "The Jewish Ghetto in Relation to Urban Quarters," 12–21; Stow, *Theater of Acculturation*; Siegmund, *Medici State and the Ghetto of Florence*; Ravid, *Studies on the Jews of Venice, 1392–1797*; and Ravid, "From Geographical Realia," 373–85.

24. Siegmund, *Medici State and the Ghetto of Florence*, 168.

25. Siegmund, *Medici State and the Ghetto of Florence*, 384–404.

26. Insofar as the ability to procure kosher meat constituted an indication of "Jewish life," the advanced skills required to slaughter cattle limited their availability, but bird-slaughtering abilities may have been more widespread, especially where performed by women. There is some uncertainty on this question: Toaff's assertion that "we may assume that during the late middle ages *every* Jewish family included someone able to slaughter chickens, capons, and pigeons" seems overstated, though on the following page he adds that "the wide dispersal of Jewish communities . . . and the small number of Jewish families in any one place made it difficult for them to maintain their usual customs, and they sometimes had to compromise in order to survive. Butchery was an area requiring just such flexibility." See Toaff, *Love, Work and Death*, 68–69. On the other hand, Stefanie Siegmund points out that the "issuance of licenses by rabbis to kosher-slaughterers was a sixteenth-century innovation." Prior to that, women had long been considered competent to slaughter. Siegmund, *Medici State and the Ghetto of Florence*, 160–61.

27. Archivio di Stato di Genova (ASG), Archivio Segreto 776. Gian Giacomo Musso, "Per la storia degli ebrei in Genova nella seconda metà del cinquecento: Le vicende genovesi di Joseph ha-Cohen," in *Scritti in memoria di Leone Carpi*, eds. Attilio Milano, Alexander Rofe, and Daniel Carpi (Jerusalem: Fondazione Sally Mayer, 1967), 110.

28. ASG, Senarega 509: "Detti hebrei sono tre fratelli Angelo, Lazaro et Anselmo de Nantua che stanno in una medesma casa sono tutti infresca et fano il loro negotio insieme. Stanno qui con molta sodisfatione della terra et masime de poveri. Sono persone quiete et i negotii che loro fanno sono di dua milia scuti. Prestano sopra pegni a dennari seii per libra il mese, et anche meno à persone di Gavi."

29. Anselmo is not mentioned in any documents after the podestà's report of 1578 in ASG, Senarega 509.

30. ASG, Senarega 553: "Gli ha dato un schiaffo da tutto suo potero in facia et fattoli sangue et enfiar un occhio."

31. ASG, Senarega 553: "non portando segno per salvo un poco di lista gialda sotto il braccio."

32. ASG, Coppialettere del Senato 1016.

33. Fifteen pages long, the inventory of their house was exhaustive and very detailed. See ASG, Senarega 553.

34. ASG, Senarega 553.

35. ASG, Senarega 553, fol. 1–3.

36. Patricia Fortini Brown, *Private Lives in Renaissance Venice: Art, Architecture, and the Family* (New Haven CT: Yale University Press, 2005), 71, 111. Whether only women sat on the *da donna* chairs in the Nantua house cannot be inferred from the inventory. The fact that they had more women's than men's chairs (eight versus six) may suggest a preference for these chairs, which were more comfortable.

37. Francoise Piponnier, "From Hearth to Table: Late Medieval Cooking Equipment," *Food: A Culinary History*, eds. Jean-Louis Flandrin and Massimo Montanari, trans. Albert Sonnenfeld (New York: Columbia University Press, 1999), 333; Ken Albala, *The Banquet: Dining in the Great Courts of Late Renaissance Europe* (Urbana: University of Illinois Press, 2007), 1–26.

38. Piponnier, "From Hearth to Table," 333–334.

39. ASG, Senarega 553.

40. Piponnier, "From Hearth to Table," 342–343.

41. Toaff, *Love, Work and Death*, 68–69.

42. Fernand Braudel, *Civilization and Capitalism, 15th-18th Century*, Vol. 1: *The Structure of Everyday Life* (Berkeley: University of California Press, 1992), 190–199; Toaff, *Mangiare alla giudia*, 37.

43. Sally Scully, "Unholy Feast: Carnality and the Venetian Inquisition," *Ateneo Veneto* 196, nos. 8–11 (2009): 84–85.

44. A staio is a bushel in English, or eight gallons. A rub corresponds to twenty-five pounds. See Ronald E. Zupko, *Italian Weights and Measures from the Middle Ages to the Nineteenth Century* (Philadelphia: American Philosophical Society, 1981), 231, 277; and John Florio, *Queen Anna's New World of Words, or Dictionarie of the Italian and English Tongues* (London, 1611).

45. Modena, *Historia de gli riti hebraici*, 49–50.

46. Toaff, *Mangiare alla giudia*, 59–72. For more on the centrality of goose meat, fat, and their association with Jews, see also Horowitz, "Remembering the Fish and Making Tsimmes," 67; Ken Albala, *Food in Early Modern Europe* (Westport CT: Greenwood, 2003), 68. Even Bartolomeo Scappi, Pope Pius V's cook, remarked

in his cookbook published in 1570 that Jewish farmers produced huge goose livers. Bartolomeo Scappi, *L'opera* (Rome, 1570), 113.

47. Toaff, *Mangiare alla giudia*, 59–72.

48. Likewise, when discussing the links between the many small Jewish settlements of Tuscany, Siegmund noted that "The Jews living in Tuscany (but not 'the Jews of Tuscany') may be considered part of a larger Jewish community based on their shared membership in a minority religion, their inevitable consciousness of "sameness" in contrast to the "otherness" of non-Jews." Siegmund, *Medici State and the Ghetto of Florence*, 147.

49. A bar is about seven pints in Genoa in the sixteenth century. See Zupko, *Italian Weights and Measures*, 19.

50. Modena, *Historia de gli riti hebraici*, 47–51.

51. Modena, *Historia de gli riti hebraici*, 51–52.

52. Pullan, *Jews of Europe*.

53. Pullan, *Jews of Europe*, 161.

54. The aggravated status of "Jewish meat" is confirmed by the rhetoric of Christian thinkers from Augustine and Chrysostom in the fourth century to di Castro and Capistran in the fifteenth century. See Freidenreich, *Foreigners and Their Food*, 191–96.

55. Pullan, *Jews of Europe*, 163.

56. Pullan, *Jews of Europe*, 164.

57. Dana E. Katz, *The Jew in the Art of the Italian Renaissance* (Philadelphia: University of Pennsylvania Press, 2008), 41.

58. David Nirenberg, *Communities of Violence: Persecution of Minorities in the Middle Ages* (Princeton NJ: Princeton University Press, 1996), 208.

59. Nirenberg, *Communities of Violence*, 214–21.

60. Efrat Tseëlon, *Masquerade and Identities: Essays on Gender, Sexuality and Marginality* (New York: Routledge, 2001), 28–29; Peter Stallybras and Allon White, *The Politics and Poetics of Transgression* (Ithaca NY: Cornell University Press, 1986), 53–55.

61. Katz, *The Jew in the Art of the Italian Renaissance*, 56–68.

62. Dursteler, *Food and Identity*, 144.

63. See, for example, the fine for "mixing with Christians" paid by Davide de Savigliano: Archivio di Stato di Torino (AST), Conti delle Castellanie, art. 2, mazzo 16, rot. 84, pec. 19. Or the one paid by Bellavinea of Geneva for eating in Rivoli without wearing the yellow badge: AST, Conti delle Castellanie, art. 65, mazzo 26, rot. 125, pec. 15.

64. For more on the symbolism of blood in Jewish and Christian discourse, see David Biale, *Blood and Belief: The Circulation of a Symbol Between Jews and Christians* (Berkeley: University of California Press, 2007).

65. Ken Albala, *Eating Right in the Renaissance* (Berkeley: University of California Press, 2002), 14–48.

66. Brian Jeffrey Maxson, *The Humanist World of Renaissance Florence* (New York: Cambridge University Press, 2014), 27.

67. Gavin I. Langmuir, "The Knight's Tale of Young Hugh of Lincoln," *Speculum* 47, no. 3 (1972): 459–82; Gavin I. Langmuir, "Thomas of Monmouth: Detector of Ritual Murder," *Speculum* 59, no. 4 (1984): 820–46.

68. R. Po-chia Hsia, *Trent 1475: Stories of a Ritual Murder Trial* (New Haven CT: Yale University Press, 1996) and the completely discredited Ariel Toaff, *Pasqua di sangue: Ebrei d'Europa e omicidi rituali* (Bologna, Italy: Il Mulino, 2007). For more on the artistic propagation of the Trent myth, see Katz, *The Jew in the Art of the Italian Renaissance*, 119–147. Blood libel accusations continued to be leveled against Jews in Italy in the sixteenth century as well. See Robert Bonfil, "The Historian's Perception of the Jews in the Italian Renaissance: Towards a Reappraisal," *Revue des Études Juives* no. 143 (1984): 59–82.

2

Global Jewish Peddling and the Matter of Food

HASIA R. DINER

Historians and other writers who have contemplated the experience of Jews in the American West in the nineteenth century have repeatedly told a story, one which they believe says much about the idea of Jews in strange places. The story, unverifiable, although its appearance in a number of memoirs gives it an air of authenticity, tells the tale of a Jewish peddler. A young man, like millions of his peers, joined in the great migration of the Jewish people, a movement which changed the profile of world Jewry. Like so many of the men, he decided that his chances for economic success depended upon his willingness to put a pack on his back and head out to the hinterlands to sell consumer goods to customers with limited access to the marketplace. He, like they, went anywhere and everywhere that people in need of material goods welcomed the arrival into their home of someone willing to bring it. Most began their careers selling by foot, graduating eventually to an animal-drawn wagon. Wherever they went they depended directly on the good will of their customers to buy the items they carried, and also to lodge them at night and to feed them.

In this narrative, one which has entered into the realm of American Jewish folklore, the peddler, a regular itinerant merchant who sold among the Cherokee Indians in Oklahoma, had been offered something to eat by his hospitable customers. Despite his hunger and after his long hours on the road, he refused to partake of the food offered to him by his customers. The food violated the Jewish dietary laws. It consisted of forbidden ingredients and had been prepared in vessels tainted by the *treife*, or impure, foods that had been cooked in them. But he did accept one item. He consumed an egg cooked in its shell. The egg conformed to the rules of kashrut; and the fact that it had never directly touched an unkosher pot—protected as it was by its hard shell—meant that the Jewish peddler could consume it. So commonly did this act of eating take place, that the story, repeated in works of history and memoir, in jokes and in theatrical renditions, went on to declare that some of the Cherokee therefore referred to all Jews, regardless of occupation or levels of religious observance, as "egg eaters."[1]

This small anecdote, whether true or not, contains within it a universe of meaning in terms of the history of Jewish migrations, Jewish occupations, Judaism as a religious system, and the role of food. In the long nineteenth century, from the end of the eighteenth into the early twentieth, millions of Jews left their places of long-term residence—Europe, the Ottoman Empire, and North Africa—and set out to a variety of new lands. Those lands stretched from the Americas to southern Africa to Oceania, taking Jews mostly to the United States but also Cuba, Mexico, Peru, South Africa, and Australia, as well as to regions of Europe like Ireland, Sweden, Wales, and Scotland, which had never had a Jewish population before.

They left for a combination of mainly economic reasons but also in order to address their anomalous status in the Christian and Muslim lands where Jews had lived for centuries. Their economic motivations reflected both crises in the lands they had lived in and the opening up of new opportunities in the lands to which they went. Most of those prospects, born of the age of colonialism, European expansion, and the

spread of consumer capitalism, involved commerce. As a broad gener-
alization, the period of Jewish on-the-road peddling in these new lands
coincided with the rise of new economic realities that put small amounts
of cash in the hands of people who had previously lived without it. With
that cash, these women and men could buy items that they had never
had before. They could afford to augment their material lives with a
variety of consumer goods that either had not existed before or which
the better-off and urban people had enjoyed. Such items as eyeglasses
and bed linens, pictures and picture frames, buttons, needles, thread, and
tablecloths could be had by ever-expanding populations of customers,
in remote places, and the Jewish immigrant men who took to the road
served as the middlemen between these neophyte consumers and the
stuff produced in the cities.

The massive transfer of Jewish people, a migration of over four million
throughout the nineteenth century, pivoted around peddling, an occupation that Jews knew and which reflected internal credit networks. While
each of the places from which Jews left and each of the places to which
they went had a separate and unique history, young men willing to peddle made up the majority of those who went, particularly in the earlier
stages of the migration. For example, the majority of Jewish men who
migrated to Lithuania at the end of the nineteenth century started out as
peddlers, known there as "weekly men." The bulk of Macedonian Jews,
men mostly from the town of Monastir, who went to the Amazon region,
began their careers there as peddlers. So, too, the Bavarian Jews—all
males, who fanned out across the United States in the 1830s and 1840s—
got launched through peddling.[2]

The history of Jewish migration cannot be disassociated from the
history of peddling, and the history of Jewish peddling cannot be understood without the matter of food. Peddlers, these Jewish men who in the
main hailed from traditional backgrounds, had to negotiate food as they
set off on their roads, and as a concern it shaped how they related to their
customers and also how it bound them to the Jews who already lived
in these places and provided the new peddlers with goods and credit.

JEWISH FOOD BEFORE THE GREAT MIGRATION

Food vexed and challenged the millions of Jewish men on the roads of these new lands in ways that it had not in their long history of peddling before the great migration. Extending backward into the Middle Ages and encompassing nearly the entire world, as known at the time, Jews engaged in the retail sale of wares from packs on their backs or from animal-driven carts. They sold to Jews and non-Jews. Both Jewish women and men developed their routes, forged relationships with customers, helped stimulate desire for new goods, and served as fixtures of many local economies. In some regions and towns peddlers outnumbered non-peddlers in the Jewish community, and the clustering of Jews in this one occupational group affected nearly all aspects of the Jewish experience.

Numbers varied from place to place and changed over time. They also could be elusive in that the peddlers came in and out of towns and regions, and many individuals peddled at some point or another in their lifetimes. But just a few samplings of efforts at counting peddlers in premigration Europe demonstrate the significance of peddling to Jewish history. In 1863 one writer for the French Jewish newspaper *L'Univers Israélite* remarked, looking backward to an earlier era, that "during the First Empire peddling was the chief occupation of Jews. Thus according to the census of 1808, 20 of approximately 26 Jewish families of Fontainebleau were so engaged: in Versailles, Orléans, and Nantes all the Jews were peddlers." In Württemberg in 1812, no fewer than 85.5 percent of the Jews made a living as "hucksters," and a study of Polish Jewry in the nineteenth century stated quite simply, "A majority of the Jewish population in Poland made their living in trade, but this principally meant peddled trade rather than retail." It may not be at all outrageous to suggest that every European Jew would have known ped-dlers, as family members, neighbors, and real presences in the ordinary course of everyday life.[3]

Notably, Jewish peddling in Europe had been different vis-à-vis its practice and its relationship to food. Jewish communities in the pre-modern and premigration settings, for example, made certain that either individual Jews or the community as a whole provided food and lodging for the Jewish peddlers. Fulfilling the fundamental religious obligation of *hachnassatorchim*, or the welcoming of visitors, took on particular salience in an environment in which vast numbers of Jews walked the roads selling goods and found themselves in need of places to eat and sleep.

The existence of hundreds of scattered Jewish communities, in relative proximity to each other, also meant that these peddlers in the Germanic states of Poland, Alsace, and elsewhere on the continent, as well in the vast stretches of the Ottoman Empire, did not have to return home every week for the Sabbath. Since they could avail themselves of Sabbath services, and Sabbath food in the towns along their route, they could traverse large regions and return home just a few times a year. They spent the weekly Sabbath and the many Jewish holidays away from their own families but still basked in the comfort of Jewish homes, resting, praying, and consuming the food items associated with the holy days. In fact Jewish peddling in Europe exposed relatively humble Jews to the foodways of Jews in towns and regions beyond their familiar ones.

But even on ordinary days, the Jews who sold goods along the roads of the premigration world had to deal with the issue of food. For the most part, these poor and generally traditional men maintained the dietary laws. They had to eat kosher food, and geographic and demographic patterns made that possible. As they plied their routes, they could depend upon Jews in the small towns to feed them and know that the food that they put in their bodies conformed to the strictures of halakhah, or Jewish law.

Particularly in some of the most important places from which Jewish peddlers left—Bavaria, Alsace, Lithuania—most Jews lived in small enclaves, scattered throughout the countryside. The existence of these little clusters meant that the Jewish peddler could always avail himself of the obligatory hospitality of the community by which the peddlers would be fed and lodged and as such dependent neither on their own wits or of their non-Jewish customers. The string of small communities, the nodes of Jewish life along their routes, meant that kashrut did not have to be negotiated, compromised, violated, or, if observed, done so with great effort and difficulty. The ability of premigration Jewish peddlers to adhere to their dietary code benefitted also from the close relationship that existed between Jews and non-Jews, neighbors for centuries.

In European and Ottoman settings, Jewish peddling played a crucial role in forging relationships between Jews and non-Jews, and these relationships existed in environments where Jews had lived for centuries. Non-Jews—whether French or German speakers, Polish, Lithuanian, Hungarian, Czech, or Arabic—knew Jews, after long eras of exposure. Jewish peddlers and their non-Jewish customers spoke the same languages, and evidence exists that the customers in many places incorporated Jewish words, particularly Yiddish, Ladino, and Judeo-Arabic, into their own lexicons as they interacted with the Jewish peddlers. Jews had been in their midst for so long that the non-Jews, Christian or Muslim, knew the intricacies of the Jewish calendar and, importantly here, they knew what Jews ate and what they could not. We learn from a variety of sources that at times Jewish peddlers did spend the night in Christian homes or in inns catering to many different kinds of wayfarers. The Jewish peddlers, as it were, taught their Christian customers something about Judaism.

Given the ubiquity of the Jewish peddlers and the familiarity non-Jews had with Jewish customs, inn keepers, non-Jews, allowed Jewish peddlers to store their cooking pots at the inns. The Jewish peddlers often impressed their marks on their own utensils so that they could be kept safely and away from contamination from non-kosher foodstuffs. Every time they returned to that establishment, they had access to the cooking vessels and could prepare food for themselves. In a family reminiscence of the peddling experience in the early nineteenth century, in Rhein-bischofsheim, a small town in Germany, Moses Kahnmann's grandson recalled his grandfather describing how he "occasionally might find in a village inn or with a friendly peasant a pan especially marked with the sign of kashrut, for the exclusive use of Jewish guests," the majority of whom came as peddlers. Others, both in personal memoirs and in historical studies, observed that "the pedlars stayed overnight with peasant acquaintances with whom they left their own kosher crockery for repeated uses." Peasant meant non-Jew, and such respectful behaviors demonstrated the possibility of Jewish-Christian amity in an otherwise hostile environment and underscored the significance of the peddlers as historical actors.[4]

In the largest sense, despite all of the many difficulties and hostility they faced from the non-Jews, particularly state officials who set up onerous restrictions on where the Jews could go and imposed steep taxes on them, as well as the poverty which most endured, they did not have to worry about food.

PEDDLING AND MIGRATION

The act of leave-taking pivoted in a number of ways around the peddling phenomenon. Notably, Jewish peddlers in their new lands may not themselves have ever peddled before their migrations. Many came from the ranks of young men unable to find a place for themselves in the local economies of the regions where they had grown up. Migration offered them a way of establishing themselves as adults. They may have been too young to have ever peddled themselves, but when they needed to find a means of migration and a means of making a living in their new homes, they turned to what they knew. After all, they would have known in their immediate families and in their villages many peddlers whose experiences and skills the potential migrant drew upon. In addition, these young Jewish emigrants abandoned precisely those places where intense competition from other Jews in the field of peddling had made it impossible for them, as young people, to get started with their lives. Finally, the young men poised to emigrate by taking up the peddlers' pack, departed from towns and regions that no longer needed peddlers because new commercial realities undercut the peddlers' —and the Jews' —longstanding modes of making a living.

Instead these young men began a process of moving outward,

discovering as Jews a number of new worlds, and peddling, the old familiar economic modus operandi of the Jews, structured that linked physical movement and the process of discovery. This new age of Jewish peddling took Jews out of continental Europe and brought them over the course of the next two-and-a-half centuries to no fewer spots around the globe than the British Isles, the Americas—North, South, and Central—South Africa, and Australia.[5]

In each one of these places, and the many specific regions within them, peddlers as the first Jews, and sometimes the first white people, penetrated these unknown spaces. In various lands the activities of the peddlers cleared the ground for the eventual formation of settled Jewish communities, while in others the peddlers—and the Jewish presence—disappeared leaving few traces.

The history of Jewish peddling in each new location has a history of its own. Each one stands as worthy of analysis. Jewish peddling in South and Central America followed a particular course no doubt different from that of Jewish peddling in South Africa or Canada. Furthermore, within any one of these continents or countries, local variations also made for many different histories of Jewish peddling and Jewish migration. For example, Jewish peddlers in Quebec, who sold to French-speaking Catholic customers who may have evinced hostility toward the idea of Canada as a modern, liberal, and British-oriented nation, had a particular set of experiences that diverged from those of Jewish peddlers who cast their lot in the Anglophone provinces—where Protestantism predominated and most women and men embraced their connections to Great Britain and its economic and political practices. Likewise in South Africa, Jewish peddlers sold at one time or another to the Afrikaner Boers and British, as well as to native customers, who had been colonized by both previously named groups.

Each constituency had a different set of reactions to the peddlers as Jews, immigrants primarily from Lithuania, and bearers of consumer goods. Each history needs to be explored and each stands on its own. Young Jewish men who showed up in the American South to peddle their wares found a particular racial landscape, one in which the black-white divide created a set of social practices not replicated in New England or upstate New York, where differences of class rather than color structured political relationships, which the peddlers had to know about and deal with. Further west, the presence of Indians and Mexicans as customers forced Jewish peddlers fresh from Posen or Lithuania to confront yet another set of on-the-ground realities as they sought to accomplish the goals of the migration: earn money, settle down, marry, or bring wives and children left behind in either Europe or some other large city, and get on with life.

Yet certain characteristics have been shared by all of these Jewish peddling histories, regardless of continent or country, and food made an appearance as an issue in all of these places. First, unlike peddling on the European continent, the immigrant peddlers sold only to non-Jews. This perhaps obvious point had tremendous historical significance, not just for the peddlers themselves but for the development of Jewish communities in these places. The young Jewish man who decided to leave Alsace or Lithuania—two important senders of Jewish migrant-peddlers—and try his luck in the Mississippi Delta, the Pacific Northwest, as well as the Transvaal, the Australian outback, the Argentine Pampas, the Irish midlands, the mining regions of Wales, or the foothills of the Andes, had no string of Jewish enclaves to turn to when the day ended, when the sun set on Friday, or when Jewish holidays punctuated the calendar.

Instead, these peddlers spent the days of the week only among non-Jews, depending upon their customers for a place to sleep and eat before setting out again on the road. Since Jewish peddlers divided up the countryside among themselves, no one encroaching upon another's territory, they lived pretty much devoid of contact with other Jews. This reality reflected the fact that the first of the peddlers, as pioneers, went to places where no Jew had been before. Those who immigrated later and entered the field took the place of the Jewish peddlers who had amassed enough savings to be able to own their shops in town. While the later peddlers sold to non-Jews who had already become acquainted with Jews, they still did not share the road or their weekday time with other Jews, and the newcomer peddlers, like their predecessors, spent days on end with no other Jews around him. After all, they spent the entire week, save the Sabbath, with non-Jews who had never had contact with Jews before.

This then meant that Jewish peddlers in their new lands, unlike their counterparts back home, did not travel as far and chose to organize their selling lives in such a way as to be able to get back to Jewish enclaves for the Sabbath. The life histories of many of these immigrant peddlers repeatedly noted that their lives marched according to a kind of weekly rhythm. They went out on their routes on Sundays and returned by Friday to whatever existed in the way of a Jewish hub for the Sabbath where they encountered Jewish food, fellowship, and rest.

Joseph Jacob, in his 1919 apologetic defense of the Jewish people, *The Jewish Contribution to Civilization*, described how in England—which in terms of Jewish migration history must be thought of as a "new world"— "it was customary for the Jews of the seaport towns . . . to send out their sons every Monday morning to neighboring villages as hawkers, who would return in time for the Friday night meal." These hawkers, the British word of choice for peddlers, came to be known within the Jewish community as "Wochers," that is, "weekly people."[6] In Ireland, to which several thousand Lithuanian Jews immigrated after the 1880s and where nearly all the men peddled at one time or another, Jews described themselves and were described by their customers as "weekly men," the ones who showed up week after week at the farmhouse doors, ready to collect payment for previously purchased goods and to show the woman of the home some new "things" to buy.[7] Throughout Spanish-speaking South and Central America, local people referred to the Jewish peddlers, whether Ashkenazim from Europe or Sephardim from the Ottoman Empire, as "semananiks," that is, weeklies. In Mississippi, as in many Southern Jewish communities, former peddlers, turned shopkeepers, provided the space for those still on the road needing a Sabbath resting place. In Natchez, the Millstein's house became the place where "many of the peddlers who came home . . . after a week's work would gather . . . for the Sabbath."[8] Simon Wolf recalled that "twenty or thirty Jewish peddlers," gathered at his mid-nineteenth-century home in Uhrichsville, Ohio, every Sabbath and that his aunt provided them with food during their weekly sojourns off the road.[9]

In other places around the Jewish peddlers' new lands, Jewish women opened up boarding houses, which served the men during the weekends when they came back to town. In the towns, peddlers not only got their chance to rest and eat home-cooked meals, prepared by Jewish women, but they also transacted business. Here they paid back the wholesalers from whom they had gotten their goods and then filled up their packs so that they could go back out onto the road.

Many of the small towns to which the peddlers went on the weekend themselves lacked facilities for kosher food. They had no ritual slaughterers, for example, and as such the peddlers who came for the Sabbath could not always get the kind of food that would have been the norm before migration. The story of Abraham Kohn, a pious young man, provides a case in point. Despite his commitment to Judaism, a theme which runs through his superb diary written in the 1840s, he spent a year peddling in western Massachusetts and then pursued the same occupation in Illinois. By the middle of that decade he had opened a store in frontier Chicago and joined together with a group of other Jewish men, all Bavarian Jews, who either had peddled, or still did so, in the founding of the village's first Jewish congregation and its first cemetery. In those early Chicago years they lived without access to kosher food. That is, these men, all of whom had spent some amount of time peddling in America, once settled down began to create the infrastructure of Jewish life. But they did not have kosher food. Only five years later, after the founding of the synagogue, when Kohn's more observant mother, Delia, arrived from Bavaria and refused to eat anything other than vegetables, did a kosher slaughterer get brought to Chicago, and it became possible to eat kosher food.[10]

For Jews, particularly those who ventured out to places with no Jews, this ubiquitous weekly cycle elevated food to a serious matter as they had to figure out how to organize their time and, even more so, had to decide on their own if the dietary laws mattered or not. It should be kept in mind that most of the Jewish immigrants of this era, whether male or female, came from traditional homes and communities; and while it is not possible to say with certainty whether all of them had formerly observed the law in a punctilious manner, these migrations, for the most part, began just at the onset of modernization and before Jews embarked on a process of rethinking what the dietary system meant and why they did not have to follow it. That is, the typical immigrant Jewish peddler, regardless of where he had come from, had before migration lived a life based on this system, which divided the world into the ritually edible and inedible. Kashrut had enveloped their lives. It had required a communal structure to supervise, certify, and make possible eating the acceptable.

It required trust and a system to enforce it that did not exist in their new homeland. Rather, as nonspeakers of the dominant language, newly arrived peddlers received detailed instructions as to how to begin their careers on the road. The seasoned Jews of Cuba, Chile, Canada, Ireland, Ohio, Alabama—wherever—would write out in Yiddish characters a variety of stock phrases for the newcomer. Among them they included variants on the question, "May I lodge in your home?"

The memoirs we have, the scraps of information which detail the day-to-day lives of the peddlers, point to a range of strategies to deal with the food problem.

Certainly some did not fret the details of kashrut. They ate what they could and may not have worried about it at all, but given the class level of most of the peddlers, it is reasonable to assume that many came from fairly traditional backgrounds and were relatively unaffected by the secularization of the Jews going on in the cities of Europe. As such their journeys on the road and into the kitchens of their customers likely offered their first encounters with "treife" and the first challenges to their own standards of observance, something that was—prior to migration—relatively unselfconscious, based on customary and familiar behavior and not ideology.

These first encounters may have played a role in loosening the bonds that tied Jews in their new countries to the formal and structural constraints of Judaism. Here they found themselves in new, alien, and utterly "un-Jewish" places, which forced them, or possibly allowed some, to decide for themselves what they wanted to do as Jews.

That is, living by themselves amid non-Jews, five days out of seven, forced them to decide on their own what to eat, and what not to eat, what constituted an obligation positively embraced or a burden which the past had imposed upon them and which they not could loosen. Either way, the decision to eat or not eat, like so many other details of Jewish life and law, now lay in their hands. Distances in time and space meant that no one could supervise what they ate.

This led many to create a new reality for observing kashrut. During the week, while out on the road, they would eat what they wanted or what they could find. On the weekend, however, when they returned to the nearest Jewish communities—where they paid back their creditors, replenished their packs, and rested—they also got the chance to eat among other Jews, and this often meant that they could eat kosher.

As such it is clear that some of these peddlers observed what we might call situational kashrut. That is, during the week as they walked the road, or rode on their horse-drawn wagons, they ate whatever came their way. If their customer who provided lodging and fare offered pork, then they ate pork; if they offered squirrel or other animals that had been hunted, they ate that. But on the weekends, when the peddlers got off the road and "rested," spending Friday night through Sunday in some kind of Jewish setting, they did eat those foods for which both tastes and modes of preparation were familiar and acceptable. Thus Monday through Friday was anything; Friday through Sunday was kosher.

Accounts of peddler-customer interactions also depict how the customers asked the peddlers about their lives back home, places they may never have heard of, like Lithuania or Alsace or Bohemia. One peddler's memoir from Georgia told how Mr. Bedford, an American farmer, questioned Mr. Yampolsky about himself and his life. Besides asking Yampolsky to write out his name, since Bedford had never heard it before, he asked the peddler "Where did [you] come from? . . . What kind of country? . . . What kind of city?"

Mr. Bedford had yet another question to ask, one which got asked nearly everywhere around the peddler's globe. He wanted to know, "What was [Yampolsky's] religion? . . . Why didn't Jews believe in Jesus Christ?" The fact of the Jews' Jewishness surfaced repeatedly. As a matter of discussion it often began over the matter of food. The wife, who had allowed the peddler to sleep over, or her husband, often times then invited the peddler eat with them as well. For the peddler this proved to be no simple matter. While some peddlers in their narratives admitted that after a day on the road, lugging a huge backpack, they would willingly eat anything, even if they preferred to observe the dietary laws, others stated categorically that they did not care about those strictures, the system of kashrut, and did not have to justify to themselves their violation.

But most of the peddlers, among that small minority whose thoughts have been recorded in some form or another, felt compelled to announce to their generous hosts that they could not eat the food. From the point of view of the customers, certainly the first time they had a Jewish peddler in their home, this seemed astounding. Why would anyone turn down pork or ham or whatever food the family put on its table? This then led them to ask the peddler why he would not eat the food that everyone else in the family would consume, and the peddler had to answer basically that his religion would not allow it. Housewives, who seemed to have liked accommodating the peddlers, would then set aside a pot for the peddler's use whenever he came. A memoir of Jewish peddling in New Zealand told the story of a peddler who, in 1863, came to a small town and faced a breakfast of ham and eggs. The peddler, eager for a sale but averse to eating the forbidden food, had to figure out a way to do nothing that seemed impolite but yet refrain from consuming the food on the plate in front of him. When his hostess left the room, "he threw [the unkosher food] into the fire. In an instant it blazed and set fire in the chimney and there was great consternation." Unfortunately the memoirist did not describe his hosts' reaction to the fire or if he had to confess what he had done.[11]

Many memoirists report that rather than being offended by the peddlers' unwillingness to eat their foods, families most often respected the Jews' religious integrity. Certainly in the United States, the most important peddler destination, a strong strain of religiosity pervaded civic life. Since the 1830s, and the famous visit to the United States of Alexis de Tocqueville, observers have noted that Americans view religion as a benign force that promotes virtue. At least as embodied in the memoirs of the peddlers and in some of the customers, the Jews' observance of the dictates of their religion won kudos from the Americans. Rather than finding fault with Judaism as a religion that had rejected Jesus and his divinity, the peddlers' customers found the practice of Judaism in their homes something positively good.

The father of Leon Schwarz came to peddle in Alabama in the post–Civil War period and on one occasion, according to family lore, he "sat down to eat in a farm house and was served pot-liquor, fried bacon and some greens served with side meat." The elder Schwarz, either because he did not care or was just very hungry "pitched in and ate heartily." His hostess, surprised at Schwarz's willingness to consume all the forbidden food, interrogated him. "Mr. Schwarz, I am surprised to see you eat pork. I thought Moses ordered the Jews not to eat any hog meat." As the story went, the peddler surveying the table and seeing nothing but pork, replied, "Ah, madam, if Moses had travelled through Perry County, Alabama, he would never have issued such an order."[12]

Most immigrant peddlers seem, however, to have gone to great lengths to adhere to the restrictions. They ate only what they could carry in their packs. They supplemented with vegetables, fruits, and the like that they knew to fit the dictates of the system. The memoirs detail the ways in which peddlers attempted to observe kashrut as best they could. Never particularly well educated or knowledgeable Judaically, they believed that they knew what was demanded of them and did what they could to adhere to a standard that seemed to them "natural" and inherent to their Jewishness. Memoirs abound with narratives of peddlers who, at fortunate times, had a favorite customer with whom they could lodge on a weekly basis, staying every Monday with the same family, every Tuesday, and so on. Most of these customers were in fact women, and they typically designated a special pot for the peddler to use. Either she cooked his acceptable foods for him in that pot, or he, the peddler, did that cooking himself.

This fairly mundane fact offers an interesting window into the potential significance of peddling for the history of Jewish integration. A customer, in Cuba, in Ireland, in Quebec and the Maritime Provinces of Canada, in the American South or West or New England, in South Africa, wherever they might be, developed a relationship, based on the transaction of commerce, with a Jewish peddler and that peddler stayed over one night every week on his route, known in the Jewish peddlers' lexicon as his *medinah*, or kingdom.

Why, the customers asked, can you not eat the same food that we are eating? Why can you, the peddler, not share from the pot, the dishes, or the cutlery that the family is using? This question, repeated in English, French, Spanish, Mayan, Afrikaans, and Cherokee, forced the peddler to say something about the nature of Judaism. Judaism, they would have to say in their stumbling version of those same languages, does not allow us to eat pork, squirrel, rabbit, or the flesh of other forbidden animals. It does not allow us to eat meat that has not been slaughtered in a very particular way, with particular equipment. We cannot consume meat and dairy products at the same time and in less than a set number of hours apart. Our religion does not let us eat food that has been prepared in pots and off plates that may once have had forbidden foods on them, and the like.

Such answers, so fundamental to the Jewish system and so familiar to the non-Jewish customers of the European continent, must on the surface and at first blush have seemed utterly absurd to people whose religion did not require them to eschew particular foods, did not define the universe of food stuffs into the forbidden and the acceptable, from a religious point of view. They would certainly know these categories from an aesthetic or cultural perspective, but not from the point of view of religious truth.

What the peddlers did, then, by explaining what they could or could not eat, involved explicating the laws of kashrut, and in the process the nature of Judaism. He, through his food practices, served as a kind of interpreter of Judaism to people who never before had known any Jews. He exposed his customers to the inner life of a religious tradition they did not know, or if they knew it, they knew it only as something from the pages of the Hebrew Bible and not as something lived by real people.

In the matter of food, the peddler helped shape the process of Jewish integration into all the various destination lands of the great Jewish migration of the long nineteenth century. In all of these places, Jewish men came to enjoy right away, or over time, a thick bundle of rights, equal to those of the other white men. Having slept in their customers' homes, having eaten at their tables, or having explained to their customers why they would not share their customers' foods, opened the door to familiarity and common citizenship.

Additionally, the fact that Jewish peddlers decided on their own, each man on his own terms, how to handle the food problem tells us something about the kinds of Judaisms that emerged in these new places, the most significant of which—the United States—became the breeding ground for religious innovation. The Judaic system does not give much room to individual negotiation, to individuals deciding what to do, or how and when to do it. It gives them a "set table." Yet our immigrant Jewish peddlers when on the road, and off, considered themselves both obliged and able to rethink the nature of Jewish practice. What, they asked themselves, was essential? To what degree did living as a

Jew require observing the dietary laws in a meticulous fashion? How important was not sitting down and eating with a non-Jew? Eating from their pots? Sharing their food?

If in the months and years on the road peddlers, each on his own, decided that it was acceptable to, at times, or in fact all the time, compromise with kashrut, then what got eaten became a matter of choice not obligation. Time on the road peddling in strange new lands empowered them to tinker with tradition, and each individual behaved as he saw fit. His decisions involved a high degree of personal choice and each one, by himself, had to go beyond the commandments as laid out in normative texts inherited from the past. Personal choice and the ability of individuals to mold Judaism as they saw fit became one of the hallmarks, surely, of American Judaism. And we can see, too, how the peddling experience, as it was played out in the realm of food, helped pave the way for a series of religious innovations that characterized the kind of religious life emerging among Jews in the United States, the single largest receiver of Jewish immigrants, with peddlers accounting for so many.

The history of every Jewish population center to which European Jews migrated—including the United States, Canada, England and the rest of the British Isles, South Africa, Australia, Mexico, Argentina, and elsewhere in South and Central America—cannot be disassociated from the global history of peddling. Common themes, common processes, and common concerns linked these places and made the history of any one place not all that different from the basic contours of another.

These universals or commonalities connected the experience of being a Jewish peddler at the tip of the Cape of Good Hope with the experience of being a Jewish peddler in, say, Newfoundland, or the tip of Cape Horn with that of Alaska. Yet local stories of Jewish migration and Jewish peddling also deserve to be told in order to enrich and complicate modern Jewish history. In each place the local contours of attitudes toward consumption, allocations of power, distribution of resources, basic religious, ethnic, and racial cleavages in the society, as well as ideas about foreigners, shaped the ways in which Jewish peddlers as immigrants and Jewish immigrants as peddlers made their way.

The long nineteenth century witnessed a Jewish migration of transformative impact, changing the face of world Jewry. Peddling spearheaded that migration, paving the way for the Jewish penetration into so many new lands and regions. Peddling, the experience of being out on the road, day in and day out, made food a central concern for the young immigrant Jewish men who willingly went out onto so many roads, taking them far away from places where they could get kosher food. Without their willingness to go and to negotiate food, the migrations would not have happened. Food functioned as a powerful element in this history as both a matter of personal crisis and choice.

NOTES

1. Mel Marks, *Jews Among Indians: Tales of Adventure and Conflict in the Old West* (Chicago: Benison Books, 1992).

2. For a fuller discussion, see Hasia R. Diner, *Roads Taken: The Great Jewish Migration to the New World and the Peddlers Who Forged the Way* (New Haven: Yale University Press, 2015).

3. Quoted in Zosa Szajkowski, "The Growth of the Jewish Population in France," *Jewish Social Studies* 8 (1946): 307; David S. Landes, "The Jewish Merchant: Typology and Stereotypology in Germany," *Yearbook Leo Baeck Institute* 9 (1974): 13; Anna Maria Orla-Bukowska, "Shtetl Communities: Another Image," *Polin: Studies in Polish Jewry* 8 (1994): 94.

4. Werner J. Cahnman, "Village and Small-Town Jews in Germany: A Typological Study," *Yearbook of the Leo Baeck Institute* 19 (1974): 112–14, 121. For other references, see Mordecai Kossover, "Inland Trade among Polish Jews in the Sixteenth–Seventeenth Centuries," *Yivo Bletter* 15, no. 3 (1940): 182. One of the best sources on Alsatian Jewish peddling is Daniel Stauben, *Scenes of Jewish Life in Alsace* (London: Joseph Simon, 1979), which originally had been published in the *Revue des Deux Mondes* in the late 1850s.

5. For the purposes of thinking about Jewish migration and peddling from the end of the eighteenth century onward, the Netherlands, despite being Continental European, functioned as a new world setting. From the beginning of the eighteenth century, German, Bohemian, and Polish Jews came to the

Netherlands to hawk their goods in towns, many of which did not allow Jews to reside there. Referred to as *smous*, a somewhat pejorative term, Ashkenazi Jews invoked the ire of merchants in Leiden and a number of other cities for their ability to sell goods door-to-door at low prices. For Jewish migrant peddling in the Netherlands, see several articles in J.C.H. Blom, R.G. Fuks-Mansfled, and I. Schöffer, *The History of the Jews in the Netherlands* (Portland: Litman Library of Jewish Civilization, 2002), 114, 117, 167, 227.

6. Joseph Jacob, *Jewish Contributions to Civilization* (Philadelphia: Jewish Publication Society, 1919), 219.

7. On Jewish peddling in Ireland and the use of the term "weekly men," see Louis Hyman, *The Jews of Ireland: From Earliest Times to the Year 1910* (London: Jewish Historical Society of England, 1972), 160–66.

8. Leo E. Turitz and Evelyn Turitz, *Jews in Early Mississippi* (Jackson: University Press of Mississippi, 1983), 26.

9. Cited in Esther Panitz, *Simon Wolf: Private Conscience and Public Image* (Rutherford NJ: Farleigh-Dickinson University Press, 1987), 19.

10. Hyman Meites, *History of the Jews of Chicago* (Chicago: Chicago Jewish Historical Society, 1924), 114–116.

11. Eliot R. Davis, *A Link with the Past* (Auckland, New Zealand: Unity Press, 1948), 18.

12. Abraham Peck, "That Other 'Peculiar Institution': Jews and Judaism in the Nineteenth-Century South," *Modern Judaism* 7, no. 1 (1987): 99–114 (106).

3

Jews among Muslims

Culinary Contexts

....

NANCY E. BERG

At the corner of the street, from a sidewalk stall, came the smell of fresh dough and of angel hair being fried on top of a large copper stand—a common sight throughout the city every Ramadan. People would fold the pancakes and stuff them with almonds, syrup and raisins. The vendor caught me eyeing the cakes that were neatly spread on a black tray. He smiled and said, "Etfaddal, help yourself." . . . The Egyptian didn't want any money. "It's for you," he said, handing me the delicacy on a torn sheet of newspaper.
—ANDRE ACIMAN, *Out of Egypt*

Early each morning, the woman who sold *geymar*, cream skimmed from buffalo's milk, would compare her fresh snowy wares to the soft untouched skin of the beloved. *Tekki a sham*, black mulberry, tasted like the forbidden lips of the desired one. *Semit* rings, pretzels, were the engagement rings the wooer dreamed of sliding onto her fingers, while onions hid sad secrets as tearful as her heart.
—MONA YAHIA, *When the Grey Beetles Took Over Baghdad*

This chapter investigates how Mizraḥi Jewish foodways—especially the customs of culinary production and consumption—reflect and foster relationships within the Jewish community and between Jews and their Arab neighbors. While there are variations among the different communities, the Mizraḥi Jewish kitchen tends to be closer to that of its non-Jewish neighbors: the cuisine it produces resembles that of their respective neighbors more than the food of Jews in other Arab countries. Collective histories, intercommunal relations, and shared identities are recorded in each local gastronomy.

Food is particularly salient in the recollections and writings that reconstruct the past. We know food to be powerfully evocative, intimate, and personal, bringing forth strong emotions, and even more so in the context of displacement. Exile's compensation is memory, and can be nourished by gustatory delights. The Jewish cuisines of Egypt and Iraq as seen in memoirs, websites, and novels, serve as case studies, revealing the respective communities' ties to the past, religion, and their host countries.

In addition to memoirs, autobiographical writing, and fiction by Jewish Egyptians and Iraqis, I also draw from cookbooks and their electronic equivalents. The case has already been made to consider cookbooks as a cultural genre worthy of study.[1] The idea of cookbook as anthology, in which choices of inclusion and thus exclusion as well as order and presentation are subject to analysis and interpretation, allows us to read it as literature. And while cookbooks on one hand capture a specific time and place in the past—especially those under discussion—they are, of course, always written and read in the present and project toward the future: the possibilities of a completed recipe. They not only instruct—allowing someone to re-create—but also record, forming a narrative of sorts. They facilitate the transmission of recipes. And while the former category tends to be more functional—performing a service for those who are less knowledgeable about the specific foods or techniques—the line between cookbooks and the food memoir becomes less distinct the more the author focuses on foods from childhood. Both genres include autobiographical and historical dimensions.[2]

A fair amount has already been written about Egyptian Jewish foodways, thanks in large part to the works of Claudia Roden, Colette Rossant, and others who develop the "language of food" in their works.[3] Roden is best known for remembering her lost past through tracking down other displaced Middle Easterners to gather recipes and compile cookbooks, checking them and reports from tales, poems, and proverbs against her own memories. She writes of the annual quail harvest from the dunes of the beaches of Agami, her aunts' date, rose, cherry, and coconut jams, her mother's recipe for *haroset*. Her memories and recipes range from the personal to the shared, just as she describes a very cosmopolitan Egypt on one hand, and the interconnections and similarities throughout the Arab lands on the other. They speak both to permanence, describing customs repeated for hundreds of years still extant in her childhood, and to ephemerality, her quest to collect and preserve these customs before they are all forgotten.

Her cookbooks are "the fruit of nostalgic longing for, and delighted savoring of, a food that was the constant joy of life in a world so different from the Western one. . . . [The recipes] have conjured up memories of street vendors, bakeries and pastry shops, and of the brilliant colours and sounds of the markets."[4] Roden's cookbooks bridge the gulf between now and then, a gustatory celebration of what was. The evocative flavors temper the bitterness of departure.

Roden writes of the multicultural nature of the Cairo in which she grew up. Her own grandparents came from Syria and Turkey; her family identified completely as European. As others have pointed out, she only discovers the foods of the majority of Egyptians once she is living abroad, when family members would gather in a nostalgia of exile. Her claim to the culture is not her own childhood, her own experiences—as she admits, it was "a part of my culture that I hardly knew"—but rather, ancestral. "Past generations of my family had lived, for hundreds of years, an integrated life in the Arab and Ottoman worlds, and something of their experience filtered down to us."[5]

Colette Rossant also makes a connection to her Egyptian upbringing through food in her culinary memoir *Apricots on the Nile*.[6] Born to a Parisian Jewish mother and a Cairene Jewish father, Rossant left France for Egypt at age five because of her father's illness. After her father's death, her mother leaves her with her grandparents in what she experiences as the first of a series of abandonments. One constant is the kitchen, where she finds her home. Her grandmother loves "all things Egyptian"; ironically many of the arguments the older woman has with her cook concern the former's insistence on Egyptian cuisine, countering the desire of the Egyptian cook—the more authentic Arab—to cook French food.

The city comes to compensate for Rossant's losses and for her life's absences: "I had lost a mother then, but at least I had had Cairo, a city and family that nurtured me and that gave me a strong sense of identity."[7] Educated at a convent school, Rossant converts to Catholicism at her mother's urging before they move back to France. As an adult she moves to New York, where being French is seen as an advantage and being Egyptian is exotic. For the first time in her life she cooks a "real Egyptian dinner," embarking on the project that her book is a part of, in reclaiming her Egyptian identity and her love of Cairo.

The belated embrace of Egyptian cuisine by both Roden and Rossant speaks to both the power the food has—to reach across time and space—and to the earlier estrangement of the (middle- and upper-class) Jewish community from their surroundings. Similarly, the food mentioned in *Kayitz Alexandroni* (Alexandrian summer), a novel by Yitzhak Goremazano, ranges from the French cake *baba au rhum* to Sephardi delicacies of *boyos*, *borekitas*, and *biscochicos*, with nary a dish of *ful* or *malukihya* in sight.[8]

Andre Aciman's memoir *Out Of Egypt* describes the young boy at the center of the story, the narrator-protagonist, insisting on an "American" breakfast. "No yogurt this morning. Instead, the smell of eggs and bacon and of butter melting on toast wafted from the kitchen. I had seen American breakfasts in movies and at school and had instructed Abdou I wanted eggs with bacon every Saturday."[9] The national breakfast—fava beans that have been cooked, mashed, and spiced into ful, with its tantalizing aroma—is rejected as food for the poor, and messy besides.[10] The same young boy is the one who delights in the *fiteer* (fried dough) depicted in the epigraph. It is the first night of Passover, and the family seder has just fallen apart. In accepting the treat, he thinks of both his aunt's disapproval—for breaking the Passover diet—and his grand-mother's: "eating fried food by Arabs on the street, unconscionable."[11] But it is also his last night in Egypt before the family's involuntary departure, and much like the distance imbues local dishes with appeal for both Roden and Rossant, the impending exile turns the simple street food into a desired delicacy.

Among the Jews of Iraq—at least according to memoirs, autobiography, and fiction—we find a similar repudiation of street food (and a similar attraction to it). However, their food was the same as the food of the Arabs in whose midst they lived, reflecting their community's longevity, rootedness, and degree of acculturation. The Egyptian Jews were more recent arrivals in the Arab world—whether coming in the wake of the Spanish exile in the fifteenth century, traveling from other parts of the Ottoman Empire in the sixteenth through twentieth, from Italy or Greece, or even Ashkenazi Jews seeking refuge from the late nineteenth-century pogroms in Eastern Europe—than were the Iraqi Jews to their homeland. Similarly, the majority of Jews in Egypt were never granted local citizenship unlike their counterparts in Iraq.[12]

The Jewish community in Baghdad in the twentieth century was the most ancient, integrated, and literary. Unlike most Jews in Arab and Islamic lands, who traced their roots back only to the Spanish expulsion and/or Ottoman Empire—or, in the case of many in Egypt, even later—the history of Babylonian Jewry begins in biblical times when Nebuchadnezzar deported the most prominent citizens of Judah to Babylon. Although those exiled—or more likely, their descendants— were allowed to return seventy years later, a critical mass stayed, and founded what would become the longest continuous Jewish settlement until its demise in the last century.[13]

In the decades before its end, however, Jews made significant contributions to modern Iraqi society, and were well integrated. Although there were Jewish neighborhoods in the larger cities, Jews lived among others in smaller cities and towns. So too, by the interwar period, Jews spread out of the Jewish quarters to the suburbs, living in mixed neighborhoods among Muslims and Christians. They formed the plurality in Baghdad in the earlier part of the twentieth century and dominated fields as disparate as business and music.[14] Commerce shut down for the week on Saturday, the Jewish Sabbath, and no live music was broadcast on Yom Kippur, the Jewish Day of Atonement.

Jews were also at the forefront of the literary renaissance; the poet Anwar Shaul and short-story writers Yaacub Bilbul and Shalom Darwishe were among those who developed modern Iraqi literature.[15] Shaul was especially effective in encouraging other writers, most prominently as editor of the *Harvest*. Eliahu Dangoor, son of the chief rabbi, was "reputedly the world's largest printer of books in Arabic."[16]

It is this literary tradition, in part, that has generated several of the sources for this discussion. These works speak to the rupture from the past as Babylonian Jewry came to an end, and Iraqi Jews left without much possibility of return. At the same time, they restore the past with re-creations of specific dishes, and memories of the cuisine.

While food among Ashkenazi Jews from different Eastern and Central Europe countries tended to be more similar to each other, and more distinctive from the respective non-Jewish cuisines of each country, this was not so among Mizrahi Jews. Even as these similarities and differences arise from a number of factors, they reveal some cultural truths. So while the climate in Eastern and Central Europe limited the variety of available foods, the reliance on pork in many of these countries, and Jewish laws of kashrut, created significant distinctions between Jewish and non-Jewish foodways. The similarities in food prohibitions among Jews and Muslims, as well as the relative abundance of indigenous ingredients, gave rise to greater distinctions between national and regional diets, than between those of Jews and Arabs.[17]

This was true, to a large extent, among the Jews of Iraq. To understand their cuisine, and what that reveals about their relationships with the larger Iraqi community, it makes sense to start with a description of the general foodscape.

It has been said that there is no Iraqi cuisine. "Iraq [is] one of the only Middle-Eastern nations to lack a unique cuisine," claims the Jewish Virtual Library.[18] Other sources concur.[19] In her memoir *Day of Honey*, Anna Ciezadlo explores this myth of Iraqi cuisine. She chronicles her first encounters with food in Iraq, finding it bland and uninspired at best. "Iraqis have really good bread," someone tells her when she asks about the food, implying, of course, that nothing else is worth the effort of mastication. She further describes Iraqi food as "a war on your taste buds" and "the real weapon of mass destruction."[20] The lack of cuisine distinctive to Iraq is explained by geography—that Iraq's location, so close to other culinarily dominant cultures, precluded the development of its own signature cooking, and instead the Iraqis borrowed dishes from Turkish, Syrian, and Iranian kitchens. Ciezadlo wonders whether the food she has eaten reflects some cultural deficit among the Iraqis or "was there something else going on?"[21]

What she discovers is that the food being served to foreigners is some distortion of pan-Mediterranean dishes, and that in fact Iraq has a strong gastronomic heritage dating back to the cuneiform tablets that hold the world's oldest extant recipes.[22] It might be said that the location of Iraq at the crossroads of Turkey, Syria, and Iran can be seen as enriching rather than effacing an already well-developed tradition. Furthermore, its position on several significant trade routes allowed its inhabitants to take advantage of different spices and other ingredients from a number of places, culminating in a very tasty and varied repertoire. Iraq, Sami Zubaida asserts, "is the receptacle of the greatest diversity of communities and cultures."[23] The mountainous geography, proximity to Turkey, and Kurdish population influenced the cuisine in the north to develop differently from the piscacentric diet in the area around Basra. The sea served as a conduit bringing spicing from India and beyond. The Shi'a population tended to follow Persian styles; the Sunnis favored the Ottoman palates. The metropolis of Baghdad absorbed inspiration from a range of cultures and traditions.

A complete description of Iraqi cuisine is beyond this chapter.[24] For our purposes, a general outline will suffice. Characteristics of the cuisine include a reliance on bulgur, barley, and rice for grains, favoring lamb as meat, featuring dates, and a flavor palate that ranges from Indian (cumin, turmeric, cardamom, coriander), to Mediterranean (oregano, thyme), and Middle Eastern spices (sumac, za'atar and baharat mixtures).[25] Mezze—small plates of salads, dips, and spreads—are similar to those found in surrounding countries, as are stuffed vegetables and dishes of minced meat cooked in pastes of grain and ground meat. Boiled meats, dates in various forms, and dried yogurtlike dishes are also common. Pacha (stomach and intestines stuffed with rice or meat and rice) could be considered a national dish.

Amba—the Iraqi version of mango chutney, adapted from the Indian kitchen—was ubiquitous. Sold on the streets, Iraqis often associated the condiment with school, as they would buy it on their way home from school, using samoon, the diamond-shaped bread unique to Iraq, to absorb the thick yellow sauce. The samoon, like a cross between ciabatta and French bread, is described as "an emblem of urbanity."[26] Khubuz or laffa, Iraqi pita, a flatbread of medium thickness that is slightly chewier than the more well-known pita, is also often used for sandwiches, but in this case wrapped around the filling.

Dairy may not be central to the Iraqi diet, but cheeses made from dried yogurt and geimar (qeymar)—a clotted cream from buffalo milk—are common in the diet and the literature.[27] Mazguuf, fish from the Tigris that is marinated and roasted, served with onions, tomatoes, and lime, is as close to being the national dish as any. It recurs in memoirs and novels alike, equally beloved by both Jews and Arabs.[28] And for dessert there were many different kinds of baked goods and sweets. I'll mention just one because of its significance, popularity, and adaptability: kleicha. "All Iraqis," asserts cultural historian Nawal Nasrallah, "irrespective of region, ethnicity, or religion, look to the kleicha as our national cookie, and no feast, religious or otherwise, is complete without it." Generally made with a flaky yeast dough and filled with dates, the kleicha appears in any number of shapes and variants. Muslims baked kleicha for their two major holidays ('Id al-Fitr and 'Id al-Adha); Christians for Christmas and Easter; Jews for Purim. They were also prepared for special occasions, usually in huge amounts. Finding possible connections throughout the Middle East, Russia, China, and South Asia, Nasrallah traces their history back to medieval cookbooks, and even to ancient Mesopotamia.[29]

"But the real food of Iraq was the dates."[30] It is not surprising that dates play a prominent role, as Iraq purportedly supplies 80 percent of the world's product. Fresh, dried, and made into syrup by pressing or boiling (known as *silaan* or *dibis*), dates are a staple of the Iraqi diet.

While the Jews of Iraq shared many of the food customs, preferences, and recipes, they had also developed some that were unique to them. Most of these were related—directly or indirectly—to religious practice. Until well into the last century, Babylonian Jewry tended to be traditional: they kept kosher, observed the Sabbath, celebrated the holidays, and married within the community. Unlike other Jewish communities that absorbed tastes for different foods or different means of preparation from the places they had lived, the majority of Jews of Iraq could trace their roots back to the original exile. Thus any outside influences of any significance on the foods eaten and on means of preparation were generally shared with their non-Jewish neighbors as well.

The laws of kashrut generally distanced Jews from their non-Jewish neighbors throughout Jewish history, and indeed, may have been the real reason behind their existence. Yet there are interesting ways in which they also led to bringing Jews closer to their Arab neighbors, as we will see later on.

Food prohibitions generally kept Jews from eating at the tables of those from outside their community and meant that when they traveled, they either stayed at Jewish homes along the way or took provisions with them. (There was not much of a restaurant culture at any rate.) Violette Shamash remembers traveling on pilgrimage during the holiday of Shavuot with a *shochet*, a kosher butcher, "so that they could be sure of eating nothing but properly slaughtered meat. . . . He took care of the ritual dispatch of whatever chicken or baby lamb they might fancy for dinner and it was then immediately grilled on a wood fire."[31]

Even Jews who did not keep kosher—a phenomenon that became more widespread as the twentieth century progressed—bought kosher meat. "The paradox was that members of some of these same families, while not hesitating for a moment to eat out of a tin of imported nonkosher corned beef...would not come near to a local nonkosher butcher."[32] Nissim Rejwan cites a proclamation issued by the British in 1919 that set daily quotas for animals to be slaughtered in Baghdad. Kosher butchers were allowed 220 sheep and all other butchers, 160. This not only attests to the official recognition of the status of the kosher butcher, but also the relative size and wealth of the capital's Jewish population at the time, and their aforementioned loyalty to the kosher butcher.

A tax on kosher meat was a significant source of funding for the organized Jewish community. The less fortunate segment of the population was especially affected by the tax, particularly when it was raised steeply following the 1936 coup. The poet Muhammad al-Jawahiri, the scion of an important Shiite clerical family in the Muslim holy city of Najaf, composed a poem protesting the increase on behalf of the poorer Jews. The poem was noted for both its sentiment and its language, having included the Hebrew words "kasher" and "trayf." Because of the poem, al-Jawahiri even served two months in prison for—as per the official charge—"sowing communal strife."[33]

Arabs were aware of Jewish food prohibitions and customs. Several sources tell of neighbors or business associates who would bring "break the bread-fast tray" to Jewish families at the end of the Passover holiday. Jewish families were delighted to receive gifts with breads, yogurts, and other items not allowed over the previous week. Because the Passover prohibitions preclude owning leavened food items, because bread takes time to prepare, and because the markets were closed by the time sunset marked the end of the holiday, having good relations with non-Jewish neighbors or coworkers was undoubtedly the fastest way to break the "bread fast."[34]

The benefit went in both directions. Nawal Nasrallah writes of families sharing foods.[35] If a slaughtered animal turned out not to meet the standards of kashrut, it would be given to neighboring Arabs.[36] The prohibition against eating pork shared by Jews and Muslims meant that such meat was largely absent. And although the laws of kashrut and halal diverge, the existence of both created a certain sensitivity toward the other.

While the Iraqi Jewish kitchen was, first and foremost, Iraqi, there were specific ways in which it was distinctly Jewish.[37] To begin with, there was the smell of the kitchen. While Arabs often used butter, Jews preferred sesame oil for frying. It made it much easier to keep meat and dairy separate (according to kosher regulations); other vegetable oils became readily available in Iraq only toward the middle of the last century. "You could tell if you were in a Jewish neighborhood on a Friday because the whole neighborhood was full of the aroma of hot sesame oil."[38]

There was also a certain rhythm to the kitchen; the weekly schedule established by the Jewish Sabbath and the annual one by the holidays. During the week, the main meal was at midday. Rice was served at nearly every meal, with a stew of lamb or fresh fish. Beef was considered less desirable because it was less fatty than mutton.[39]

Preparations for the Sabbath began on Thursdays, the day that a simple—and inexpensive—dish of rice and lentils would be served. Known variously as *kicheree*, *kedgeree*, and *khichdi*, the dish originated in India, spreading throughout the Middle East, with variations in spicing, perhaps added onions, tomatoes, and in Egypt, stretched with macaroni to become koshary. Rejwan describes how garlic and cumin would be fried in sesame oil in a separate pan and added to the rice and lentils. Those less poor might cook with butter instead of oil; the wealthy would have fried eggs on top, or a cup of yogurt.[40] Thursdays were also when households would bake bread for the week.[41]

On Friday night, Jewish families would welcome the Sabbath with a feast that included fried fish, the dark meat of the chicken and/or chicken soup, *arook* (fritters) and/or kebab, fishcakes coated with rice and herbs. According to Violette Shamash, the kebab was prepared according to the season: a sweet-and-sour dish with beets in the winter, and with mint and lemon in the summer.[42]

On Saturday mornings, quick foods that did not need to be heated—in order to abide by the prohibition of cooking on the Sabbath—were eaten: salad, fried slices of eggplant, boiled or steamed potatoes, the Sabbath egg, all eaten at room temperature and flavored with amba. This dish, today known as *sabich*, would become popular in Israel when put into pita like falafel.[43]

Similar to the cholent of Eastern European Jews, and the hamin of Sephardim, the Jewish Iraqis also had a casserole-like recipe that was cooked overnight and eaten for the main meal of the Sabbath, allowing families to enjoy hot food while observing the Sabbath. T'beet (tebeet, itbeet, tibayt, and so on) was the stuffed skin of chicken stewed in rice.[44] "No Jewish Iraqi Sabbath table is complete without tebit."[45] The dish is iconic, and often remembered longingly by Iraqi Jews.[46] An article in the *Jerusalem Post*, titled "The Jewish Palate: T'beet—Flavors of Iraqi Jewish Exile," encourages the reader to "learn about the Iraqi Jewish Community through one of its renowned recipes."[47] A similar article in *Haaretz* defines it as "an Iraqi-Jewish Shabbat overnight stew of chicken and rice. The chicken will turn out so moist," food blogger Vered Guttman declares, "you'll be eating the bones."[48] Just eighteen months later, the same writer mentions that the dish was adopted by non-Jewish Iraqis; recipes for its preparation are included in the first Iraqi cookbook from 1946 (written in English) and the first one in Arabic.[49]

The author of the definitive book on Iraqi cuisine tasted tebeet for the first time in the early '60s, when a Jewish neighbor would send them the dish as thanks for lighting their stove on the Sabbath. "I used to love those brown eggs they would arrange on top of the cover of the dish to cook all night. . . . The tabyeet became part of our cuisine," she added, and the Jewish dish continues to be prepared in an Iraq that no longer houses Jews.[50]

The traditional foods of Babylonian Jewry celebrated in cookbooks, recipe websites, and culinary memoirs, attest to the longevity of the community—several of the dishes find their origins dating back many centuries—and to its level of integration; with the few exceptions noted above, the Jews of Iraq ate the foods of Iraq. These dishes also play a significant role in the fiction as well. Sami Michael's celebrated novel *Victoria*, for example, could be considered a gastronarrative; food is used in multivalent ways to add layers to characterizations, relationships, and plot. The book tells of a young Jewish girl growing up in early twentieth-century Baghdad. Food is used as currency: as a peace offering between sparring spouses, as appeasement for a neglected child, as a form of courtship, as payment for entertainment at celebrations. It can be used to symbolize rank in the family, the hold of tradition, openness to Westernization. Its preparation implies the expertise (and thus value) of the cook, and the affection the cook has for her diners. It can express love, friendship, affection, anger, disgust, and desire.

The appetite for food is especially telling. When a Zionist emissary visits, his message is undermined by his hunger: "I saw you yesterday licking your lips from the fish," he is told. "You polished off a whole dish of dates. What harm have we done you, that you want to cart us off to a land of starvation?"[51]

It is, indeed, hunger that is woven throughout the novel in a powerful motif. Victoria's hunger as a young mother, virtually abandoned by her husband, is foreshadowed by the hunger of others earlier in her life. Hunger does not ennoble; rather it dehumanizes the sufferers.

Eliahu's children, emaciated from their long hunger, had invaded the kitchen and they were snatching the food straight from the boiling pits and devouring it in blind greed. One of them choked on a bone and vomited. They chewed with their mouths full; they burned their thieving fingers. The girls lifted their skirts shamelessly and shoveled pieces of lamb and joints of chicken and scalding rice into their dresses. Their hands dripped with oil, gravy ran down their chins. . . . Pots were overturned. Bare feet were scalded by the steam. In the end, the children fled, their mouths and pockets crammed with meat and rice.[52]

The hunger serves to temper the nostalgic returns to Iraq, adding a reminder of the reality of many Iraqis — Jews and non-Jews alike — who faced poverty and times of extreme need.

When the Grey Beetles Took Over Baghdad takes place in Baghdad years later, a generation after the mass departure of Iraqi Jewry. We find the same traditional foods — geymar, *masguf*, amba, salt cucumber and Kurdish cheese, Mosul kibbe and *zingula* — but we also find imported Swiss and Belgian chocolate, French wine, Italian ravioli and German sausage. Hospitality still dictates that one serves guests, and mothers still rail against buying food from the street.[53] Food is currency here too, buying good will, offering consolation. The family buys from the grocer they think is a government spy to get on his good side; a young man buys out the semit vendor, hoping to buy his silence; the cat named Curry(!) gets treated to a chicken dinner their last night, the long-awaited sign of the family's departure from Iraq.

At least since Proust, we have recognized the power of food to bring back memories, and since Lévi-Strauss, the idea of food having meaning. Food remembered and inscribed reveals identity, history, and communal relations. While Egyptian Jews belatedly lay claim to the cooking of Egypt as their heritage, the Jews of Iraq cooked alongside their neighbors, distinguished only by the sesame oil, the rules of kashrut, and the specific calendric rhythms. Whereas the food of the Egyptian Jews spoke of their peripatetic past, that of the Iraqi Jews attested to their rootedness. Looking forward we see the contributions they have made, from Roden's and others' cookbooks chronicling Middle Eastern food, memoirs, and novels, to the tibeet given to Iraqis, and sabich to Israelis.

NOTES

1. See, for example, Rafia Zafar, "The Signifying Dish: Autobiography and History in Two Black Women's Cookbooks," *Feminist Studies* 25, no. 2 (1999): 449–69.
2. See, for example, Carol Bardenstein, "The Gender of Nostalgia," *Signs: Journal of Women in Culture and Society* 28, no. 1 (2002): 353–87; Nefissa Naguib,

"The Fragile Tale of Egyptian Jewish Cuisine: Food Memoir of Claudia Roden and Colette Rossant," *Food and Foodways* 14, no. 1 (2006): 35–53; Jopi Nyman, "Cultural Contact and the Contemporary Culinary Memoir: Home, Memory, and Identity in Madhur Jaffrey and Diana Abu-Jaber," *Auto/Biography Studies* 24, no. 2 (2009): 282–98.

3. Nefissa Naguib, "Tastes and Fragrances from the Old World: Memoirs by Egyptian Jewish Women," *Studies in Ethnicity and Nationalism* 9, no. 1 (2009): 122–27; Carol Bardenstein, "Transmission Interrupted: Reconfiguring Food, Memory, and Gender in the Cookbook-Memoirs of Middle Eastern Exiles," *Signs: Journal of Women in Culture and Society* 28, no. 1 (2002): 353–87.

4. Claudia Roden, *A Book of Middle Eastern Food* (New York: Penguin, 1984), 11–12.

5. Claudia Roden, *The New Book of Middle Eastern Food* (New York: Knopf, 2008), 5.

6. Colette Rossant, *Apricots on the Nile* (New York: Simon and Schuster, 2004).

7. Rossant, *Apricots on the Nile*, 159.

8. Yitzhak Goremazano, *Kayitz Alexandroni* (Tel Aviv: Am Oved, 1978). The baba au rhum is translated as "Sabrina cake," in the Hebrew; likely a more familiar variant to the Israeli reader.

9. Andre Aciman, *Out of Egypt* (New York: Farrar, Straus and Giroux, 1994), 305–6.

10. Aciman, *Out of Egypt*, 262.

11. Aciman, *Out of Egypt*, 338.

12. See, for example, Joel Beinin, *The Dispersion of Egyptian Jewry: Culture, Politics, and the Formation of a Modern Diaspora* (Berkeley: University of California Press, 1998); Aron Rodrigue, *Jews and Muslims: Images of Sephardi and Eastern Jewries in Modern Times* (Seattle: University of Washington Press, 2003); Victor Sanua, "The Vanished World of Egyptian Jewry," Foundation for the Advancement of Sephardic Studies and Culture, http://www.sephardicstudies.org/vanished.html.

13. The long history and tragic end of Babylonian Jewry are well documented. See, for example, Nissim Rejwan, *The Jews of Iraq* (London: Weidenfeld and Nicolson, 1985); Orit Bashkin, *New Babylonians: A History of Jews in Modern Iraq*(Stanford CA: Stanford University Press, 2012); Meir Basri, *A'lam al-Yahud fi al-'Iraq al-hadith* (Jerusalem: Rabitat al-Jami'iyin al-Yahud al-Nazihinmin al-'Iraq, 1983); Yusuf Rizq Allah Ghanimah, *Nuzhat al-mushtaq fi tarikhYahud al-'Iraq* (London: Dar al-Warraq, 1997); Haim J. Cohen, "A Note on the Social Change among Iraqi Jews 1917–1950," *Jewish Journal of Sociology* 8 (1996): 204–18; Shlomo Deshen, "The Jews of Baghdad in the Nineteenth Century: The Growth

of Social Classes and Multicultural Groups," (Hebrew) *Zemanim* 73 (2001): 30–44; Maurice Sawdayee, "The Impact of Western Education on the Jewish Millet of Baghdad 1860–1950" (PhD dissertation, New York University, 1976); Abbas Shiblak, *Iraqi Jews: A History* (Al-Saqi Books, 2005); David S Sassoon, *A History of the Jews in Baghdad* (New York: AMS Press, 1982).

14. By one account, Jews made up 98 percent of the professional musicians in Iraq. Both the famous Jewish School for Blind Children, which taught music, and the celebrated Kuwaity brothers contributed to this statistic. Yeheskel Kojaman, "Jewish Role in Iraqi Music," *Scribe*, no. 72, 42, http://www.dangoor.com/72page42.html. See also Edwin Seroussi, "Jewish Musicians in the Lands of Islam," *Tapasam: A Quarterly Journal of Kerala Studies* 1, no. 3 (2006): 596–609.

15. See Sasson Somekh, *Bagdad, Etmol* (Tel Aviv: Hakibbutz Hameuchad, 2003) and Nissim Rejwan, *The Last Jews in Baghdad: Remembering a Lost Homeland* (Austin: University of Texas Press, 2004), for descriptions of the café culture where established and aspiring writers, Arabs and Jews, would meet and discuss literature. See also Ahmad 'Abd al-Ilah, *Nash'at al-qissahwa-tatawwuruha fi al-Iraq, 1908–1939* (Baghdad: Matba'atShafiq, 1969).

16. Joel Millman, "Iraq's Forgotten Exiles Seek Redress," *Guardian*, July 5, 2003.

17. Jennifer Berg, "Food in Jewish American Culture," in *Jews and American Popular Culture*, ed. Paul Buhle (New York: Praeger, 2006), 164–65.

18. http://www.jewishvirtuallibrary.org/jsource/Food/Iraqtoc.html.

19. "Iraqi food is so strongly influenced by its neighboring countries, Turkey and Iran, it is one of the few nations of the Middle East to lack a unique cuisine. Like the Turks, Iraqis like to stuff vegetables and eat a lot of lamb, rice, and yogurt. Like Iranians, they enjoy cooking fruits with beef and poultry." http://www.foodbycountry.com/Germany-to-Japan/Iraq.html.

20. Anna Ciezadlo, *Days of Honey: A Memoir of Food, Love, and War* (New York: Free Press, 2012), 66.

21. "[W]as it because they were uncivilized, lizard eating Bedouins who had never mastered the culinary arts? Or was there something else going on?" Ciezadlo, *Days of Honey*, 67.

22. See, for example, Jean Bottéro, *Textes culinaires Mésopotamiens* (Winona Lake IN: Eisenbrauns, 1995); Jean Bottéro, *The Oldest Cuisine in the World: Cooking in Mesopotamia* (Chicago: University of Chicago Press, 2004), cited in Alice L. Slotsky, "Cuneiform Cuisine: Culinary History Reborn at Brown University," *SBL Forum*, http://sbl-site.org/Article.aspx?ArticleID=703.

23. Sami Zubaida, "National, Communal, and Global Dimensions in Middle Eastern Food Cultures," in *A Taste of Thyme: Culinary Cultures of the Middle East*, ed. Sami Zubaida and Richard Tapper (New York: I. B. Tauris, 1994), 33–45.

24. The most comprehensive discussion of Iraqi cuisine to date, Nawal Nasrallah's *Delights from the Garden of Eden: A Cookbook and History of the Iraqi Cuisine* (London: Equinox, 2013), stands at 574 pages.

25. Sami Zubaida, "Rice in the Culinary Cultures of the Middle East," in *A Taste of Thyme*, ed. Zubaida and Tapper, 93–104. Za'atar refers to hyssop (an herb related to thyme and oregano) and the mixture made with hyssop, sesame seeds, sumac and salt. Baharat is similar to the Indian spice mix garam masala, in both ingredients and range of variation; it commonly includes a mixture from among the following: black pepper, cumin, coriander, allspice, cinnamon, cardamom, cloves, nutmeg, chili, ginger, turmeric, and rose petals.

26. Nasrallah, *Delights*, 70.

27. Mona Yahia, *When the Grey Beetles Took Over Baghdad* (New York: George Braziller, 2007), 57.

28. See, for example, Avraham Zilkha, "By the Rivers of Babylon" and Maysoon Pachachi, "East West," in *Remembering Childhood in the Middle East: Memoirs from a Century of Change*, ed. Elizabeth Warnock Fernea (Austin: University of Texas Press, 2002), 120–26, 275; Oded Halahmy, "Delicious Memories," in *Iraq's Last Jews*, ed. Tamar Morad, Dennis Shasha, and Robert Shasha (New York: Palgrave MacMillan, 2008), 60.

29. Nawal Nasrallah, "The Iraqi Cookie, *Kleicha*, and the Search for Identity," *Repast* 24, no. 4 (2008): 4–7, 10.

30. Zilkha, "By the Rivers of Babylon," 120–26.

31. Violette Shamash, *Memories of Eden: A Journey Through Jewish Baghdad* (Chicago: Northwestern University Press, 2010), 160.

32. Rejwan, *Last Jews in Baghdad*, 29.

33. Although chances are that the Bakr Sidqi government was more concerned with sending a message to the politically active poet than it was with an internal dispute within the Jewish community. Somekh, *Bagdad, Etmol*, 164.

34. Such a custom was not unique to Iraq. Jews who lived in mixed communities in prestate Israel/Palestine also tell of their neighbors bringing them baked goods at the end of Passover. See Effi Banay's documentary film *Ga'agu'a* (2012). So too the Mimouna festival in Israel has its roots in similar neighborly generosity in Morocco. See, for example, Alexandra Audrey Galef, "The Evolution of the Moroccan Judeo-Muslim Relationship and the Mimouna Festival" (honor's

thesis, Wesleyan University, 2013); Namratha Somayajula, "Seeds of Peace: Visible Cooperation between Jews and Muslims in Morocco" (independent study project, Oregon State University, 2015).

35. Nasrallah, *Delights*, 2–3.

36. See, for example, David Kazzaz, *Mother of the Pound* (New York: Sepher Hermon, 1999).

37. The edible equivalent of Senator Ezra Menachem Daniel's famous proclamation that "We are Iraqis before we are Jews" (*Nahnu 'arabqablaannakunyahudan*). See Rejwan, *Jews of Iraq*.

38. Oded Halahmy, "Delicious Memories," 64. See also Claudia Roden, "Jewish Food in the Middle East," in *A Taste of Thyme: Culinary Cultures of the Middle East*, ed. Sami Zubaida and Richard Tapper (New York: I. B. Tauris, 1994), 154.

39. According to Rejwan, only poor Muslims ate beef. Rejwan, *Last Jews in Baghdad*, 35.

40. Rejwan, *Last Jews in Baghdad*, 35.

41. Kazzaz, *Mother of the Pound*.

42. Shamash, *Memories of Eden*, 43.

43. The origin of the name is unclear; explanation stories range from the apocryphal—that the name of the first person to sell the sandwich was Sabich—to the acronymic—in Hebrew, the main ingredients are salat (salad), baytzim (eggs), khatzilim (eggplant)—to the linguistic—coming from the word for morning (*sabakh*). See, for example, Neal Ungerleider, "Hybrid Power: The Iraqi-Israeli Sabich," *Saveur*, March 31, 2011; Yael Gerty, "Ayn Kmo, Ayn Kmo Amba: Madrikh Ha Sabikh—Me Dan V'ad Eilat," *Yediot Ahronot*, November 12, 2006; Sala Levin, "From Iraq with Love," *Moment*, September–October 2012.

44. The skin, stuffed with pieces of chicken, other meat, tomatoes, spices, and rice was baked in a stew of rice and tomato paste overnight. Unshelled eggs were placed on top and were eaten in the morning (known as Shabbat or T'beet eggs).

45. Rivka Goldman, *Mama Nazima's Jewish-Iraqi Cuisine* (New York: Hippocrene, 2006), 121.

46. Salim Sassoon, *Iraq's last Jews* (New York: Palgrave Macmillan, 2008), 41; Rejwan, *Last Jews*, 20.

47. Dennis Wasko, "The Jewish Palate—T'beet—Flavors of Iraqi Jewish Exile," *Jerusalem Post*, November 22, 2010. *Tabayit* is described as "spicy chicken stuffed with different meats and rice and is cooked over a bed of rice mixed with zesty tomato sauce." See also: http://www.tastebook.com/recipes/3475522-Nana-s

-Tibeet; http://www.tasteofbeirut.com/iraqi-jewish-chicken-and-rice-tibeat/; http://www.tabletmag.com/jewish-life-and-religion/124026/best-cholent -ever-an-iraqi-stew; OrlyPelli-Bronstein, "Arukha Mishpakhtit—T'beet-Ha Gersa Ha Mikutzeret," http://food.walla.co.il/item/2603905. Linda Dangoor, "Shabbat Meals: T'beet, Fragrant Iraqi Chicken and Rice," *Forward*, May 4, 2011.

48. Vered Guttman, "Modern Manna Recipe Tbeet—Adapted from Victoria Levy," *Haaretz*, January 17, 2012.

49. May Beattie, ed., *Recipes from Baghdad* (Baghdad: Indian Red Cross, 1946); Vered Guttman, "Offerings from the Treasure Trove of Babylonian Cuisine," *Haaretz*, July 27, 2013.

50. Guttman, "Offerings from the Treasure Trove of Babylonian Cuisine."

51. Sami Michael, *Viktoriyah* (Tel Aviv: Am Oved, 1993), 241.

52. Michael, *Viktoriyah*, 50–51.

53. "[T]hey never wash these bowls. Do you know how many mouths drink from them every day?" Yahia, *When the Grey Beetles*, 280–81.

PART 2

The Politics of Jewish Food

Culinary Articulations of Power, Identity, and the State

4

Mosaic or Melting Pot

The Transformation of Middle Eastern
Jewish Foodways in Israel

....

ARI ARIEL

This chapter links changes in Middle Eastern Jewish foodways after the
establishment of the State of Israel to Ashkenazi forms of Orientalism
and civilizing mission. It outlines the Israeli melting pot ideology and
its impact on the food culture of Middle Eastern immigrants and particularly highlights the importance of table manners in socialization.
It also delineates transformations in the taste and methods of preparation of "traditional" foods and highlights culinary continuities, for
example, in the use of spices. The chapter concludes by arguing that the
dominant role of Middle Eastern foods and flavors in the construction
and promotion of modern Israeli cuisine is not a sign of Middle Eastern
Jewish social or political ascendancy.

ETHNIC TENSION IN ISRAEL

Between 1948 and 1951 almost 700,000 immigrants reached Israel, quickly
doubling the country's Jewish population. As important as the increased
demographic strength was to the new state, however, the most profound
impact of this migration was on the ethnic makeup of the population.

In the prestate period, most Jewish immigrants had come from East-ern Europe. Zionism was, after all, a European ideology and its target audience was European Jewry; its impact on Middle Eastern Jewish communities was initially minimal. Some Middle Eastern Jews were, in fact, interested in Zionism, but primarily as a movement for Jewish cultural renaissance, unrelated to migration to Palestine or the estab-lishment of a Jewish state. Moreover, the World Zionist Organization did little to encourage Middle Eastern Jewish interest in the movement, preferring to focus its resources on European Jewry. As a result, before the establishment of the State of Israel, Middle Easterners accounted for only about 12 percent of Jewish migrants.[1]

World War II and then the establishment of the State of Israel radically changed this situation. The Nazi genocide in Europe eliminated much of the potential immigrant reservoir that the Zionist movement had hoped to attract. The Israeli government, therefore, began to encourage and sometimes provoke Middle Eastern Jewish immigration. By the time of the declaration of Israel's independence in May 1948, Muslim-Jewish relations throughout the Middle East had been tense for some time. The clash of Arab nationalism and Zionism made Jewish life in the region precarious. Neither the Zionist movement nor the new Arab governments distinguished sufficiently between Jews and Zionists. As Arab popula-tions and states rallied around the Palestinian cause, Middle Eastern Jews appeared, to some, to be a potential fifth column. Centuries-old Jewish communities were forced to question the viability of their futures in the region. This, not surprisingly, led to large-scale emigration, much of it to Israel. By the mid-1950s Middle Eastern Jews would account for about half of the Jewish population of Israel.

As immigrants from Europe and the Middle East continued to pour into Israel, Zionist ideologues began to worry about how the newcomers would be assimilated into the new Jewish nation. David Ben-Gurion in particular was concerned that the post–World War II migrations, because they were not ideologically driven, would negatively impact the culture and spirit of the new state. Borrowing the idea of a melting pot from the American experience, Ben-Gurion called on immigrants to shed their distinctive identities and behaviors.[2] In theory, this melting pot ideology applied equally to all immigrants. They would all take part in the formation of a new Hebrew society, which required the negation of their diasporic cultures and identities. In practice, however, all Jews were not equal. Some would have to change more than others. European Jews, who controlled the new state, viewed their Middle Eastern co-religionists with the typical prejudice and Orientalist attitudes common at the time. Worse, they feared that if they did not acculturate the Middle Eastern Jews, they themselves might be Levantized. Ben-Gurion spoke of fighting against the spirit of Levant and stressed that he didn't want Israel to become Morocco.[3]

As late as 1969, Abba Eban would write about the cultural danger posed to Israel by the large number of Middle Eastern Jewish immigrants. "Our object," he said "should be to infuse them with an Occidental spirit, rather than allow them to drag us into an unnatural Orientalism."[4] The melting pot process was, therefore, largely experienced by Middle Eastern Jews as a humiliating attempt to civilize them. In the words of Moroccan Jewish scholar, poet, and activist Sami Shalom Chetrit: "When reasonable Ashkenazi people talk to me about integration or melting pot, or the integration of the exiles and other national sugar-coated candy, I want to ask them in all seriousness—why are you troubled with the fact that I want to stay Mizraḥi? Or what elements of my Mizraḥi culture and identity do you wish to adopt or to bestow to your children? . . . In other words, what is left of Mizraḥi identity after integration? Nothing!"[5]

THE ISRAELI PRESSURE COOKER

Middle Eastern Jews were not passive in the face of the melting pot ideology. Although they adopted some aspects of the new Israeli culture, they resisted ethnic assimilation and Ashkenazi hegemony. Yehiel Hibshush exemplifies both accommodation and resistance. Hibshush, a merchant from a prominent family in Sanaa, immigrated to Palestine in 1930, where he was active in Zionist organizations, like *ha-noʻar ha-ʻoved*, and in the organized Yemeni community. In 1945 with his brother he established the firm Sons of Aharon Hibshush.[6] After the establishment of the State of Israel, Hibshush petitioned the Office of Business and Industry (later part of the Ministry of Economy) for permission to import *samna* (clarified butter) and small dried fish called *wazif* from Yemen.[7] The Office of Business and Industry, in turn, referred him to the rabbinate to obtain a certificate of kashrut. The rabbinate rejected his request, saying that these foods were not kosher because they were produced by non-Jews.[8] Hibshush, still intent on importing these items, asked a Yemeni community rabbi to intervene on his behalf. That rabbi, however, refused to help him because he was afraid to come into conflict with the Ashkenazi rabbinate. In fact, in his account of these events, Hibshush specifically states that he is not naming the rabbi because he doesn't want to shame him. Hibshush then turned to Rabbi Shalom Yitzhak Ha-Levi, the son of one of the last chief rabbis of Yemen. Ha-Levi himself was the chief Yemenite rabbi of Tel Aviv (1925–61) and was from 1956 to 1973 a member of the Chief Rabbinical Council of Israel.[9]

The idea that Hibshush had been refused this certificate enraged Ha-Levi and he immediately scheduled a meeting with the rabbinate. The chief rabbi of Tel Aviv, Rabbi Unterman, presided over the meeting, held in a room "full of long bearded distinguished rabbis."[10] All of them rejected giving the certificate to Hibshush. Rabbi Ha-Levi, undeterred, rose defiantly and said, "If my father, the head of the community, and all my forefathers ate *samna* made by Arabs and the fish *wazif*, my community and I eat, and will [always] eat, them. You must give Mr. Yehiel Hibshush the required certificate. If you forbid [them], forbid them only to yourselves and your community."[11] After a bit of debate, Rabbi Unterman ruled in Hibshush's favor, but conceded only that it was permissible for members of the Yemeni community to eat these products.

A few things are immediately clear from this account. Firstly, Jews from Yemen wanted to preserve their foodways and saw them as an inseparable part of their culture and tradition. Neither their migration nor the establishment of the State of Israel signified a complete break with Yemen or with Yemeni Muslims. Yemeni Jews used food to maintain this connection and to preserve Yemeni identity. Secondly, food marked distinctions between ethnicity communities in Israel. It functions here as a boundary marker between Yemeni and other Jews. Finally, in the unnamed Yemeni rabbi's reluctance to challenge the Ashkenazi rabbinate, and in the rabbinate's decision to register these comestibles as kosher for Yemeni Jews only, we observe the extension of ethnic hierarchy into Israeli food culture.

The melting pot, and the Orientalist attitudes that accompanied it, extended to Middle Eastern Jewish foodways. Government officials believed that the new immigrants had to be taught to eat appropriately, and in accordance with the new disciplines of hygiene and nutrition, in order to be successfully assimilated into Israeli society. Nutritionists encouraged the use of some Middle Eastern foods, particularly local vegetables, which they thought were appropriate for the climate of Israel. However, cooking techniques and spicing had to be changed and new ingredients introduced.[12] This was particularly important because during the first decade of the state's existence, many foods were rationed.[13] To achieve this, the Women's International Zionist Organization and Israel's Ministry of Welfare together sent instructors into the transit camps set up for new immigrants to teach them to plan menus and cook, particularly how to use widely available ingredients like cheese, milk, powdered eggs, and new and unfamiliar vegetables.[14]

The attempt to get immigrants to change how and what they ate was, of course, met with some resistance. However, studies done from the 1950s to the 1970s suggest that Middle Eastern Jewish foodways did change.[15] A study conducted by the Israeli Institute of Applied Social Research and the Department of Preventive Medicine of the Hebrew University–Hadassah Medical School in 1958 asserts that Middle Eastern Jews altered their food habits in an effort to emulate Western Jews, whom they considered a "prestige group."[16] Similarly, Meir-Glitzenstein has noted that for at least a segment of young middle-class Iraqi Jew-ish immigrants to Israel, the adoption of Western foodways was an important measure of modernization.[17]

Middle Eastern Jewish adoption of Western food habits was posi-tively correlated to both the length of time that they had been in Israel and the amount and intimacy of contact they had with Western Jews. Children, through their exposure to new foods outside of their homes, played an important role in this transformation. According to the 1958 study: "Not only does the child take his values from outside the culture of the parents but he becomes, in turn, the agent through which the mother acquires the new culture."[18] This aspect of the immigrant expe-rience is almost universal. Immigrant children, and children born to immigrant parents in the receiving country, are intermediaries between the private culture of their homes and the public sphere.[19] In the Israeli case, the state aggressively encouraged this process. For example, in the transit camps established for new immigrants, families were separated. Children and adults slept in separate quarters and dined separately, in spite of the protest of parents, who insisted they had the right to decide what to feed their children. This was done in part because of Ashkenazi stereotypes. Middle Eastern parents were criticized for putting their needs above their children's, for example, taking the best portions of food for themselves. Middle Eastern men in particular were thought to neglect their children and were accused of selling their children's rations to buy arak.[20] Transit camp staff believed that feeding children separately ensured that they would receive appropriate amounts of food and nutrients. Moreover, they would learn proper table manners and could later pass these on to their parents.[21]

KNIFE, FORK, AND PLATE TECHNOLOGY ENTERS THEIR LIVES

Western dining manners were an essential aspect of the civilizing mis-sion applied to Middle Eastern Jews. Meals were to be eaten sitting upright at a table, with a knife and fork. Eating with one's hands was marked as primitive.[22] Middle Eastern Jewish foodways didn't always conform to these norms. In Yemen, for example, people ate seated on floor cushions. Food was served on shared straw or metal plates, either on mats on the floor or on low tables, and was consumed by hand. As part of the process of immigration and assimilation, Yemeni Jews were expected to give up these habits. Even prior to their arrival in Israel, in the transit camp in Aden, Israeli educators taught Yemeni Jews to use a knife and fork. *Exodus from Yemen*, published by the United Israel Appeal in 1950, portrays this reeducation as part of a larger process of acculturation.²³ The book describes Yemen as outside of history, its Jews in a perpetual state of bondage. Yemen is depicted (quite inaccurately) as barren, and Israel as fertile. The spatial shift, from Yemen to Israel, marks the Yemeni Jews' emergence into modernity. This move, however, requires their transformation. They must be "imbued with concepts of hygiene and social life which were unknown to them in Yemen."²⁴ One of the most important things they must learn is how to eat properly.²⁵ Among the photos in the book, three are related to food and speak quite directly to the modernization of Yemeni Jews. As a series they represent the "before and after" of Yemeni migration. The first picture shows a nurse, perhaps herself a Yemeni Jew from an earlier period of migration, teaching three men how to use cutlery; the caption below the photograph reads "Knife, fork, and plate technology enters their lives." The two postmigration pictures, by contrast, represent modern, socialized Yemeni Jews. In the first, two women wearing skirts are standing outside of a grocery store. The modernization of Yemeni women, as portrayed in this image, involves their adoption of Western clothing and styles of consumption. The caption below the image reads "Their new-found peace." In the second image, a small Yemeni family—a husband, wife, and child, dressed in Western clothing—is sitting at a table and eating with knife and fork; the caption reads: "The meaning of home." These two images take up the final two pages of the book; they are its closing statement, and their meaning is clear. Taken together these photographs present the transformation of primitive Yemenis into modern Israelis.

FIG. 4-1. "Knife, fork, and plate technology enters their lives." *The Exodus from Yemen* (Jerusalem: Keren Hayesod–UIA, 1950). Used with permission by Keren Hayesod–UIA.

FIG. 4-2. "Their new-found peace." *The Exodus from Yemen* (Jerusalem: Keren Hayesod, 1950). Used with permission by Keren Hayesod–UIA.

A fictional movie made in 1952, entitled *To Save One Life*, contains similar images of Yemeni Jews.[26] The film is about two Yemeni sisters, fifteen-year-old Tamar and four-year-old Yael. Their mother passed away just after they reached Israel, and since then they have been trying to sneak from the transit camp, where they live with their aunt, into a Youth Aliyah village, Mossad Greenbaum. Yael soon takes ill and is admitted to the hospital. Tamar is then brought to the Mossad where she awaits Yael's recovery. The majority of the film revolves around Tamar's contact

FIG. 4-3. "The meaning of home." *The Exodus from Yemen* (Jerusalem: Keren Hayesod, 1950). Used with permission by Keren Hayesod–UIA.

with Western Jews, which enables her transformation from a primitive Yemeni to a modern Israeli. Mossad Greenbaum officials replace her "traditional" Yemeni garb with Western clothing and shoes, and we soon see her wearing short-shorts. In one scene, we see Tamar seated in the Mossad cafeteria. She begins to eat with her hands, but a friend quickly stops her and places a fork in her hand, showing her how to use it. She finds this difficult, and we hear her think: "Fingers are cleverer than a fork, yet see how the fork defies them. I feel like a child, learning how to walk." Triumphant horns sound as Tamar succeeds at eating with the fork. The significance is clear; eating by hand is represented as childlike; modernity requires utensils.

The Israeli melting pot process demanded that Middle Eastern Jews alter their foodways. They would have to change what they ate, so that it would conform to contemporary understandings of nutrition. Perhaps even more importantly, they would have to adopt Western table manners. In short, to contribute to the Zionist project, Middle Eastern Jews would have to become Western. Ironically, the 1958 study cited above suggests that food might be an important aspect of their contribution. However, the ethnicity of their foodways marked them as primitive. They would have to be transformed before they could be of any value.

THERE THE FOOD WAS MORE TASTY

In addition to changes in foodways made under the civilizing pressure of the Israeli authorities, some food products fell out of use because they were hard to get or expensive in Israel. During the first decade of the state's existence, many foods were rationed. Also, local production and importation were controlled by the Israeli government, which was largely Ashkenazi, and therefore provided foods important to European Jews. Moreover, the implementation of the Arab League boycott of Israel in 1950 made importing items from the Arab world more difficult. The samna and wazif that Yehiel Hibshush was so insistent on importing, therefore, fell out of common use. Culinary substitutions were made. Iraqi Jews, for example, ate less mutton, rice, and fresh fish after migration, despite the fact that these were important and favored items in the Iraqi diet. They substituted noodles and potato flour for rice because during Israel's austerity period the amount of rice rationed per family was small and it was often saved for special occasions.[27] In general, Middle Eastern Jews consumed more vegetables and dairy, and often less meat, in Israel than before migration. Margarine largely replaced oil and samna, noodles replaced rice, and white flour replaced wheat flour and other grains that had been used for making breads. In keeping with current understanding of nutrition, margarine was promoted as a healthy product. According to one researcher, children "brought margarine into the family's diet from their experience with school meals."[28]

Middle Eastern Jews continued to cook many traditional dishes, but adapted them as necessary. For example, *kubane*, a Sanani Sabbath yeast bread had been made with whole wheat flour and samna in Yemen. In Israel it was (and is) generally made with white flour and margarine and is often enriched with eggs and sugar. According to Yosef Qafih, *kubane* was so important to Sanani Sabbath celebration that if one didn't eat it, it was "as if he didn't observe Shabbat according to the halakha."[29] Despite its importance in local practice, however, it was necessarily altered in Israel.

Migration also impacted cooking techniques. Previously used utensils and methods were often unavailable or difficult to reproduce in Israel. In Yemen, for example, cooking had been done in clay pots in traditional ovens. In Israel, most cooking was done in metal pots on a primus kerosene stove. This change obviously impacted the flavor of food. One Yemeni participant in the 1958 survey described the change as follows: "In Yemen we had earth vessels and cooking was done on [sic] the oven. Here, in Israel, the pots are aluminum and the fire is provided by kerosene stoves. It is easier here, but there the food was more tasty [sic]."[30] In fact, according to that study, a large majority of Yemeni and Iraqi housewives (82 percent of Yemenis and 73 percent of Iraqis) had trouble preparing traditional foods in Israel. Moreover, almost all respondents preferred the taste of their own cuisines to that of Western food. This means that the change in Middle Eastern Jewish foodways appears to have been accompanied by a loss of pleasure in food.

Two kinds of comestibles were particularly resistant to change. Middle Eastern Jewish cooks insisted on using traditional spices and spice mixtures. In addition to being important flavoring agents, spices aren't very perishable and would have been similar to what was available in Palestinian markets. Moreover, Middle Eastern Jewish merchants had been importing spices since before the state was established. The Hibshush family had been importing spices thorough Aden since the 1930s.[31] Likewise condiments resisted change. For example, Iraqi Jews continued to eat *amba*, a pickled mango chutney, and Yemeni Jews, *shug*, a spicy, garlicky, cilantro paste. Not only have these condiments continued to be eaten in their ethnic communities, but they have now entered the mainstream Israeli diet; today most falafel stands offer them. Here, too, we should note a technical change; although *shug* would have traditionally been made with a mortar and pestle, today it is usually prepared in a food processor.

LEVANTIZATION?

At the same time that Middle Eastern Jewish foodways were being Westernized, Ashkenazi Israelis were eating more and more Middle Eastern foods. Earlier Ashkenazi immigrants had adopted some Palestinian foods. For ideologically driven settlers this was a way to mark themselves as local.[32] Nutritionists also promoted some Palestinian foods, for example falafel and hummus, as appropriate meat substitutes.[33] As conflict between Jewish immigrants and Palestinians increased, these foods were de-Arabized and attributed instead to Middle Eastern Jews. Yemenis, who began immigrating to Palestine earlier than most Middle Eastern Jews, had been operating falafel stands since the 1920s.[34] Falafel could therefore be redefined as Yemeni, despite the fact that it was not a food commonly eaten in Yemen. After the establishment of the State of Israel, with the influx of Jews from the Arab world, this process was expanded. The more Middle Eastern Jews opened "Oriental" restaurants, the more comfortable Ashkenazi Jews could feel incorporating "Oriental" dishes into their repertoires.[35] By the late fifties, even the Israeli army, which played such a key role in Ben-Gurion's "melting pot" ideology, was serving some Middle Eastern foods.[36]

Two distinct processes worked to fashion new cuisines in Israel. Specific ethnic cuisines (Yemeni, Moroccan, etc.) had to be homogenized and defined. For example, a single Yemeni cuisine could only be conceptualized after migration to Israel. In Yemen, village, city, and regional identities were more important than a general concept of Yemeni-ness. Once in Israel, however, people from different parts of Yemen came to see themselves, first and foremost, as Yemeni. Their distinct cuisines could then merge. Perhaps the best example of this is the elevation of *jaḥnun* from a regional specialty to the paradigmatic Yemeni food in Israel.

Jaḥnun is a Sabbath dish that was made in part of southern Yemen, between Baadan and Aden. It is a cylindrical baked good made by rolling a fat between layers of flour dough, in a manner similar to the process used to make puff pastry. It is then slow-baked overnight. In Sanaa, jaḥnun was made with samna and was baked in a traditional clay vessel. In Israel it is made with margarine and is baked in an aluminum pot. Jaḥnun was not known to Jews in other parts of Yemen. For example, Sarah Amiti, from the Khawlan region of Yemen, notes that she first saw jaḥnun in Aden, while her family was waiting to immigrate to Palestine.[37] Today, however, it is the most well-known Yemeni food in Israel, and is eaten by all Yemenis, regardless of region of origin. It is also now popular among Israelis of all ethnic groups. It is mass-produced and sold frozen in most Israeli supermarkets. In short, a single unified, Yemeni cuisine was constructed and then entered the Israeli mainstream.

At the same time that specific Middle Eastern Jewish ethnic cuisines were homogenized, Middle Eastern Jews opened an increasing number of "Oriental" restaurants. In these establishments, a pan–Middle Eastern cuisine emerged, which included Palestinian Arab street foods, like falafel and hummus, and the culinary highlights of other Middle Eastern Jewish communities, for example, Sephardi *bourekas*, Moroccan cigars, and Tunisian *shakshuka*. These all became universal—at first in the Middle Eastern community and in Middle Eastern restaurants—and then for all Israelis. Despite all the pressure placed on Middle Eastern Jews to Westernize their foodways during the first decades after migration, it is these foods that today form the basis of modern Israeli cuisine.

NEW ISRAELI CUISINE

As of late, official Israeli institutions have been promoting "New Israeli Cuisine" internationally. This cuisine is based largely on Palestinian and Middle Eastern Jewish foods. Elements of Ashkenazi cuisine are present, but clearly play a secondary role. "New Israeli Cuisine," therefore, is fertile ground on which to explore how changes in foodways are linked to ethnic relations. It also allows us to interrogate the outcome of the Israeli melting pot. One particularly instructive example was an online seminar sponsored by the consulate general of Israel in New York in 2010 in conjunction with the *New York Times* Knowledge Network. The course offered "a tour through the fascinating evolution of Israel's culinary scene." The instructors were two prominent food writers, Joan Nathan and Janna Gur. Nathan, an award-winning cookbook writer, has written numerous books on Jewish cooking and is frequent a contributor to the *New York Times*. Gur, is the founder and editor of *'Al ha-Shulḥan*, an Israeli food magazine. Both have published cookbooks on Israeli food: Nathan's *The Foods of Israel Today* was first published in 2001 and Gur's *The Book of New Israeli Food: A Culinary Journey* was published in 2007.[38] Along with online materials, these two books served as the texts for the course.

According to Liora Gvion, in Israel, as in the United States, "Jewish food" is Ashkenazi food, while "Israeli food" refers to a hybrid Middle Eastern cuisine.[39] The course materials refer somewhat disparagingly to Ashkenazi food. For example: "In the past three decades, Israeli cuisine has been one of the fastest-changing kitchens. A melting pot of more than 60 different ethnicities from India through Morocco to Argentina has helped create a true synthesis of flavors. This is not your Mother's matzo ball or chopped liver but rather a sophisticated Mediterranean flavor that rests on local ingredients with international flavoring."

The melting pot metaphor suggests that the diverse cuisines, and by extension the people, of the Israeli population, have shed their distinctive qualities and have assimilated into a single, unified national culture. However, the course materials do not distinguish melting pot from multiculturalism. In fact, the diversity of New Israeli Cuisine is stressed throughout. Ethnic tension in Israel is mentioned briefly; we are told that migration to Israel "was especially traumatic for Sephardi and Middle Eastern Jews. Many came from affluent backgrounds, with fine cooking and lavish hospitality an important part of their lifestyle. They were now practically destitute, cut off from their heritage and looked down on by settlers of European origin, both newcomers and veteran. In the eyes of the Ashkenazi, the Sephardi Jews didn't look at all like Jews—they had dark skin, spoke strange languages and followed strange customs."

This trauma, however, is presented as short-lived. The lesson section titled "The Melting Pot of Immigrant Cuisines," describes the transformation of immigrant foodways that has been the topic of this chapter thus far. Borrowing from the discourses noted above, this section describes Ashkenazi cuisine as heavy and inappropriate for the climate of Israel. It then links the increased popularity of Middle Eastern cuisines to a decrease in Ashkenazi prejudice:

Though at the time of their arrival, the old timers (who were predominantly Ashkenazi) regarded their [Middle Eastern] cooking styles as foreign and dubious, they were quickly seduced by Bulgarian *bourekas*, Tunisian *chreime* (spicy fish stew), Morrocan couscous soup, Lybian *shakshuka* (spicy tomato and egg stew), Yemenite *jachnun*, Iraqi *kubbe* and many other dishes which are now considered all-Israeli favorites and are served in many households as well as in restaurants. But to regard these two culinary cultures as adversarial (or even competing) would be a gross misunderstanding of the Israeli society. In spite of a considerable amount of prejudice and separatism, typical for every immigrant society, the amount of cross marriages was constantly on the rise. In fact in present day Israel, it is the norm. On the culinary level, this means that recipes, ingredients, and techniques are swapped, mixed and reshuffled even on a single plate. A typical Israeli lunch might include Viennese schnitzel happily coexisting with a side dish of couscous and spiced with a dash of Iraqi *amba* (mango pickle) or Yemenite *zehug* (hot sauce).

Here the course materials make an assertion about the relationship between food, bodies, and subjectivity. As these dishes became Israeli, it claims, so too did the immigrants that cooked and consumed them. Culinary fusion equals intermarriage, which equals the reunification of the Jewish people. Food, then, produces the triumphant arc of Zionist history and the regeneration of the Jewish nation. Ella Shohat has observed this same motif in the genre of Israeli cinema, perhaps not coincidentally, called "bourekas" films, after a stuffed pastry called borek, common in former Ottoman and Sephardic communities. In these films, Shohat notes, "ethnic/class tensions and conflicts are solved by a happy ending in which equality and unity are achieved by means of the unification of the mixed couple."[40] The theme of intermarriage, in fact, develops throughout the online course. The last lesson states: "With cross-cultural marriage the norm in a country so small, ethnic cooking traditions are constantly mixed and reshuffled. An Eastern European chicken soup can be spiced with Yemenite hawaij and Austro-Hungarian schnitzel shares the place with Moroccan couscous."

Although intermarriage is an important phenomenon in Israeli society, it is crucial to note that it has done little to close the persistent socioeconomic gap between Middle Eastern and Ashkenazi Israelis. According to Chetrit, Middle Eastern Jews in Israel still "suffer the consequences of prolonged economic oppression, as evident in the data on the three main areas of inequality: education, occupation, and quality of life (income and housing density)."[41] Furthermore, this invocation of culinary diversity seems, at times at least, to empower Ashkenazi cooks. In *The Book of New Israel Food*, Gur writes: "Paradoxically, as Israeli society becomes more cosmopolitan and sophisticated in its tastes, local ethnic food traditions have become more pronounced. Family heritage is often the primary source of inspiration for local chefs. . . . *Regardless of their ethnic origin*, leading Israeli chefs all offer some kind of personal take on Mediterranean and Middle Eastern cuisines [emphasis added]."[42] As Middle Eastern foods become Israeli, then, Middle Eastern Jews potentially lose ownership over them.

Gvion notes a similar problem. On one hand, Middle Eastern Jewish chefs can use the current global interest in ethnic food to empower themselves. On the other hand, their authority in the culinary scene does not extend to other realms. Perhaps the need to appeal to Ashkenazi customers stifles their political potential. Gvion states: "Although it has taken three or four generations of Mizrachim in Israel to take the lead in the process of creating a national cuisine, very few chefs have dared to express discontent with the position that Mizrachim as an ethnic group have occupied in Israel. Neither do they protest against the persistent economical and educational gaps between Mizrachim and Ashkenazim. The majority of my interviewees disregarded a possible connection between food, ethnicity and politics of identity."[43]

The invocation of diversity in New Israeli Cuisine is also in keeping with a larger global trend embracing multiculturalism. Increasingly, states have turned away from the goal of forming a single culturally homogeneous nation. Cultural diversity within a nation is now a sign of modernity and cosmopolitanism. For Israel to position itself as modern, it now needs a national cuisine that is diverse and ethnic. Its ethnicities, however, must mix harmoniously. Given the enduring socioeconomic gap between Ashkenazi and Middle Eastern Jews, and between Jews and non-Jews, in Israel, culinary mixing does not indicate integration and is not necessarily benign. Gunew has noted that cuisine is often the "acceptable face of multiculturalism."[44] She argues that "we don't simply become like each other by eating each other's food (akin to donning each other's clothing) but that eating each other's food is a barely sublimated way of simply eating each other." As these relate to language and power, she notes, "Thus, the dominant culture engages in multicultural cuisine as a way of not acknowledging multicultural words."[45] Perhaps, then, the rise of Middle Eastern Jewish food in Israel should not be understood to represent successful immigrant assimilation or the emergence of a more equal Israeli society. The link between prejudice against Middle Eastern Jews and changes in their foodways were described earlier in this chapter. If, in New Israeli Cuisine, the role of Middle Eastern Jewish food is to provide material for the creation of a single national cultural product, this is simply the continuation of an older pattern that calls on Middle Eastern Jews to serve the nation. And if this national cuisine is to be exported, who will benefit?

The promotion of New Israel Cuisine internationally is a claim that Israel is a modern cosmopolitan nation. Israeli cuisine must, therefore, be able to compete in reputation with the cuisines of France and Italy and must be served in international capitals like New York and London. Therefore, as Israeli cuisine is becoming more global, its distinctiveness must be emphasized. Its value must be recognized by non-Israelis. Ferguson has suggested that this is one of the defining features of culinary nationalism in the twenty-first century; recognition must come from outside the nation.[46]

The value of New Israeli Cuisine, on the international stage, is found in its ethnic diversity, but before this diversity is exported, it must be filtered through a normative Israeli screen. The Israeli nation can thereafter be presented as unified and varied simultaneously. In this scheme, diversity is not a detriment to the formation of national identity. On the contrary, it bolsters it. Arjun Appadurai, in his seminal food studies essay "How to Make a National Cuisine," shows that a national cuisine emerges "because of, rather than despite, the increasing articulation of regional and ethnic cuisines. As in other modalities of identity and ideology in emergent nations, cosmopolitan and parochial expressions enrich and sharpen each other by dialectical interaction."[47] Perhaps for this reason, the focus on Middle Eastern and Sephardic foods in the course New Israeli Cuisine should not be taken as in any way subversive. Distinct Middle Eastern cuisines, and a developing pan–Middle Eastern cuisine, are marked as ethnic in this dialectical process. On one hand, these cuisines are a form of social capital that might be used to challenge ethnic hierarchies, but at the same time they must be mediated through Ashkenazi and international cosmopolitan tastes if they are to be of value to the nation. Israeli foods may be multicultural, but to become a cuisine they must merge, and those with greater access to power remain the arbitrators of what emerges from the melting pot as Israeli.

NOTES

1. Sammy Smooha, *Israel: Pluralism and Conflict* (Berkeley: University of California Press, 1978), 57.

2. Yosef Gorny, "The 'Melting Pot' in Zionist Thought," *Israel Studies* 6, no. 3 (2001): 65. For more on immigration to Israel, see Dvora Hacohen, *Immigrants in Turmoil: Mass Immigration to Israel and Its Repercussions in the 1950s and After*, trans. Gila Brand (Syracuse NY: Syracuse University Press, 2003).

3. Alexandra Nocke, *The Place of the Mediterranean in Modern Israeli Identity* (Leiden, The Netherlands: Brill, 2009), 190; Gershon Shafir and Yoav Peled, *Being Israeli: The Dynamics of Multiple Citizenship* (New York: Cambridge University Press, 2002), 72; Smooha, *Israel*, 88.

4. Smooha, *Israel*, 88.

5. Shoshana Madmoni-Gerber, *Israeli Media and the Framing of Internal Conflict* (New York: Palgrave Macmillan, 2009), 181.

6. For more information on the Ḥibshush family, see Yeḥiel ben Aharon Ḥibshush, *Mishpaḥat Ḥibshush* [The Ḥibshush Family], 2 vols. (Israel: Ofset Ha-Omanim, 1985) and Alan Verskin, "Ḥabshūsh Family," in *Encyclopedia of Jews in the Islamic World*, ed. Norman Stillman, http://referenceworks.brillonline.com/entries/encyclopedia-of-jews-in-the-islamic-world/habshush-family-SIM_000413.

7. For Ḥibshush's account see Yeḥiel ben Aharon Ḥibshush, *Shene ha-meorot* [The Two Luminaries], (Tel-Aviv: The Ḥibshush Family, 1987), 183–84. See also Aharon Gaimani, "Le-foʻaloshel ha-rav Shalom Itzhak Ha-levive-yahso le-minhageteyman" [The Work of Rabbi Shalom Itzhak Ha-Levi and his Attitude to the Customs of Yemen], in *Ha-Rav'Uziel u-venezemano: pirke'iyun be-hagutamshelḥakhme ha-mizraḥ be-yisraelba-meah ha-'esrim* [Rabbi Uzziel and his Peers: Studies in the Religious thought of Oriental Rabbis in Twentieth-Century Israel], ed. Zvi Zohar (Jerusalem: Ha-vaʻad le-hotzaatkitve ha-rav Uziel, 2009), 46–47.

8. Ḥibshush's uses the word *treif* in his account.

9. For more about Ha-Levi, see Gaimani, "Le-fo'alo."

10. Rabbi Unterman later became the chief Ashkenazi rabbi of Israel.

11. Ḥibshush's, *Shene ha-meorot*, 183.

12. For example, one doctor, E. Rigger, wrote that "in our hot climate country the appetite can be damaged and many combat this by using hot spices, the people of Oriental sects in particular tend to overdo this." Quoted in Yael Raviv, "Recipe for a Nation: Cuisine, Jewish Nationalism, and the Israeli State" (PhD dissertation, New York University, 2002), 190–91.

13. For more on rationing see, Yael Raviv, *Falafel Nation: Cuisine and the Making of National Identity in Israel* (Lincoln: University of Nebraska Press, 2015), 64–74; Orit Rozin, *The Rise of the Individual in 1950s Israel: A Challenge to Collectivism*, trans. Haim Watzman (Waltham MA.: Brandeis University Press, 2011), 4–19.

14. It is worth noting that Ashkenazi immigrants also had to learn to use new ingredients. For example, they were less likely than Middle Eastern Jews to be familiar with local Palestinian vegetables. For more on culinary and nutritional reeducation, see Raviv, *Falafel Nation*, 100–109, 140–43; Rozin, *Rise of the Individual*; Dafna Hirsch, "'We are Here to Bring the West, Not Only to Ourselves': Zionist Occidentalism and the Discourse of Hygiene in Mandate Palestine," *International Journal of Middle East Studies* 41, no. 4 (2009): 577–94.

15. Israel Institute of Applied Social Research and the Department of Preventive Medicine of the Hebrew University of Jerusalem-Hadassah Medical School, *Changes in Food Habits in the Yemenite and Iraqi Communities in Israel* (Jerusalem, 1958); Sarah Bavly, "Food Intake of Yemenite and Kurdish Jews in Israel," *Philosophical Transactions of the Royal Society of London* 266, no. 876 (1973): 121–26; Moshe Prywes, ed., *Medical and Biological Research in Israel* (Jerusalem: Hebrew University of Jerusalem; New York: Hadassah, The Women's Zionist Organization of America, 1960). See also Michael A. Weingarten, *Changing Health and Changing Culture: The Yemenite Jews in Israel* (Westport CT: Praeger, 1992).

16. Israel Institute of Applied Social Research, *Changes in Food Habits*, 4.

17. Esther Meir-Glitzenstein, "Kanokhlim be-sakin u-mazleg" [Here They Eat with a Knife and a Fork], in *Society and Economy in Israel: Historical and Contemporary Perspectives*, eds. A. Barely, D. Gutwein, and T. Friling (Jerusalem: Ben-Gurion Research Institute and YadItzhak Ben-Zvi Press, 2005), 615–44.

18. Israel Institute of Applied Social Research, *Changes in Food Habits*, 23.

19. Rozin, *Rise of the Individual in 1950s Israel*, 169; Raviv, *Falafel Nation*, 97; Simone Cinotto, *The Italian American Table: Food, Family, and Community in New York*

City (Urbana: University of Illinois Press, 2013), 41; Hasia R. Diner, *Hungering for America: Italian, Irish, and Jewish Foodways in the Age of Migration* (Cambridge MA: Harvard University Press, 2001); Susan Kalcik, "Ethnic Foodways in America: Symbol and the Performance of Identity," in *Ethnic and Regional Foodways in the United States: The Performance of Group Identity*, eds. Linda Keller Brown and Kay Mussell (Knoxville: University of Tennessee Press, 1984), 40–41.

20. Rozin, *Rise of the Individual in 1950s Israel*, 148. See also *The Black Panthers (in Israel) Speak*, directed by Eli Hamo and Sami Shalom Chetrit (2003). One interviewee in this documentary film notes that the stereotype of Middle Eastern Jewish men spending all their earnings on arak was a common trope and was used by the media as a way of discrediting the Israeli Black Panther movement.

21. Rozin, *Rise of the Individual in 1950s Israel*.

22. Rozin, *Rise of the Individual in 1950s Israel*. Esther Meir-Glitzenstein, "Longing for the Aromas of Baghdad: Food, Emigration and Transformation in the Lives of Iraqi Jews in Israel in the 1950s," in *Jews and Their Foodways*, ed. Anat Helman (New York: Oxford University Press, 2016), 89–109. Writing specifically about Iraqi Jews Meir-Glitzenstein states, "Use of a fork and knife became a test of modernity and progress, regular meals at regular times were presented as being ideal, force-feeding became an educational principle, and eating with the hands symbolized primitive behavior. The intervention of the Israeli system was total, to the point where, even in the culinary sphere, the Iraqi Jews were no longer their own masters."

23. *The Exodus from Yemen* (Jerusalem: Keren Hayesod, 1950).

24. *The Exodus from Yemen*.

25. Israeli officials also thought it was necessary for Yemeni Jews to replace traditional remedies with Western medicine and to learn to wear Western shoes. Two other photographs in *Exodus from Yemen* are illustrative. In the first, a group of men stand around a shoe, looking baffled. The caption reads: "The puzzle in hand is one of the least problems of adaptation to Western life with which they will have to grapple." In another picture, a camp doctor is giving a vaccination to a scared child. The caption reads: "Inoculation against disease will replace his faith in an esoteric amulet."

26. *To Save One Life*, produced by Hazel Greenwald (1952), Jewish Film Archive, Hebrew University.

27. Israel Institute of Applied Social Research, *Changes in Food Habits*; Meir-Glitzenstein, "Longing for the Aromas of Baghdad."

28. Weingarten, *Changing Health and Changing Culture*, 56.

29. Yosef Qāfiḥ, *Halikhotteman: haye ha-yehudim be-tzanʿaʾ u-venoteha* [Yemeni Ways: Jewish Life in Sanaa and its Surroundings], (Jerusalem: Ben Zvi Institute, 1961), 278.

30. Israel Institute of Applied Social Research, *Changes in Food Habits*, 34.

31. Ḥibshush, *Mishpaḥat Ḥibshush*.

32. Oz Almog, *The Sabra: The Creation of the New Jew*, trans. Haim Watzman (Berkeley: University of California Press, 2000); Yael Zerubavel, "Documenting Israeli Folk Culture," in *Documenting Israel: Proceedings of a Conference Held at Harvard University on May 10-12, 1993*, ed. Charles Berlin (Cambridge MA: Harvard College Library, 1995), 171.

33. Raviv, *Falafel Nation*, 17.

34. Yael Raviv, "Falafel: A National Icon," *Gastronomica* 3, no. 3 (2003): 22; Zerubavel, "Documenting Israeli Folk Culture," 178-79.

35. Dafna Hirsch, "Shel Mi Le-Azazel Ha-Hummus Ha-Ze?" [Whose Damn Hummus Is This?], *Adkan* no. 52 (2010).

36. Raviv, "Recipe for a Nation," 177-78.

37. Sarah Amiti interview in Ben Zvi Institute, Goitein Box 1, Tziporah Greenfield's Notebook, 71.

38. Joan Nathan, *The Foods of Israel Today* (New York: Knopf, 2001); Janna Gur, *The Book of New Israeli Food: A Culinary Journey* (New York: Schocken, 2008).

39. Liora Gvion, "Two Narratives of Israeli Food: 'Jewish' versus 'Ethnic,'" in *Jews and Their Foodways*, ed. Anat Helman, 126-41.

40. Ella Shohat, *Israeli Cinema: East/West and the Politics of Representation* (Austin: University of Texas Press, 1989), 122.

41. Sami Shalom Chetrit, *Intra-Jewish Conflict in Israel: White Jews, Black Jews* (New York: Routledge, 2009), 154. On the continuing socioeconomic gap, see Shafir and Peled, *Being Israeli*, 74-95.

42. Gur, *Book of New Israeli Food*.

43. Gvion, "Two Narratives of Israeli Food."

44. Sneja Gunew, "The Melting Pot of Assimilation: Cannibalizing the Multicultural Body," in *Transnational Asia Pacific: Gender, Culture, and the Public Sphere*, ed. Shirley Geok-lin Lim, Larry E. Smith, and Wimal Dissanayake (Urbana:

University of Illinois Press, 1999), 146. See also Sneja Gunew, "Introduction: Multicultural Translations of Food, Bodies, Language," *Journal of Intercultural Studies* 21, no. 3 (2000): 227–37; Heike Henderson, "'Strange' Foods, Taboos, and German Tastes," *Rocky Mountain Review of Language and Literature* 65, no. 2 (2011): 148–67.

45. Gunew, "Melting Pot of Assimilation," 147.
46. Priscilla Parkhurst Ferguson, "Culinary Nationalism," *Gastronomica* 10, no. 1 (2010): 102–9.
47. Arjun Appadurai, "How to Make a National Cuisine: Cookbooks in Contemporary India," *Comparative Studies in Society and History* 30, no. 1 (1988): 21–22.

5

Soviet Jewish Foodways

Transformation through Detabooization

....

GENNADY ESTRAIKH

By the time of the 1917 revolution, Lenin and his cohort of Bolsheviks did not have any coherent strategy for the future of Russia's Jews; and, it seems, they seriously believed that, in a socialist environment, all issues associated with this group of the population should be solved just by themselves. When it became clear that the postrevolutionary reality nevertheless demanded special attention to this population segment, the establishment and activity of the People's Commissariat for Jewish Affairs (1918–24) and the Jewish sections of the Bolshevik Party (1918–30) set the tone for the state-cum-party policy: a radical ideological, cultural, and social modification of Jewish forms of life in the country and a transition from "parasitic" occupations in shtetls, typically market towns, to productive work in socialist society. As a reflection of this strategy, the shtetl, or *mestechko* in Russian, disappeared from the territorial structure of the Soviet state. The construction and sustainment of a new Jew, an urbanite or (much rarer) village dweller, able to fit in with advanced members of society, continued almost until the collapse of the Soviet Union in 1991. To this end, Soviet ideologists sought to eliminate all religious facets of traditional Jewish life. At the same time, they tended to consider the Yiddish language, literature, and theater worthy of limited preservation and even further development. Any activity in the secular cultural field fell under an unwritten, but unbroken, ban only during several years in the late 1940s and early 1950s.

Jewish foodways also found appreciation as a valuable form of cultural expression. For a short while, the Commissariat for Jewish Affairs shared premises with Moscow-based Zionist organizations, and the commissariat's staff, headed by Shimon Dimanstein, a former student of a Lubavich yeshiva, did not see a problem in eating at the same kosher canteen.[1] Elissa Bemporad's analytic portrayal of Soviet Minsk shows that throughout the 1920s the city continued to consume almost exclusively kosher meat.[2] The rebranding of the shtetls into towns and villages certainly did not bring immediate changes in the foodways of their residents. In general, however, communists as well as other "politically conscientious" segments of the Jewish population were not supposed to burden themselves with following the "obscurantist" dietary rules, although the new regime tried (albeit not consistently) to show its readiness to tolerate some vestiges of religious traditions, especially if they survived exclusively among the ancients.

Critical food shortages in the early years of the Soviet regime, most notably during the Military Communism period (1918–1921), made it onerous to observe any dietary restrictions. A memoirist of the period recalled that, in their hungry desperation, Moscow-based Jewish intellectuals were happy to get horse beef or—"as a treat"—even cat and dog meat.[3] In Moscow, no flour was available for baking matzo, so during Passover many observant Jews followed the local rabbi's advice, eating rice and peas instead.[4] In 1919 they could receive some amount of matzo as their bread ration allowance.[5] The situation improved with the commencement of the New Economic Policy (1921–1929), during which the government permitted opening of private enterprises.[6] It again became a challenge to keep kosher in the 1930s, when forced collectivization of agriculture led to a great loss in production of grain, meat, and milk.

Cows had been confiscated by the state and their slaughter was heavily regulated, therefore kosher beef remained almost inaccessible. Legal kosher butchers continued to exist in certain localities, specializing in slaughtering chickens and other fowl. For instance, in 1935, Kiev had twenty-one butchers for the Jewish population of over 220,000.[7] In 1939 the American chess player Samuel Reshevsky experienced problems with finding kosher food when he participated in a tournament in Moscow and Leningrad (with Jewish populations of 250,000 and 200,000 respectively). The *New York Herald Tribune* reported:

> The hospitable Soviet authorities find complying with the orthodox kosher diet an unsolvable problem, and the champion has been reduced to a diet something like Mahatma Gandhi's one of goat's milk. Last week in Leningrad, Reshevsky, tired of milk, tea and fruit, visited the last remaining synagogue there and found a family whose observance of the dietary laws he considered acceptable after personal investigation. He tasted meat for the first time in many weeks. . . . He will have to contend with the food problem for the remainder of his month's stay in Moscow, since the sole restaurant serving Jewish dishes complies with the hygienic regulations rather than the traditional kashruth rules.[8]

In the 1930s, Jewish dishes—cooked following Jewish recipes rather than religious dietary laws—were supposed to add national spice to the Jewish Autonomous Region (JAR), established in the Far Eastern corner of Siberian Russia as a constituent of the ethnoterritorial patchwork of the Union of Soviet Socialist Republics. A late-Soviet cookbook, William Pokhlebkin's *National Cuisines of Our Peoples*, represented Jewish fare (gefilte fish, carrot stew, or *tzimmes*, and chopped herring, or *forshmak*) as an ethnoterritorial phenomenon—in a chapter dedicated to food traditions of the Far East.[9] This reflected the Birobidzhan-centered ideological model, which dogmatically linked the entire Soviet Jewish population to its "heartland" in the JAR. Characteristically, according to the universal system developed for Soviet library catalogues, Yiddish books and their translations were placed among the "literatures of Far Eastern Peoples."[10]

The JAR was built to house a militantly secular society, so a Polish Jewish activist who visited the area in 1934 found, or chose to see, there only several men who observed Sabbath and abjured pork. Ironically, all of them were *subbotniks*, or Judaized Russians.[11] According to David Khait, a Russian Jewish writer, by the mid-1930s young Birobidzhaners knew very little about Jewish traditions and were bemused when a group of *subbotniks* settled in one of the collective farms of the JAR. Some local Jews even offered in jest their services as *shabes-goyim*, or gentiles, hired to perform domestic chores forbidden to Jews (and the godly converts) on the Sabbath.[12] It did not mean, however, that Jewish re-settlers had forgotten the recipes of their traditional dishes.

In February 1936, when Lazar Kaganovich, Stalin's Jewish lieutenant, visited Birobidzhan, the administrative center of the JAR, housewives cooked for him gefilte fish, a staple of Jewish holiday dinners. In the event, the guest—who traveled in style, accompanied by a cook—did not touch the local food. Nevertheless, next year, when the secret police arrested the party boss of the JAR in the wave of Stalinist "purges," his wife was grotesquely accused of trying to poison Kaganovich with her gefilte fish. The issue of gefilte fish also emerged during the visit of another Jewish guest, Polina Zhemchuzhina (Perl Karpovskaya), whose non-Jewish husband, Viacheslav Molotov, would in August 1939 carve for himself a notorious place in history by signing the Soviet-German Pact. Zhemchuzhina, herself a high-ranking state functionary (at that time she headed a department at the Ministry of Food Industry), expressed her disappointment that this quintessential Jewish dish did not appear on the menu of the—apparently only—Birobidzhan restaurant.[13]

Although the Soviet food mainstream had absorbed some elements of Jewish cuisine, and tzimmes had even enriched the Russian language with the word "tsimes" (meaning "a very good/nice thing"), they never became as important to the pan-Soviet national palate as, for instance, the Caucasian Style *shashlik* (shish kebab) or the Central Asian *plov* (conglomeration of rice, vegetables and meat bits swimming in meat fat—traditionally lamb—and oil). In any case, *khala*, or challah, Jewish-style braided bread, could be bought in many Soviet food stores at least as late as the 1950s or even later.[14] A 1955 textbook for students of food merchandising describes the variety of porkless sausages known as *evreiskaiakolbasa* ("Jewish sausage").[15] I (born in 1952) also have childhood memories that *evreiskaiakolbasa*, with a bit of a garlic taste, and *khala* could be bought in my home city of Zaporizhia and its neighboring city of Dnipropetrovsk (now Dnipro), in Ukraine.

Esther Markish, widow of the Soviet Yiddish writer Peretz Markish, recalled that in the late 1940s and early 1950s, during the "campaign against the pernicious influence of the West," the "Jewish sausage" was renamed "dry sausage."[16] The poet Lev Druskin felt sorry that *khala* would be sold under a different name, that of *pletenka* (*pletionka*), or "braid."[17] Alice Nakhimovsky, the American scholar of Russian and Jewish literature and culture, wrote:

Jewish foods that made it into the public sphere tended to be renamed. Challah was sold in stores in Leningrad and Moscow under the public name pletenka [braid], though in some bakeries you could ask for it by its Yiddish name. A similar public disguise was given to a classic Jewish recipe for stuffed cabbage included in a Soviet cookbook of 1973. The recipe is recognizable as Jewish because it is sweet-and-sour—a combination that has no place in Russian cuisine—and because the sauce for the meat-stuffed cabbage rolls is not enriched with the otherwise ubiquitous sour cream. The cookbook codes the recipe as 'Stuffed Cabbage. Oriental Style [*golubtsypovostochnomy*].'[18]

The 1952 edition of *The Book about Delicious and Healthy Food*, including an epigraph with Stalin's words that the revolution had "given the people not only freedom but also material goods as well the opportunity of a prosperous and cultured life," does not contain any direct mention of Jewish dishes, although it has a recipe for stuffed fish, essentially gefilte fish.[19] By contrast, the first edition of *The Book about Delicious and Healthy Food*, published in 1939, mentions in passing or describes recipes for the "Jewish sausage," "Jewish pretzel (*krendel*')," and strudel—"one of the most nourishing and delicious Jewish sweets." It also has a recipe for "denationalized" stuffed pike.[20] The same year, 1939, saw the publication of a small book—in effect, a pamphlet of only thirty-two pages—entitled *50 Dishes of Jewish Cuisine*. This cookbook, brought out by the State Trade Publishing House (rather than, say, the Moscow Jewish publishing house Emes) as part of the series of books in Russian explaining how to cook dishes of national cuisines, features a recipe for *kneydlakh*, known in English as matzo balls. However, the Soviet variety of matzo balls does not contain any matzo—its main ingredient is semolina.[21]

Significantly, the 1952 cookbook came out at the time when all quasi-civic, cultural, and educational Jewish-related organizations in the entire country had been closed and rumors circulated about a forthcoming summary deportation of Jews to Far Eastern regions. On August 12, 1952, the Stalinist repressive machinery executed thirteen leading members of the disbanded Jewish Anti-Fascist Committee (1942–48). They were accused of being part of seditious plots hatched by foreign "imperialists." The Yiddish prose writer Shmuel Gordon, who was arrested during this case but survived the imprisonment, drew the watchful attention of the JAR's party leadership (despite demonstrating their vigilance, they also did not evade arrest) by showing his sympathies toward "old national and religious traditions." The denouncement referred to Gordon's description of Birobidzhan of the late 1940s, where he recognized some features of traditional shtetl life. Thus, he unwisely wrote that from the open doors and windows of Birobidzhan houses one could savor a strong sent of gefilte fish and tzimmes. By that time, however, Birobidzhan dwellers should have shed any association with their former life in the shtetl.[22] While David Hofshteyn's (executed in the August 1952) lyric hero asked "tiger meat / Could it possibly be kosher?" the poetic alter ego of his younger colleague, Aron Vergelis, was a "young daredevil, /

who spent his life at a camp-fire" and did not ask questions, but rather "went with a knife at a tiger."[23] Following Stalin's death, some elements of Jewish traditions resurfaced in the JAR. In the 1970s, the restaurant of the Birobidzhan hotel Vostok could serve a "dinner described as 'Jewish cuisine', which included something that might be called Siberian gefilte fish, chicken soup and smoked salmon."[24]

All in all, no information is available to pinpoint the year when such commodities as challah and "Jewish sausage" permanently vanished from Soviet store shelves or lost their "ethnic identity." It also remains unclear whether this was a result of a directive formulated by top ideologists and bureaucrats. Historians still know little about decision making on Jewish-related issues. Most probably, "Jewish" food products simply became a sore in the vigilant eyes of local administrators. Some parallel can be drawn, for instance, with the tacit and widely violated ban on the public performance of Jewish music.[25] The story "And Now Enters the Giant," written by the Soviet Russian writer Konstantin Vorob'ev, illustrates the fact that the word "challah" did not have to vanish from usage. The protagonist of the story, a Soviet Russian man of the 1960s or early 1970s, goes to a local store to buy a challah. He does it in 1971, the year of the story's first publication, and continues to do it in numerous later reprints of this work.[26]

Challah might have disappeared, at least temporarily, from bakeries during food shortages in 1962 and 1963, when white bread generally became a rare commodity.[27] During the same period, which saw an intensive antireligious campaign, all forms of organized production of matzo fell under a ban.[28] In the 1970s and 1980s, matzo would be produced only in a few Soviet cities, including Moscow and Odessa.[29] Earlier, in 1956, a delegation of the Rabbinical Council of America reported that in Moscow and Leningrad a state-run bakery was allowed to bake matzo under rabbinical supervision, while in some other cities people would purchase flour and bring it to the synagogue, where a small bakery had been set up.[30] The ban introduced in the early 1960s hardly affected our and many other families, who baked matzo themselves at home.

In those years, my mother, who had a gastrointestinal disease, would get, by her doctor's prescription, a few slices of white bread per day at a "diet canteen" in our neighborhood. Canteens of this type, run under medical supervision, emerged in the Soviet urban landscape in the early 1920s, thanks to the initiative of the prominent gastroenterologist Mikhail Pevzner.[31]

In their drive to transform the Jewish foodways, Bolsheviks reaped the fruit of secularization that had ripened before the 1917 revolution, when an increasing number of young, modernized (and often radicalized) Jews rejected *kashrut*, and eating non-kosher often became a sort of an initiation ceremony during their gatherings.[32] In fin-de-siècle Kiev and other Russian cities, many Jews, especially those on the higher rungs of the socioeconomic ladder, transgressed religious laws, including the ultimate taboo of eating pork.[33] In the late 1880s, radical groups among Eastern European Jewish immigrants in England and North America began to entertain themselves with food and dancing on the Day of Atonement, the most solemn and holy day of the Jewish year. The tradition of organizing "Yom Kippur balls" endured for a couple of decades.[34] The 1909 book *Kosher and Treyf, and Other Obligations to Observe*, written by the influential American Jewish socialist Benjamin Feigenbaum, called for discarding old segregating traditions.[35] It seems that most Jewish cookbooks that appeared in the United States before World War I were not kosher. For the Reform Jews who used such cookbooks it was an ideological statement: they sought to emphasize their integration into modernity and American society by eating oysters, shrimp, and ham.[36]

In the Soviet Union, de-kosherization was likewise rooted in ideology, which was of a more antitraditionalist nature than the ideology of Reform Judaism. Disguised or undisguised, Jewish dishes had to be liberated from the restrictions of kashrut, because Jewish religious laws concerning the ritual suitability of food were deemed an obstacle to building a collective, ethnically variegated socialist society. For purely practical reasons, a nondenominational cuisine simplified catering in the army, children's and youth camps, factories, and other public canteens.

Thus, Red Army soldiers' religious or cultural differences did not impact what kind of food they would receive.[37] In addition, Jewish communists, overzealous in their antireligious campaigns, viewed kosher butchering "as ideologically repulsive, primarily because it created a source of income for the rabbis."[38] Still, Jewish butchers continued to operate and, it seems, were the only butchers who knew how to make a profit from collecting down and feathers.[39] In the 1920s and 1930s, the authorities would tolerate kosher slaughtering if the Jewish butchers, or *shokhtim*, were united into cooperatives, paying taxes to the state rather than to the religious community. There were instances, particularly in the later postwar decades, when *shokhtim* continued to give part of their profits to the congregation. In general, however, the local authorities preferred allowing them to do their kosher slaughtering as workers of Soviet enterprises.[40]

I remember that in the late 1950s or early 1960s, two slaughterers, presumably employed by the market administration, shared a hut at the Old Market of Zaporizhia. One of the slaughterers was Jewish. A religious slaughterer was also at hand at the Birobidzhan market.[41] The situation was different in some "outskirts" of the Soviet Union, especially among non-Ashkenazi Jews. Thus, the 1956 delegation of the Rabbinical Council of America reported that Georgia was the only place in the Soviet Union where they saw kosher butcher shops. In general, the Georgian Jews "were maintaining their ancient religious customs, hardly touched by the Soviet regime."[42] In the 1950s, in Frunze (then the name of the capital of the Kyrgyz Republic) a state-run *gastronom* (food store) sold kosher meat.[43] In Tadjikistan and Uzbekistan, the powers-that-be tended to not interfere with Jewish ritual slaughtering.[44]

Significantly, Soviet functionaries deemed kosher food nonessential for religious rituals and preferred to categorize it as simply a variety of food consumed by a certain segment of the Jewish population.[45] In other words, the state, whose constitution promised to guarantee "freedom of conscience," could claim that it did not carry legal responsibility for facilitating production or import of such food, especially as demand for it was declining. Two decades after the revolution, Jews, most notably Ashkenazi Jews—who quantitatively vastly dominated over the less modernized Georgian, Bukharan, and Mountain groups in the Soviet Jewish population—showed the most dramatic decline in religiosity: believers in their fifties outnumbered believers aged sixteen to nineteen by more than 21:1, whereas the ratios for ethnic groups associated with the Russian Orthodox Church and Muslims were 2.4:1 and 1.8:1, respectively.[46]

Peretz Markish's documentary story "Family," published on the Proletarian May Day of 1935 in the second-most important Soviet daily, *Izvestiia*, is set in Leningrad, in a Jewish household whose head is a sixty-seven-year-old factory worker and a veteran of the revolutionary movement. Here is Markish's description of this family's dinner table: it "blossomed with the most exquisite choice of traditional Jewish dishes. [There was] excellently stuffed fish, chopped liver, amazingly prepared horseradish, and pork cutlets of an unparalleled fatness."[47] Thus, "pork cutlets" already feature as part of the new Jewish *tradition*. In his last novel (Markish was one of the cultural figures executed in August 1952), the writer devotes considerable space to showing the social adjustment of Polish Jews who fled to the Soviet Union at the beginning of World War II. Some of his characters, former shtetl dwellers, wind up in a Ural industrial city, where the majority of them manage, inter alia, to quell their prejudice against tomato, which they previously regarded as a gentile variety of food. (Tomatoes, a late arrival to Europe, reached some areas of Poland only in the early twentieth century, and there was no full consensus as to whether an observant Jew could eat this fruit.)[48] In general, the dietary preferences of Markish's literary characters change so much that in the spring of 1942 they celebrate the Passover with Siberian dumplings, *pelmeni*, rather than with traditional food.[49]

Old symbols of Jewish life became outdated in Soviet reality. Thus, in the early twentieth century, Russian Jewish artists consistently turned the goat into a distinctive symbol of the shtetl.[50] In the words of the historian of Russian Jews John Klier, "The animals of the stereotypical shtetl—the Jewish goat, the non-Jewish pig—were indicators of differences in dietary practice, exemplified by the Jewish rules of kashrut."[51] By the mid-1930s, however, these differences were disappearing, and a goat, a cheap milk-giving animal, became, in Soviet appraisal, "a hallmark of Jewish poverty."[52]

I know, but don't remember, that my family kept a goat in the early 1950s, though by that time we lived in a big urban center rather than in a shtetl. The decision to keep a goat in the backyard had nothing to do with Jewish symbolism. The reasons were purely practical, namely, to have an independent supply of milk in an environment notorious for food shortages. The year of my father's demobilization, 1947 (after the war he served as an officer in East Germany, where my mother and older siblings joined him), brought a severe food crisis. Although food supplies began to recover in 1948, average daily diets met full physiological requirements only by the mid-1950s.[53] Significantly, my mother knew how to deal with domestic animals: she was born and grew up in a Jewish village, Nay-Zlatopol, where she graduated from an agricultural college (with Yiddish as the language of instruction) and worked for some time as an animal-rearing specialist. When I was two years old, our family moved from a first-floor apartment to a much better and bigger apartment on the seventh floor in one of the first elevator-equipped buildings in our city, so the goat could no longer stay with us.

The famine of 1946–47 affected the Soviet population less severely than the famines in the postrevolutionary years and then again in the early 1930s, when many thousands of Jewish (and non-Jewish) lives were saved thanks to the extraordinary efforts of the American Jewish Joint Distribution Committee (JDC). On April 29, 1922, the *Reform Advocate*—based in Chicago and which, according to the journal's masthead, was "published every Saturday in the interests of reform Judaism"—came out with an advertisement (page 311) entitled "Have You Relatives in Russia? Send Them Food." It made known that "for ten dollars the Joint Distribution Committee will transmit through the American Relief Administration [under which auspices the JDC initially worked in postrevolutionary Russia] to your starving relatives in Russia a package of nutritious kosher food weighing 117 pounds." Similar advertisements appeared in other periodicals.

Indeed, some of the JDC-sponsored Soviet Jewish institutions, notably old-age homes, had kosher kitchens, and this situation continued at least until the late 1920s.[54] Still, the JDC did not act as a religious crusader. Moreover, the JDC representatives tended to be people of radical background and therefore were at times of one mind with Soviet ideologists. For instance, they saw pig-breeding as an apotheosis of modernization advocated by Jewish activists since the end of the nineteenth century, when some of them began to see farming communities of uncompromising atheists as way stations on the journey of Eastern European Jews journey to a bright future. In line with this ideological orientation, the JDC contributed to the encouragement of pig-breeding among Soviet Jewish famers by supplying them with piglets.

Historically, it was not the first Jewish involvement in pig-breeding. It is known, for example, that as early as the sixteenth century some Jewish owners of taverns in Poland raised pigs, which could be fed from the byproducts of brewing and distilling.[55] The motif of rationality also featured in the Soviet Jewish discourse, which presented the cultivation of pigs as an effective way of solving food problems rather than a religious anathema. The number of Jewish farmers involved in this branch of animal breeding kept growing. In 1938 the Kalinindorf Jewish National District, founded in Ukraine in 1927 as the first of five Jewish territorial units in the European part of the Soviet Union, boasted twenty-seven pig farms and three rabbit farms. An agronomist named M. Druianov published several pamphlets, instructing Yiddish-speaking collective farmers how to work with pigs and rabbits (another non-kosher animal).[56] Pig-breeding gained traction in my mother's native Nay-Zlatopol, which became the center of a Jewish national district, formed in 1929, and in other areas of Jewish agricultural activity, including the Jewish Autonomous Region. The Russian play *The Frontier Guard*, written by Vladimir

Bill'-Belotserkovskii, contains the following discourse between a kidnapped Jewish Red Army soldier (Kogan) and his interrogator (Captain):

CAPTAIN: Jewish?

KOGAN: Yes. A Jew of the Soviet land.

CAPTAIN: Why this emphasizing? Is the Jew of our land any worse?

KOGAN: Maybe he is not worse, but he is worse off.

CAPTAIN: How about pork, do you eat it?

KOGAN: Ask my father.

CAPTAIN: Why father?

KOGAN: He is the best pig-breeder in Birobidzhan.[57]

Incidentally, Zionist youth did not lag behind in this respect. In the 1920s in the Crimea, Zionist pioneers (*halutzim*) organized several communes, in which they prepared themselves for life in Palestine. The biggest of these communes carried the name of Tel Hai, the Galilee settlement where Joseph Trumpeldor, the founder of the Halutz movement, met with a tragic death. In 1926, Israel Joshua Singer, the elder brother of Isaac Bashevis Singer (the 1978 Nobel Prize winner for literature) and a popular Yiddish writer in his own right, visited the Soviet Union. In his travel notes, he hailed the Crimean Tel Hai as the best Soviet Jewish agricultural settlement he had seen. Singer was particularly impressed by the halutzim's achievements in rearing pigs. A former member of the commune, Zvi Uman, reminisced later how their pig-breeders had been awarded the first prize at the all-Crimean agricultural exhibition. Their unusually large and fecund Yorkshire pigs, presented to them by the JDC, became objects of general attention.[58] But then again, the Muslim Crimean Tatars could not be very strong competitors in this field. During the entire Soviet period, pig-breeding in Muslim republics remained at a negligible level compared with the rest of the country.[59]

Joseph Opatoshu, an American Yiddish writer, who also visited the Soviet Union, witnessed in one of the Jewish villages a conflict between a farmer and his wife: the man wanted to get a cow instead of a hog, whereas his wife and the local agronomist tried to convince him of the rationality of keeping pigs.[60] The situation appears somewhat different in the family portrayed in the 1928 short story "A Pig," by the Soviet Yiddish writer Abraham Cahan. Its protagonist, Yoylek, fifty-five, a recent re-settler from a shtetl to a Jewish village, gets a pig as a gift of the local department of the Agro-Joint (a subsidiary of the JDC). This happens on the eve of Yom Kippur, and the next day Yoylek fasts and prays together with other elderly men while the women and younger villagers continue to work. In the meantime, Yoylek cannot stop thinking about the pig. He knows that the animal remains unfed, because his wife still does not want to pay any attention to the Agro-Joint's present, regarding it as fundamentally wrong to keep a pig in a Jewish household. When Yoylek comes home after nightfall on the day of Yom Kippur, he feeds the pig first, before eating something himself, and his wife eventually relents, accepting her husband's cogent arguments.[61]

Students of Soviet Yiddish literature and culture paid special attention to pig-related topics in the poetry of Leyb Kvitko, one of the most popular of Soviet writers for children, whose poems sold many millions of copies, especially in posthumous editions (he was a victim of the August 1952 execution). Kvitko's versified image of the swine herder Anna Vanna and her pink-and-white suckling pigs, translated into Russian, Ukrainian, and some other languages, became a favorite poem for several generations of Soviet children.[62] Tsodek Dolgopolski, a prolific Minsk-based writer who wrote satiric poetry under the pseudonym of Horodoker, argued in one of his poems that "pigs represent for us a new problem, / 'pigs' (particularly of the Yorkshire breed) / is a new word, / introduced only last year." Indeed, Yiddish did not excel at pig-related lexical nomenclature, so Soviet language lanners had to equip it with terms for "to farrow," "sow," and other related notions. Meanwhile, many Jews did not want to hear about pigs in any language, particularly in Yiddish, traditionally referring to this animal as *davaraher*, or "another thing" — something not to be mentioned. Peretz Hirschbein, Opatoshu's colleague as a contributor to the New York Yiddish daily *Tog*, spent almost a year in the Soviet Union and wrote the following in the form of a monologue of an elderly Jewish colonist:

> Why was it necessary to bring a pig into our village? . . . You can imagine what kind of a mood it created. Have you seen such a thing happen anywhere in this world, that into a Jewish village, thoroughly Jewish, someone suddenly brings a pig, may the devil take it? . . . Do you want to know what happened later? It was destroyed. . . . How? We simply kept praying quietly. . . . A few observant men, including me, prayed until the pig died. Its body was found in the morning — stretched out in the very middle of our village![63]

Yet despite the resistance of the traditional segment of the population, the Soviet Jew increasingly became, in the words of Menshevik Grigori Aronson, a *khazeyrim-yid*, or "pigs-Jew," crossing the important line that divided cultivation of pigs from eating pork.[64] Even in cities, such as Vinnytsia, some Jews kept pigs in their household farms.[65] Kvitko, whose mid-1930s poem about Anna Vanna does not mention eating pork, several years later wrote another poem, "The Piglet Eats to Make Himself Edible."[66] As Anna Shternshis found out in her oral-history research, a number of her respondents, Jews from the former Soviet Union, mentioned a separate pan for frying pork.[67] This was certainly a very radical addition to — or, most commonly, replacement of — the traditional mandatory separation of *fleyshik* (meaty) and *milkhik* (milky) products. There were also other "tricks" to make eating pork "less harmful." For instance, to eat it on a windowsill without using any cutlery and plates, or to take a piece of the front part rather than from the back, especially as Jews usually did not consume the hindquarters of any carcass, even of a kosher animal.[68] At the same time, non-Ashkenazi Soviet Jews seldom ate pork. Importantly, the majority of them lived among Muslims in Central Asia and the Caucasus, whose revulsion to pork remained deeply ingrained during the entire Soviet period.[69]

As I have already mentioned, I was born and grew up in the Ukrainian city of Zaporizhia. My extended family combined "Soviet and kosher," to borrow Anna Shternshis's term. My father was a member of the Communist Party, a commissar during World War II, a history teacher before and after the war. My pious grandfather, with whom we lived in the same apartment, unofficially practiced as a religious butcher. His father, my great-grandfather, was a rabbi, who published two books, in Hebrew, discussing various issues of kosher slaughtering. Yet the revolution interrupted the family tradition of piety. My mother and all her siblings were completely secular. In general, only many years later, when I already lived in Moscow, did I meet several seriously observant Jews who belonged to the generation of my parents, born in the first two decades of the twentieth century.

As long as my grandfather lived with us — that is, the first ten years of my life — we ate kosher-slaughtered chickens as well as, sometimes, ducks, geese, and turkeys. The fowls would be bought alive at the market. Sometimes my mother would keep a goose on our balcony, force feeding it for a while before asking her father to take the bird to the bathroom, which functioned also as his slaughterhouse. The aim of force feeding was to get better *grivenes* (or *gribenes*), cracklings, and *schmaltz*, or fat, rather than foie gras (nobody in our surroundings ever heard about it). Grivenes, or *shkvarki* in Russian, with mashed potatoes was a popular dish in our family. My mother also cooked an excellent *heldzl* — chicken neck skin stuffed with flour, schmaltz, onion, and some other ingredients. On our menu there was a virtual item: *martsepanes*, or marzipan. If I did not want to eat something cooked by my mother, she would react by asking the same rhetorical question: "Do you prefer to eat marzipan?" It is worth mentioning that my mother never saw *real* marzipan, and I learned its taste many years later, outside the Soviet Union.[70]

No Jewish and general Soviet holiday or birthday passed without such special-occasion dishes as gefilte fish, and *salat Olivier*. This salad was claimed to be invented in the 1860s by Lucien Olivier, a Russian chef of Belgian origin.[71] It was made with diced boiled potatoes, carrots, pickles, green peas, eggs, and diced boiled chicken (in our family, recipes with ham or bologna sausage was considered *goyish*). The salad contained mayonnaise, a newcomer in our cuisine. In the early 1950s, my mother bought it for the first time, but, after tasting it, chucked the jar into the bin, and only later she and the entire family learned that this "inedible substance" had to be added as dressing. This revelation brought onto our table various salads, most notably the Olivier one. "Birthdays, engagements, dissertation-completion bashes, farewell parties for Jews who were emigrating (these sometimes felt like funeral wakes) — there was no special 'table' without salat Olivier."[72]

Our food was not kosher even when my grandfather slaughtered fowl. In fact, he and my grandmother kept kosher, but all other members of the family mixed *milkhik* with *fleyshik*, and hitherto tabooed pork also increasingly became part of our diet. My mother preserved some red lines uncrossed: we did not have on our table rabbits, game, or seafood. I remember that once or twice mother cooked wild pigeons shot by our neighbor, an amateur hunter, but she abstained from eating them. Her, and my aunts', cuisine differed significantly from the cuisine of our non-Jewish neighbors. Apart from cooking Jewish fare, my mother and her generation of women incorporated numerous non-Jewish dishes, but in a "Judaized" form. For instance, our borscht did not contain pork *salo*, or cured slabs of fatback, an important item in the Ukrainian cuisine. Significantly, meat would be soaked in water before cooking, which was a residue of the traditional process of koshering meat by soaking the blood out of it.

The change of the main ingredient in the recipe of the so-called Jewish *salo* illustrates the transition from kosher to pork. Jewish cuisine had an answer to the Ukrainian *salo*: sheep fatback, boiled until ready, then spiced with black pepper, garlic, salt, and bay leaves, and placed for a couple of days under a heavy iron or some other heavy things. My older sister remembers the "sheep *salo*" period in our family history of the "Jewish *salo*." In my memory, the Jewish *salo* was already made using, as a rule, pig *salo* with strips of ham. For many years, before I heard about the initial recipe of the Jewish *salo*, I was sure that it was garlic that made this dish "Jewish."

Not only did pork become a staple of Soviet Jews' diets, but it seems that some Soviet Jews (in my own experience I never met such people) even began to believe that there used to be Jewish butchers who knew how to make pork kosher. Anna Shternshis reproduces her conversation with several former Soviet citizens:

"You should try some of our food, it is all kosher," explains Gary, the manager of an old-age home in Berlin, as he leads me to the cafeteria. Every day its residents, most of whom are Jews from the former Soviet Union, gather here for lunch. . . . I sit next to an elderly gentleman . . . Grigorii. He looks at me . . . and says, "When I was a little boy, I ate real kosher meat, not like this. It was tasty, it was greasy, and it was great." "What kind of meat was it?" I ask. "It was pork," replies Grigorii. "There are special butchers for pigs. Otherwise their meat is not kosher. Ordinary butchers cannot slaughter pigs." "That is right," says Lyubov, who is sitting at the end of the table. "I heard about it," she adds. "One also needs special butchers for rabbits. I like rabbit meat. . . . But there are no butchers in Germany who can slaughter them right."[73]

Non-kosher "Jewish food," including dishes with pork, became a marker of post-Soviet Jewry in the former USSR, Israel, the United States, Germany, and other countries.[74] Striking hybrids of Jewish tradition and Soviet-style Jewishness can be observed in Brighton Beach. For instance, during the Passover some local restaurants don't serve bread, although the menu otherwise remains the same as on ordinary days. As a result, matzo may accompany seafood and pork. The bulk of Brighton Beach restaurants remain closed on Yom Kippur and open after the nightfall for a completely non-kosher break-fast, or *prazdnichnyiuzhin*, "festive dinner," as the restaurants market such meals.

It is hard to agree fully with Alice Nakhimovsky's conclusion that by the 1950s and 1960s "Jewish food was part of a hidden world."[75] In fact, Jewish food certainly was not particularly hidden in such places as the former Ukrainian shtetl of Shargorod, where Jews "formed the most visible and influential group in the town."[76] Weddings, with tables loaded with Jewish dishes, would be organized as public events rather than secret gatherings. Thus, guests at my wife's and my wedding, in 1976, at the restaurant of the Moscow hotel Mentropol, situated just a couple of hundred yards from Red Square, were regaled with various "general dishes," prepared by the chef, but also with gefilte fish of my mother-in-law's cooking and with her aunt's strudel. The institute of Jewish caterers, known in Yiddish as *sarverns* or *sarverkes*, survived in some areas, notably in Moldova. For all that, Nakhimovsky is certainly right that the Jewish food tradition transformed and endured in the Soviet Union, by and large in private kitchens rather than in public spaces. Ultimately, this modified tradition, free from religious dietary restrictions, moved to public spaces, both in the former Soviet Union and the countries where former Soviet Jews had opened food stores, restaurants, and catering businesses.

NOTES

1. Bentsiyon Katz, "Der nayer alter komisar Shimen Dimanshteyn," *Haynt*, October 3, 1930, 5; Daniel Charney, *A yortsendlikaza, 1914–1924* (New York: Tsiko, 1943), 212–13.

2. Elissa Bemporad, *Becoming Soviet Jews: The Bolshevik Experiment in Minsk* (Bloomington: Indiana University Press, 2013), 126.

3. Menashe Halpern, *Parmetn: zikhroynes un shilderungen* (São Paulo, Brazil: Alveltlekheryidisher kultur-kongres, 1952), 323–24.

4. Bentsiyon Katz, "Peysekh in Moskve in der tsayt fun militerishnkomunizm," *Haynt*, April 8, 1925, 7.

5. Osaf Litovskii, "Staroesredstvo," *Izvestiia*, April 15, 1919, 1.

6. See, for example, Zalman Vendrof, "Peysekhkumt," *Der moment*, April 24, 1925, 5.

7. Jeffrey Veidlinger, *In the Shadow of the Shtetl: Small-town Jewish Life in Soviet Ukraine* (Bloomington: Indiana University Press, 2013), 142.

8. "Lack of Kosher Food in Moscow Checks Reshevsky, Chess King," *New York Herald Tribune*, January 17, 1939, 19.

9. Adrianne Kathleen Jacobs, "The Many Flavors of Socialism: Modernity and Tradition in Late Soviet Food Culture, 1965–1985" (PhD dissertation, University of North Carolina, 2015), 129–30.

10. Gennady Estraikh, *Yiddish in the Cold War* (Oxford: Legenda, 2008), 51.

11. Osher Perelman, *Birobidzhan: shilderungen fun a rayze in yuli-oygust 1934* (Warsaw: Groshn-bibliotek, 1934), 184.

12. David Khait, "Storona Birobidzhanskaia," *Bezbozhnik* 6 (1936): 8–9.

13. Robert Weinberg, "Purge and Politics in the Periphery: Birobidzhan in 1937," *Slavic Review* 52, no. 1 (1993): 27; Ekaterina Libinzon, "Birobidzhan: Moialiubov' i moiabol'," *Korni* 34 (2007): 26; Motl Sirota, "Vospominaniia: Zapiskiaktera," *Lekhaim* 7 (2008): 37. See also, for example, E. A. Rees, *Iron Lazar: A Political Biography of Lazar Kaganovich* (London: Anthem Press, 2012), 215; Geoffrey Roberts, *Molotov: Stalin's Cold Warrior* (Washington DC: Potomac Books, 2011), 9.

14. See, for example, Iakov A. Kaminskii, *Organizatsiia i tekhnikasovetskoitorgovli* (Moscow: Gostorgizdat, 1954), 503.

15. Vasilii A. Fedotov, *Tovarovedeniegastronomicheskikhtovarov* (Moscow: Gostorgizdat, 1955), 61.

16. Esther Markish, *The Long Return* (New York: Ballantine, 1978), 137.

17. Lev Druskin, *Spasennaiakniga* (St. Petersburg: Gelikon, 2001), 292.

18. Alice S. Nakhimovsky, "You Are What They Ate: Russian Jews Reclaim Their Foodways," *Shofar: An Interdisciplinary Journal of Jewish Studies* 25, no. 1 (2006): 67.

19. O. P. Molchanova et al., eds., *Kniga o vkusnoi i zdorovoipishche* (Moscow: Pishchepromizdat, 1952), 136; Robert Service, *A History of Modern Russia from Nicholas IIto Vladimir Putin* (Cambridge MA: Harvard University Press, 2013), 320.

20. E. L. Khudiakov et al., eds., *Kniga o vkusnoi i zdorovoipishche* (Moscow: Pishchepromizdat: 1939), 84, 193, 240, 282.

21. Edward Geist, "Cooking Bolshevik: Anastas Mikoian and the Making of the *Book about Delicious and Healthy Food*," *Russian Review* 71, no. 2 (2012): 304.

22. Estraikh, *Yiddish in the Cold War*, 42.

23. Boris Kotlerman, "The Image of Birobidzhan in Soviet Yiddish Belles Letters," *Jews in Eastern Europe* 3 (2002): 58; Estraikh, *Yiddish in the Cold War*, 55.

24. Albert Axelbank, "A 'Jewish National State'?," *Present Tense: The Magazine of World Jewish Affairs* 4, no. 1 (1976): 20.

25. Zeev Khanin, *Documents on Ukrainian-Jewish Identity and Emigration, 1944–1990* (Portland OR: Frank Cass, 2003), 32.

26. See the first publication: Konstantin Vorob'ev, "Votprishelvelikan," *Nash sovremennik* 9 (1971): 36.

27. See, for example, Ilia E. Zelenin, "Agrarnaiapolitika N. S. Khrushcheva i sel'skoekhoziaistvo," *Trudy Institutarossiiskoiistorii* RAN 2 (2000): 394–425; Nataliia B. Lebina, "Khleb—imiaprilagatel'noe," *Noveishaiaistoriia Rossii* 2 (2011): 210–220.

28. Mikhail Mitsel, "Moskovskaiakhoral'naiasinagoga, vlast' i zarubezhnyekontakry: period pozdnei 'ottepeli' i perekhoda k 'kollektivnomurukovodstvu' (1960–1965)," in *100 let: Moskovskaiakhoral'naiasinagoga*, ed. Alexander Lokshin (Moscow: Dom evreiskoiknigi, 2006), 215–17.

29. See, for example, Israel V. Shvartsblat, "Pravda dolzhnabyt' slyshna," *Literaturnaiagazeta*, March 3, 1971, 9; Adolf Shaevich and Eteri Chalandziia, *Evreiskiivopros* (Moscow: ANF, 2011), 256.

30. *The Status of the Jews behind the Iron Curtain: What the Delegation of the Rabbinical Council of America Found in Its Survey inside Russian and the Satellite Nations* (New York: New York Journal American, n.d.), 21.

31. Vladimir I. Borodulin and Aleksei V. Topolianskii, "Kistoriigastroenterologii v SSSR: o nauchnoishkole M. I. Pevznera," *Problemysotsial'noigigieny, zdravookhraneniia i istoriimeditsiny* 6 (2012): 47.

32. See, for example, Inna Shtakser, *The Making of Jewish Revolutionaries in the Pale of Settlement: Community and Identity during the Russian Revolution and Its Immediate Aftermath, 1905–1907* (New York: Palgrave Macmillan, 2014), 43.

33. Natan Meir, "From Pork to *Kapores*: Transformation in Religious Practice among the Jews of Late Imperial Kiev," *Jewish Quarterly Review* 97, no. 4 (2007): 628–30.

34. Rebecca E. Margolis, "A Tempest in Three Teapots: Yom Kippur Balls in London, New York, and Montreal," in *The Canadian Jewish Studies Reader*, eds. Richard Menkis and Norman Ravvin (Calgary, Canada: Red Deer Press, 2004), 141–63.

35. Benjamin Feigenbaum, *Kosher un treyf un anderemitsves* (New York: Frayergedank, 1909).

36. Barbara Kirshenblatt-Gimblett, "Recipes for Creating Community: The Jewish Charity Cookbook in America," *Jewish Folklore and Ethnology Review* 9, no. 1–2 (1987): 8.

37. Brandon Schechter, "The State's Pot and the Soldier's Spoon: Rations (*Paëk*) in the Red Army," in *Hunger and War: Food Provisioning in the Soviet Union*

during World War II, ed. Wendy Z. Goldman and Donald Filtzer (Bloomington IN: Indiana University Press, 2015), 110–11.

38. Bemporad, *Becoming Soviet Jews*, 123.

39. "Aktivnost' popov i bezdeiatel'nost' profsoiuzov," *Pravda*, April 24, 1929, 3; Abram Agranovskii, "Chestnaiasovetskaiakoshka," *Izvestiia*, December 16, 1929, 2.

40. Mordechai Altshuler, *Religion and Jewish Identity in the Soviet Union, 1941–1964* (Waltham MA: Brandeis University Press, 2012), 164.

41. Iosif Brener, *Lekhaim, Birobidzhan!* (Krasnoyarsk, Russia: Krasnoiarskiipisatel', 2007), 126.

42. "Some Soviet Jews Free to Worship," *New York Times*, August 8, 1956, 2.

43. Aleksandr P. Iarkov, *Evrei v Kyrgyzstane* (Bishkek, Kyrgyzstan: Menora, 2000), 128.

44. Yaakov Ro'i, "The Religious Life of the Bukharan Jewish Community in Soviet Central Asia after World War II," in *Bukharan Jews in the Twentieth Century: History, Experience and Narration*, ed. Ingeborg Baldauf, Moshe Gammer, and Thomas Loy (Wiesbaden, Germany: Reichert Verlag, 2008), 67–69.

45. Altshuler, *Religion and Jewish Identity in the Soviet Union*, 161.

46. Felix Corley, "Believers' Responses to the 1937 and 1939 Soviet Censuses," *Religion, State and Society* 22, no. 4 (1994): 407–8.

47. Peretz Markish, "Sem'ia," *Izvestiia*, May 1, 1935, 6.

48. See, for example, Norman Salsitz and Richard Skolnik, *A Jewish Boyhood in Poland: Remembering Kolbuszowa* (Syracuse NY: Syracuse University Press, 1999), 177; P. Berman [Max Weinreich], "Ven hot ir tsum ershtn mol gegesn a 'treyfenem epl'," *Forverts*, July 7, 1951, 8; idem, "Vi azoy yidn hobn zikh oysgelernt esn 'treyfene epl'," *Forverts*, August 9, 1951, 2, 7; Gennady Estraikh, "Nokh a molvegn di pomidorn," *Forverts*, January 6, 2012, 11.

49. Gennady Estraikh, "Anti-Nazi Rebellion in Peretz Markish's Drama and Prose," in *A Captive in the Dawn: The Life and Work of Peretz Markish*, ed. Joseph Sherman et al. (Oxford: Legenda, 2011), 181.

50. Hillel Kazovsky, "Jewish Art between *yidishkayt* and Civilization," in *The Shtetl: Image and Reality*, ed. Gennady Estraikh and Mikhail Krutikov (Oxford: Legenda, 2000), 81–82.

51. John Klier, *Russians, Jews, and the Pogroms of 1881–1882* (New York: Cambridge University Press, 2011), 72.

52. "Predsel'soveta," *Izvestiia*, July 11, 1935, 3.

53. Donald Filtzer, *The Hazards of Urban Life in Late Stalinist Russia: Health, Hygiene, and Living Standards, 1943–1953* (New York: Cambridge University Press, 2010), 163–69.

54. Michael Beizer and Mikhail Mitsel, *The American Brother: The "Joint" in Russia, the USSR and CIS* (New York: JDC, 2004), 57.

55. Glenn Dynner, *Yankel's Tavern: Jews, Liquor, and Life in the Kingdom of Poland* (New York: Oxford University Press, 2014), 65–66.

56. M. Druianov, *Krolik-tsukht in der yidisher kolektivervirtshaft* (Moscow: Tsentral-farlag, 1930); M. Druianov, *Hodevanye fun khazeyrim* (Moscow: Tsentralfarlag, 1931); M. Druianov, *Khazeyrim-fermes* (Moscow: Emes, 1933).

57. Gennady Estraikh, "Pig-Breeding, *Shiksas*, and Other *Goyish* Themes in Soviet Yiddish Literature and Life," *Symposium: A Quarterly Journal in Modern Literatures* 57, no. 3 (2003): 163.

58. Estraikh, "Pig-Breeding, *Shiksas*, and Other *Goyish* Themes," 163–64.

59. James Critchlow, *Nationalism in Uzbekistan: A Soviet Republic's Road to Sovereignty* (Boulder CO: Westview Press, 1991), 21.

60. Gennady Estraikh, "Soviet Dreams of a Cultural Exile," in *Joseph Opatoshu: A Yiddish Writer between Europe and America*, ed. Sabine Koller, Gennady Estraikh, and Mikhail Krutikov (Oxford: Legenda, 2013), 41.

61. Estraikh, "Pig-Breeding, *Shiksas*, and Other *Goyish* Themes," 161.

62. Anna Shternshis, "May Day, Tractors, and Piglets: Yiddish Songs for Little Communists," in *The Art of Being Jewish in Modern Times*, ed. Barbara Kirshenblatt-Gimblett (Philadelphia: University of Pennsylvania Press, 2008), 94.

63. Gennady Estraikh, "From 'Green Fields' to 'Red Fields': Peretz Hirschbein's Soviet Sojourn, 1928–1929," *Jews in Russia and Eastern Europe* 1 (2006): 70. When the authorities tried to set up a pig-breeding farm in a Chechen village, within hours locals had killed the entire herd. David Motadel, *Islam and Nazi Germany's War* (Cambridge MA: Harvard University Press, 2014), 135.

64. Grigori Aronson, *Di yidishe problem in sovetrusland* (New York: Veker, 1944), 172.

65. Aron Erlikh, "Posledniedni Erusalimki," *Pravda*, May 22, 1935, 4.

66. Leyb Kvitko, *Nayelider* (Moscow: Emes, 1939), 50. For an interpretation of this poem as a metaphorical one, see Velvl Chenin, "Ispoved' porosenka," *Ierusalimskii zhurnal* 23 (2006): 186–92.

67. Anna Shternshis, "Salo on Challah: Soviet Jews' Experience of Food in the 1920s–1950s," in *Jews and Their Foodways*, ed. Anat Helman (New York: Oxford University Press, 2015), 15.

68. Maria Kaspina, "Folk Judaism: Variations of Religious Practices among the Jews of Ukraine and Moldova," *State, Religion and Church* 3, no. 1 (2016): 75–76.

69. Yaacov Ro'i, *Islam in the Soviet Union: From the Second World War to Gorbachev* (New York: Columbia University Press, 2000), 463–64.

70. Led-Pensil, "Martsepanes," *Forverts*, October 28, 1940, 3.

71. See also Anna Kushkova, "V tsentrestola: zenit i zakat salata 'Oliv'e'," *Novoe-literaturnoeobozrenie* 6 (2005): 278–313.

72. Anya von Bremzen, *Mastering the Art of Soviet Cooking: A Memoir of Food and Longing* (New York: Crown, 2013), 176.

73. Anna Shternshis, *Soviet and Kosher: Jewish Popular Culture in the Soviet Union, 1923–1939* (Bloomington: Indiana University Press, 2006), 1. See also Shternshis, "Salo on Challah," 16–17.

74. See, for example, Julia Bernstein, "Symbolic Meaning of Pork Crossing National Borders in the Migration Process: From a National Collective Anti-Key Symbol to the Manifestation of Russian Jewish Identity in Israel," *Hagar: Studies in Culture, Polity and Identities* 10, no. 2 (2012): 17–47.

75. Alice Stone Nakhimovsky, "Public and Private in the Kitchen: Eating Jewish in the Soviet State," in *Food and Judaism*, ed. Leonard J. Greenspoon, Ronald A. Simkins, and Geral Shapiro (Omaha NE: Creighton University Press, 2005), 153.

76. Charles E. Hoffman, *Red Shtetl: The Survival of a Jewish Town Under Soviet Communism* (New York: American Jewish Joint Distribution Committee, 2002), 117.

6

The Embodied Republic

Colonial and Postcolonial French Sephardic Taste

....

JOËLLE BAHLOUL

Paris, November 15, 2015: two days after the terrorist attacks that killed 130 civilians in the heart of Paris, many French people pay homage to the memory of the murdered citizens by gathering at the Place de la République, the sanctified site for the veneration of the French Republic. They are young and old, seem to be of various social, ethnic, and religious backgrounds, and they are here to pay tribute to the Republic they feel has been deeply hurt on that terrible Friday, November 13. People bring flowers; blue, white, and red flags; images of Marianne, female figurative symbol of the Republic; and in silence, they expressed their profound attachment to the republican values of France, liberty, equality, fraternity.[1] Since that time, the French military has experienced a record number of voluntary enrollments, French flags have appeared on windows and balconies, and the spirit and values of the Republic have been defended vigorously by a large number of citizens in the media, in demonstrations in support of the victims' families, and in various commemorative events. The Republic is strong and protective,

139

said French president François Hollande, and the citizens have demonstrated that as well.

A number of religious communities and organizations have expressed similar support for the victims of the attacks and the values of the Republic. The national Jewish community has been one of them, although they had already demonstrated that support for about two centuries, because the Republic accorded them equal citizenship and social and political emancipation, and they still remember it. That process has been experienced by Jews of all origins, especially those whose families have immigrated from North Africa and the Middle East since the 1950s.[2] Starting in the early twentieth century, Jews of colonial North Africa and the Middle East have slowly but surely expressed their desire to become full-fledged members of the French Republican nation in a number of ways. This process started with the schooling of their children in public French schools, the Frenchification of their language practices, and even that of their bodily practices, from dressing to food, which they generally viewed as forms of emancipatory modernization and "Europeanization."[3] Thus even before their massive postcolonial migration to Europe (and France in particular) in the 1950s and 1960s, those Jews had been moving to France through their bodily practices, including diet.

My goal in this chapter is to provide ethnographic evidence of this North African Jewish fervor for the Republic in the colonial and postcolonial period, unfolding in the intimacy of food and language practices. To that end, I will use the ethnographic data I have collected for forty years among North African Jews living in France.[4]

FRENCH SEPHARDIC JEWS

Within the world's third-largest Jewish population, after Israel and the United States, Sephardim from North Africa and the Middle East make up a modest majority of a little over 50 percent of France's Jewish community; that is, about 250,000 persons. They also are the second largest Sephardic population in the world, after the Israeli Sephardim, thus the largest Sephardic diaspora in the world. This demographic situation gives this population an important status in the development of Jewish affairs worldwide. Their recent history is also closely related to mid-twentieth century colonial French and European history. The colonial wars of the mid-twentieth century have forced a large majority of Jews of North Africa and the Middle East to the migratory roads, toward North America for a small proportion, to Israel to a moderate extent, and to Europe and France in particular, in a large proportion.[5] Those who arrived in France settled mainly in large cities of the Mediterranean and southern regions and in Paris. Migration to France has thus been the culmination of the Frenchification and Europeanization of these Mediterranean Jews who, in the process, had partly secularized, although some religious life has been preserved as a form of collective memory, especially in the kitchen, around the table, and in specific festive menus.

THE COLONIZED JEW AND HIS OR HER FOOD

In his groundbreaking book, *Colonizer and the Colonized* (1967), Albert Memmi elaborated for the first time on the complex political relations between the two protagonists of the colonial system. His primary goal was to decipher the effects of colonialism on the colonized peoples, as evidenced in the initial French title of the book, *Portrait du colonisé* (Portrait of the Colonized). Albert Memmi is a ninety-five-year-old Tunisian Jewish writer and social thinker who has been living in France for some sixty years and is one of the leading French intellectuals of the second half of the twentieth century. His oeuvre is broadly concerned with the Jewish experience of colonialism in North Africa, although his book took a universal approach to this particular part of Jewish history. The book, which in various parts specifically deals with the Jews in North African colonial society, thus considers them colonized peoples, even though some elite members of their communities might have had special entrée into the local European societies.

The book was groundbreaking for two main reasons. First it was definitely written—and read—as the testimony of a native colonized author.[6] Memmi's literature is composed as a native voice. Secondly, the book was first published in France in the late 1950s, at the peak of decolonization and the colonial wars in North Africa. As Memmi took a portrait approach to the dual relation between the colonized and the colonizer, much like Sartre's portrait of the anti-Semite, he points to the personal, somehow psychological, aspects of the colonizer's view of the colonized, including the latter's culture expressed in bodily facts.[7] To be sure, Memmi's goal is to underline the racist attitude and views inscribed in the colonial system. Some pages highlight the physical disgust that the colonizer entertains toward the colonized's sensory world, including the latter's domestic food and odors:

> The little strains of daily life will support him [the colonizer] in his decisive discovery more than great intellectual convulsions will. Having first eaten *couscous* with curiosity, he now tastes it from time to time out of politeness and finds that "it's filling, it's degrading and it's not nourishing." It is "torture by suffocation," he says humorously. Or if he does like *couscous*, he cannot stand that "fairground music" which seizes and deafens him each time he passes a café. "Why so loud? How can they hear each other?" He is tortured by that odor of old mutton fat which stinks up many of the houses. He is unable to conceal the revulsions he feels.[8]

I argue that this colonial relation, intruding into the very intimacy of domestic life and flavors, is also at work in "taste," understood as general lifestyle and as it applies to the body broadly conceived.[9] Language plays a large part in the colonial relation between colonized and colonizer. Memmi writes: "The colonized is saved from illiteracy only to fall into linguistic dualism. . . . The entire bureaucracy, the entire court system, all industry hears and uses the colonizer's language. Likewise, highway markings, railroad station signs, street signs and receipts make the colonized feel like a foreigner in his own country. In the colonial context, bilingualism is necessary."[10]

Memmi describes the development among some of the colonized of a persistent strategy of effacing the parts of their lifestyle that repel the colonizer's dominant culture, in an effort to gain recognition and cultural legitimation. Memmi again: "The first attempt of the colonized is to change his condition by changing his skin. . . . A blonde woman, be she dull or anything else, appears superior to any brunette. A product manufactured by the colonizer is accepted with confidence. His habits, clothing, food, architecture are closely copied, even if inappropriate. . . . One must resemble the white man, the non-Jew, the colonizer."[11]

In writing these words, Memmi was clearly thinking of the North African Jews' attempts to assimilate into European culture: "[The Jews]' constant and very justifiable ambition is to escape from their colonized condition, an additional burden in an already oppressive status. To that end, they endeavor to resemble the colonizer in the frank hope that he may cease to consider them different from him. Hence their efforts to forget the past, to change collective habits, and their enthusiastic adoption of Western language, culture and customs."[12]

No approach to the food practices of French Jews of North African origin can avoid taking into consideration their colonial background. It is in this historical context that Jews have developed specific bodily and social tastes, which they eventually consolidated after their immigration into France. Their children and grandchildren have reproduced and often innovated upon this taste, confirming the potent mark of colonialism on their parents' and grandparents' current bodily practices and collective memory. Part of my social cultural approach in this chapter will thus be ethnohistorical in nature. It will also point to food as an important dimension in Jewish immigrants' experiences, that is, its political and historical organization. How culture, history, and politics evolve in culinary preparations and in gatherings around the table constitutes the major interrogation of the "cultural intimacy" of French Sephardic Jews' postcolonial kitchen and personal identity.

THE REPUBLICAN CONTRACT AROUND THE TABLE

The historical specificity of North African Jewish immigrants and their descendants in twenty-first-century France lies in their particular political and cultural relation to French colonialism and its aftermath. Their history as French citizens began in the last quarter of the nineteenth century, as the Napoleonic system of French citizenship was becoming strictly enforced throughout the French territory and its colonies in compliance with the rules of the colonial Republic. Under these rules, Jews are integrated into the French nation as equal citizens, who are obligated by the Republican contract.[13] The ideological foundation of this social contract requires that all aspects of particular ascription, whether religious, linguistic, or ethnic, be displayed within the limits of private life, that is, the domestic and family domain. Outside of the private realm, in public life, adopted citizens are obligated to display signs of their membership in the French nation and its secular culture. In public life, they should demonstrate their willingness to participate in the free, equal, and fraternal French nation and culture. The French Republic thus endows Jews with every part of French citizenship in public life, under the condition that no sign of religious affiliation and belief is displayed. The Republic establishes a clear boundary between private and public in the expression of the Jewish minority identity. Jews in France and in French colonies have responded with fervor to these civic requirements, especially throughout the second half of the twentieth century. Some have interpreted the Republican contract in terms of substantial erasure of any Jewish sign of religious affiliation, both in public and in private, producing forms of "Marranism" in modern and postmodern life.[14] Nevertheless, the majority of Jews of North African origin have utilized the division between the private and public domains to achieve a dual historical, political, and social goal: the need to retain some religious observance within the limits of the domestic and family domains while making sure they are considered full-fledged French citizens in their professional and social public lives.[15] Despite occasional public displays of Judaic religious practice in contemporary

French social life, this attitude among French Jews, both Sephardic and Ashkenazic, remains in effect in the early twenty-first century.[16] Postcolonial French Jews have turned the application of the Republican requirements into the essential condition for their emancipation and integration into civil society. Consequently, religious observance has withdrawn into the core of domestic and private life, as elaborated in food. To this day, the kitchen and the table are used as dramatic scenes for the politics of Jewish identity in the French nation, behind the porous gates of domestic life.

In its practical execution, the Republican contract has resulted in the creation of strictly delineated boundaries — in time, in social structures, and in space — for the practice of religion and tradition in Sephardic French Jewish life. In effect, these boundaries often result in making a strong distinction between the religious and the secular realms. Secularization has indeed been one of the consequences of the Frenchification (Europeanization) of formerly colonized Jews in North Africa. The process — viewed by many, at least in the first decade following migration, as a certification of citizenship — has affected the observance of Judaic dietary laws. In any event, the social advantage of this dialogical system is that it allowed identity to evolve by crossing boundaries in both ways, depending on alternative strategies of reproduction and integration. I have chosen to underline the structural scheme of the boundary system in food practices, in their timing, their spatial itemization, and their social dimension.

TIME BOUNDARIES

Sacred time and ordinary time demarcate the Republican contract in the kitchen and on the menus as they reflect the temporal flow of daily life. The principle is to make a material opposition between the ordinary days of the week and the unordinary schedule of festive reunions around the table. The most recurrent distinction happens between the secular lifestyle of the week's working days and the sacred time of Sabbath. The distinction is to be found in culinary preparations, in the social characteristics of the gathered eaters, and in the ingredient and recipe contents of the menus. During the week, as one is involved in professional experiences and social relationships with gentile friends and colleagues, the diet tends to be Frenchified, composed of French or Western recipes, often prepared outside the family house, and can even include non-kosher items, for the most secular families. For the average traditional Sephardic families, not including the most Orthodox ones, this part of daily life pertains to the register of the secular. By contrast, Sabbath and holiday menus are in general strictly kosher. They are also composed of dishes of the traditional North-African Judeo-Arabic culinary repertoire and include a variety of spices, herbs, and vegetables commonly used in North African cuisine. Festive food is thus spicier, more flavorful, richer in fats, gluten, and ingredients, heavier in volume, and is often served once a year (for some special ritual dishes), or less frequently than the ordinary dishes of the weekly routine. This forceful opposition has sensory consequences that associate festive religious meals with more intense senses, odors, and bodily warmth, while ordinary weekday eating is less bodily fulfilling.[17] Sacred food is more flavorful and socially dense, while secular food feels utterly flavorless. Ritual food that has withdrawn into the limits of domesticity is thus frequently associated, in people's memory of their childhood, with this bodily sense of the sacred. Together with it, North African Jewish identity is most intensely expressed in these private sensory events, while their identity as French citizens remains more intensely expressed in publicly eaten secular food, flavors, and social encounters.[18]

Three recipes of the traditional North African culinary repertoire represent the sensory depth of homemade festive food. They are the world-famous couscous, the dafina, a typical Sabbath dish, and the challah, or Sabbath and festive bread.

Couscous is a complete meal mainly characterized by the steaming of the grain over a broth composed of a main meat ingredient (typically beef), a variety of leaf, green, and root vegetables (typically turnip, celery or cardoon, zucchini, and carrots), and beans (typically chickpeas). There are various types of couscous related to place of origin and depending on the specific ritual in which the dish is served. Sweet couscous is served in all three North African Jewish communities during Passover meals, as it does not include regular wheat grain but a matzo substitute, in observance of the prohibition of fermented grain consumption during the weeklong Jewish spring ritual.

Dafina, also called t'fina (among Jews of Algeria) or s'khina (among Jews of Morocco), is a complete meal as well, served most commonly at Saturday lunch.[19] This dish epitomizes the observance of Sabbath religious rules, especially those that forbid the lighting of fire for a day, since the beginning of Sabbath on Friday night until its end on Saturday night. Traditionally, it was cooked for the entire night on low fire and would include meats, beans, vegetables, and grains or potatoes, spices, and herbs. The Sephardic equivalent of the Ashkenazic *tshulent*, dafina is still cooked traditionally among Orthodox Jews, although some less Orthodox cooks would use a pressure cooker for this dish, for claimed reasons of practicality.

Dafina is also served at religious holiday meals, such as the Rosh Hashana dinner (Jewish New Year). In families originating in eastern North Africa, dafina includes a main leaf vegetable (typically spinach or Swiss chard), beef, and chickpeas.

Challah, also called in French *pain juif* (Jewish bread), is a bread loaf of specific shapes that is baked in most traditional Jewish families, both Sephardic and Ashkenazic, using similar baking and shaping techniques. This bread is generally required for Sabbath and festive religious meals, for the recitation of the bread blessing. Preparation of the Sabbath bread is part and parcel of the welcoming of the weekly ritual gathering, and as such, it is highly ritualized.

SPATIAL AND SOCIAL BOUNDARIES

The Republican rule of separation between public and private social life results in the distinction between foods prepared and consumed at the family home and those eaten outside the home. Though some French recipes would be allowed inside the house during weekdays, and most certainly outside the family home, traditional North African kosher cuisine is imperative on Sabbath and religious holiday menus. Serving nonkosher food at a ritual festive meal would be an "abomination" for those who do observe some religious traditions on these occasions.[20] Traditional Sabbath and festive cuisine is not only prepared at home, it is also consumed at home, primarily by family members gathered for these ritual occasions.

To be sure, Sephardic traditional cuisine has been modified in the past few decades, especially in adjusting to French food markets after the immigration into France. It has changed in its ingredient composition and in its flavors, but the symbolic boundary structure remains intact. In particular, traditional festive cuisine is most often prepared at home by members of the family, typically adult women. This continues to happen despite the development, in the past couple of decades, of a market of prepared North African traditional cuisine, usually sold in kosher butcher shops and by kosher caterers, mainly in large cities like Paris, Lyon, and Marseilles, where the Sephardic population dominates the Jewish scene.

It should be noted here that when nonkosher food is consumed during weekdays at home, it most likely is not cooked at home but purchased as prepared food items. Thus, one rarely finds nonkosher items cooking in family pots. The distinction between home/sacred/traditional and nondomestic/secular/French is a separation between the cooked and the raw, to refer to the classic Lévi-Straussian culinary triangle.[21] Dafina constitutes the most representative culinary evidence of this process. A result of the Napoleonic Republican contract, it actually turns ritual homemade food—because it is highly cooked and for a long time— into a highly cultured matter, one that most dramatically expresses the religious and cultural identity of these Jews in civil society.

TRANSLATING NORTH AFRICAN CULINARY TERMINOLOGY INTO FRENCH FOOD LANGUAGE

As Albert Memmi reminded his readers in his 1967 book, an important part of colonial domination is channeled through language power. The

North African formerly colonized Jews are still, to various degrees, bilingual. The former vernacular Jewish languages used for centuries in North Africa were various forms of Judeo-Arabic, popular Arabic, and Ladino. Today that too has withdrawn to the limits of private domestic culture. The boundaries mentioned above are manifested in language as well, and table and kitchen practices consequently bear the mark of culinary bilingualism. At home, traditional dishes are more likely to be called by their past Judeo-Arabic names. So our Sephardic eaters do not only eat traditional cuisine, they also eat words of their native language. But with the progressive passing of the generation of native Judeo-Arabic speakers, these names will eventually fade away. One notices, though, that food names are the last native words to disappear. They function as memorial linguistic and cultural lexicons.

In some cases, Judeo-Arabic food names have been translated into French, mainly in the postmigration period. One typical case (and my favorite) is the *blanquette de veau*. The original traditional dish is in fact a lamb soup, simply cooked with garlic, and in which a beaten egg mixed with fresh mint is thrown seconds before serving. Its original Judeo-Arabic name is *m'hatsar* among eastern Algerian Jews. Although it does look white like the blanquette, it definitely belongs to a different culinary category because it is a soup and because it uses lamb rather than veal. The blanquette also includes butter and cream, as opposed to the kosher lamb soup that does not allow the combination of meat and dairy ingredients. What has happened here is a process of linguistic legitimation of a dish that is usually served during the Rosh Hashana dinner, and as such is a prestigious and festive dish. Thus the analogy to the blanquette consists in identifying the traditional Judeo-Arabic dish with one of the most prestigious French culinary items.[22] Further evidence of the legitimation at work here is the switch from lamb to veal, the latter representing a modern meat, less fatty than lamb, though still strong in flavor. As a matter of fact, many cooks have indeed replaced lamb with veal in the traditional dish for health-oriented reasons.

DAFINA GETS ON SOCIAL MEDIA

From the heart of the kitchen, many traditional dishes have moved out into new media in the past two to three decades. In this process, collective memory is operating as the recorder of traditional North African vernacular language. Indeed, the websites created by associations of Sephardic Jews in France have all been given the Judeo-Arabic names of traditional dishes. The main websites are harissa.com (for Tunisian Jews), zlabia.com (for Algerian Jews), and dafina.net (for Moroccan Jews).[23] They feature a large volume of information on the original local communities in Morocco, Algeria, and Tunisia. There one can find a treasure of photos of the main cities and the synagogues, public parks, and religious celebrations in these locales. Culinary photos and recipes are also posted by users in interactive formats, allowing both Muslim and Jewish users to compare their recipes and discuss the "authenticity" of their mothers' and grandmothers' culinary contributions.

COLONIALISM, NORTH AFRICAN JEWS, AND MUSLIMS ON THE CULINARY SCENE

The decolonization of North African Jews, both in North Africa and in France, has affected their relationships with their Muslim neighbors, even in culinary taste. Frenchification of the kitchen and the palate has progressively separated the Jews from their native Muslim neighbors. Yet despite the widespread post–World War II de-ghettoization of the Jews in North Africa, specific forms of Jewish-Muslim cohabitation persisted until the very last years of the colonial era, the 1950s and early 1960s, especially at the lowest levels of the social ladder. Domestic life has long been an area of exchange, especially for ritual occasions.[24]

The main actors of these dense interreligious exchanges were women. On the Muslim side, their presence has been dominant inside the home for quite a long time, and due to the resistance of their society's patriarchal rule, their role in the domestic sphere continues to be dominant in many contemporary Arab-Muslim societies, even in those where the female levels of education have dramatically increased in recent years.

On the Jewish side, women had been emancipated earlier, as soon as they had entered the labor market. But due to the sexual division of domestic and culinary labor, Jewish women continued until recent times to be the principal actors of food acquisition, cooking, and ritual preparation.

In many small towns in North Africa, the politics of Jewish-Muslim relations have unfolded during colonial times, first in private life, and then in the neighborhoods and the towns through the dense fabric of commercial, family, and personal ties and exchanges. In modern history, those relations were particularly rich and cohesive in two areas of cultural life: food and music. The latter was activated by women and the former primarily, though not exclusively, by men. During Jewish holidays, Muslim women were often quick to give a hand to their Jewish neighbors in the preparation of complex dinners for large family ritual gatherings. Every week on the eve of Sabbath, Muslim women would help turn cooking stoves off and on when their Jewish neighbors were not allowed to do so by religious law. Just before the holiday of Passover, Jewish women would give leftovers of leavened food to their Muslim neighbors until the end of the ritual week, when the latter would either return the food or restitute some type of food item to celebrate the beginning of the new Jewish spring.[25]

I have personally experienced these types of Jewish-Muslim cultural and food exchanges while conducting ethnography in North Africa. In 1979, I traveled to the eastern Algerian town of Sétif where my maternal relatives had lived until their postindependence migration to France, in 1962. This was a part of an ethnographic observation of a Jewish pilgrimage in Constantine, some seventy kilometers east of Sétif. I visited the house that my relatives had shared with Muslim neighbors, some of whom were still living there seventeen years after the Jews' departure. The courtyard gate opened into the same private world occupied mainly by women. Everyone introduced herself, and after an animated session of ululations and emotional remembrances, the women took me on a memory visit of the house in which every corner contained a historical reminder of the former Jewish neighbors.

Before I left, I received two "memory presents" from the house community to be given to my relatives in France: a female house robe and a large piece of challah. Although both presents were given in a highly symbolic gesture, the bread drew my special attention.[26] It had obviously not been baked in preparation for my unannounced visit. It was different from the bread that most local Muslim women baked on a daily basis. It was offered as a sample of Jewish bread and in memory of the former Jewish neighbors. Indeed, by the late 1970s, only two kinds of breads were available on the Sétifian market and in local kitchens. The first one was a flat round bread grilled on a small tripod coal burner and inside a terra-cotta pan, the *kanun*. That bread was generally made by housewives in their home kitchens. The other most commonly eaten bread was the French baguette, usually available in neighborhood bakeries. The former was native homemade bread, while the latter was a culinary remnant of colonial times. To honor my 1979 visit, the challah was thus presented as a typically native Jewish bread that used to be prepared by Jewish housewives, under their Muslim neighbors' eyes, every Friday morning and baked in the kosher community oven before the beginning of Sabbath. The braided challah gift was the Muslim women's narrative of remembrance of the weekly Jewish ritual and of their participation in the baking process.

THE COLONIZED PALATE, EMANCIPATION, AND INTEGRATION

Colonialism in North Africa has opened the door to emancipation for Jews and also to some other native groups on their way to upward mobility. The process is a sort of oddity in the history of Jewish emancipation, in a sense, in that it took Jews out of colonial domination and brought them to equality with their non-Jewish, French fellow citizens. To be sure, this process unfolded slowly and included a number of political obstacles.[27] The Jewish response to colonialism in North Africa has been ambiguous and, as some have said, "neutral." This characterization is, in my view, due to the way many scholars and ideologues understand the colonial system as a mere dual relationship with two unequivocally opposed and antagonistic parties. Memmi's book is probably responsible for that view, even though he placed Jews of colonial countries in the "colonized" camp. The historical reality has been more complex, and the Jews, in various historical situations, have been at the core of this complexity. In North Africa, there were more than two parties to the colonial system of domination. It took the Jews almost a century to understand that their future was to melt into European culture and society in order to acquire equality and integration into civil society, and into a secular culture that had dominated and oppressed them, similarly to other native peoples, for several decades. They adopted European culture to the extent of embodying it, literally incorporating it. Once they arrived on European soil, they encountered another type of Jewish relation to Europe, that of Ashkenazim who had experienced a different trajectory and tragedy in their efforts to melt into European identity and to be recognized as full-fledged Europeans, if not *the* ultimate Europeans. For these reasons, I argue that postcolonial Jews constitute the most Europeanist among the peoples of Europe, even those who reached this ideological shore by being previously subjected to colonial domination.

In the early twenty-first century, more than half a century after decolonization and the Holocaust, couscous has become the favorite dish among French people and one of the vibrant symbols of French gastronomy, according to the most recent surveys conducted on French culinary taste by diverse culinary media. Jewish immigration from North Africa in the 1950s and 1960s is partly responsible for this gustative reality.

I argue that the structure of the dichotomy separating private from public in the taste system of colonial and postcolonial North African Jews is founded and orchestrated by the collective memory of the challenges of colonial history and decolonization, what Janet Carsten calls "the Ghosts of Memory."[28] Indeed, that remembrance of taste allows for a complex balance between integration and cultural preservation. In recreating or reinventing the Maghrebi culinary system, Sephardic eaters make efforts to re-create the sensory landscape of their colonial origins and the social system that created it. Sensory memory sets a bridge between past and present. But it also creates a vibrant political relationship to their present and future status in the realm of the French Republic, a supreme value for Jews and other French citizens, even at the beginning of the third millennium, two centuries after the rules of their emancipation were set under the Napoleonic empire and Voltairean ideology of citizenship. Jewish eating is a multilayered political and historical agenda.

NOTES

I use the term "Sephardic" similarly to my informants when they identify themselves in the French Jewish cultural landscape. This term designates all Jews originating in North Africa and the Eastern Mediterranean. They mainly include former Ladino and Judeo-Arabic speakers.

1. See the columns of *Le Monde, Le Figaro,* and *Libération* in the days following the attacks (week of November 14).

2. Pierre Birnbaum, *Les Fous de la République: Histoire politique des Juifs d'État, de Gambetta à Vichy* (Paris: Fayard, 1992). In this volume, the author explores the Jewish dedication to the values of the French Republic, up to the 1940s. For historical reasons, North African Jewish immigrants are barely included in his analysis, as they have immigrated in the years following the end of World War II.

3. This term has been used by my informants in a number of the qualitative interviews and life histories I conducted in the last decades of the twentieth century.

4. These data include close to a thousand hours of recorded qualitative interviews with a few hundred first- and second-generation Jews from Morocco, Tunisia, and Algeria living in the Parisian metropolitan region, as well as along the Rhône River and the Mediterranean shore, in Marseilles, Lyon, and Nice. This ethnography was conducted in numerous fieldwork operations between 1976 and 2014 and also included participant observation as well as audiovisual recording in personal homes and public locations (cafés, bookstores, food stores, and associations' meetings).

5. The exception is the situation of Moroccan Jews who have migrated to Israel in large numbers starting in the late 1950s. For details about this historical process, see Charles-Robert Ageron, *Histoire de l'Algérie contemporaine* (Paris: Presses Universitaires de France, 1979); Joëlle Bahloul, *Parenté et ethnicité: La famille juivenord-africaine en France* (Paris: Ministère de la Culture, 1984); Joëlle Bahloul, "La famille sépharade dans la diaspora du XXème siècle," in *La Société juiveà travers l'histoire*, ed. Shmuel Trigano (Paris: Fayard, 1992); Joëlle Bahloul, "The Sephardi Family and the Challenge of Assimilation: Family Ritual and Ethnic Reproduction," in *Sephardi and Middle Eastern Jewries: History and Culture in the Modern Era*, ed. Harvey E. Goldberg (Bloomington: Indiana University Press, 1996), 85–95; Doris Bensimon-Donath, *L'intégration des juifsnord-africains en France* (Paris: Mouton, 1971); André Chouraqui, *La Saga des Juifs en Afrique du Nord* (Paris: Hachette, 1972); Maurice Eisenbeth, *Les juifs de l'Afrique du Nord: démographie et onomastique* (Algiers, Impr. du Lycée, 1936); Heller-Goldenberg, "Judeo-Moroccan Memory in Québec," in *Textualizing the Immigrant Experience in Contemporary Québec*, ed. Susan Ireland and Patrice J. Proulx (Westport CT: Praeger, 2004); Haim Zeev Hirschberg, *A History of the Jews in North Africa*. 2 Vols. (Leiden, The Netherlands: E. J. Brill, 1974–81); Laskier, *North African Jewry in the Twentieth Century: The Jews of Morocco, Tunisia, and Algeria* (New York: New York University Press, 1994); Jean-Claude Lasry and Claude Tapia, eds., *Les Juifs du Maghreb: diasporas contemporaines* (Paris: L'Harmattan; Montréal: Presses de l'Université de Montréal, 1989).

6. The book hence encouraged other native colonized intellectuals to write about colonialism and decolonization in essays and novels, throughout Africa but especially among Maghrebi authors. The election of Algerian-born Assia Djebar at the Académie Française in 2005 was a culmination of this literary trend initiated by Memmi in the 1950s.

7. Jean-Paul Sartre, "Portrait de l'antisémite," in *Réflexions sur la question juive* (Paris: Gallimard, 1946). The chapter was originally published in 1945 in *Les Temps Modernes*, a review founded by Jean-Paul Sartre and Simone de Beauvoir that same year.

8. Albert Memmi, *The Colonizer and the Colonized* (Boston: Beacon Press, 1967), 25.

9. I am using the concept of "taste" in reference to the work of Pierre Bourdieu, in *Distinction: A Social Critique of the Judgment of Taste* (Cambridge MA: Harvard University Press, 1984).

10. Memmi, *Colonizer and the Colonized*, 106–107. For more details on this linguistic aspect of colonialism, see Johannes Fabian, *Language and Colonial Power* (New York: Cambridge University Press, 1986), and most importantly Jacques Derrida, *Monolingualism of the Other: or, The Prosthesis of Origin* (Stanford CA: Stanford University Press, 1998).

11. Memmi, *Colonizer and the Colonized*, 120–22.

12. Memmi, *Colonizer and the Colonized*, 15.

13. Birnbaum, *Les Fous de la République*, and Pierre Birnbaum, *La République et le cochon* (Paris: Éditions du Seuil, 2013).

14. Memmi had already mentioned this emerging attitude among Jews in their search for emancipation in his book *The Colonizer and the Colonized*.

15. The professional experience has been, for formerly colonized Jews, in the principal areas of social and political emancipation, in that many of them were able, mainly in the post–World War II period, to exit the ghettos of traditional Jewish livelihood and to enter liberal professions and even government jobs as functionaries. That is why they have made major efforts in expressing their gratitude toward the French Republic by erasing their traditional Jewish practices and by sitting around the table with non-Jewish colleagues and friends, even if it required the consumption of non-kosher foods.

16. I am thinking, in particular, of the frequent exposition of Lubavitcher rituals in the streets of Paris, especially in the Old Jewish Quarter located in the Marais. In December 2015, Lubavitcher rabbis installed an imposing menorah under the Eiffel Tower, which was lit up during the Hanukah week-long celebrations in dramatic expression of the "no fear" outcry following the attacks of mid-November.

17. I am inspired here by David Sutton's anthropology of the senses, as elaborated in his book *Remembrance of Repasts: An Anthropology of Food and Memory* (New York: Oxford University Press, 2001), and in particular by his concept of synesthesia.

18. I should add that this dietary distinction between the weekdays and Sabbath is characteristic of the average North African family in France; that is, those located in the middle class rather than at the extremities of the social ladder, and also those whose religious life follows the "traditionalist" religious scenario roughly equivalent to the American Conservative and Reform denominations.

19. These three Judeo-Arabic terms refer to the cooking mode of the iconic Jewish dish. *Dafina* or *t'fina* are words commonly meaning "the buried." They relate to the traditional, pre–high tech mode of cooking these dishes.

Ingredients were assembled in terra-cotta pots that were buried in hot coals for the night, allowing the dish to cook slowly and to produce an overcooked culinary item. The term S'khina has a similar signifying function in that it means "the hot dish," thus referring to the high heat in which the pot was placed for a long time.

20. See Mary Douglas, "The Abominations of Leviticus," in Purity and Danger: An Analysis of the Concepts of Pollution and Taboo (New York: Routledge, 1966), 41–57.
21. Claude Lévi-Strauss, Mythologiques. Vol. 1: The Raw and the Cooked (Chicago: University of Chicago Press, 1983).
22. The blanquette de veau was first introduced in French culinary arts in the eighteenth century and evolved throughout the nineteenth century as a gastronomic characteristic of the rising urban bourgeois lifestyle. See details in Jean-Louis Flandrin, La Blanquette de veau: Histoire d'un plat bourgeois (Paris: Jean-Paul Rocher, 2002).
23. Harissa is a hot sauce used to season many stews of the North African culinary repertoire, in all religious communities; zlabia is a fried honey covered pastry. We have described in previous pages the Moroccan Sabbath stew called dafina.
24. Joëlle Bahloul, The Architecture of Memory (New York: Cambridge University Press, 1996).
25. Harvey Goldberg has documented this tradition of Judeo-Muslim exchange in his study of the Mimuna ritual in Morocco, Harvey Goldberg, "The Mimuna and the Minority Status of Moroccan Jews," Ethnology 17, no. 1 (1978): 75–87.
26. Those are the terms used by my hosts to characterize the presents.
27. One of the major obstacles to this Jewish emancipation in the twentieth century evolved during the interwar period, especially in the early 1930s, when antisemitism in French colonial Algeria was at its peak. During that period, Jews saw the emerging antisemitic political parties in Algerian national and local elections and the resulting crises that burst out around the country, notably in the eastern city of Constantine, where a pogrom killed dozens of Jews in the summer of 1934, including women and children. Richard Ayoun and Bernard Cohen, Les Juifs d'Algérie: deux mille ans d'histoire (Paris: Jean Claude Lattès, 1982), 160–67; Benjamin Stora, Les Trois exils: Juifs d'Algérie (Paris: Stock, 2006), 60–64.
28. Janet Carsten, Ghosts of Memory: Essays on Remembrance and Relatedness (Oxford UK: Blackwell Publishing, 2007).

PART 3

The Kosherization of Jewish Food

Playing Out Religion, Taste, and Health in
the Marketplace and Popular Culture

7

Appetite and Hunger

Discourses and Perceptions of Food among Eastern
European Jews in the Interwar Years

....

RAKEFET ZALASHIK

Food is central to our sense of identity. Food tells us not only how people live but also how they think of themselves in relation to others by
asserting diversity, hierarchy, and organization. A people's cuisine—a
particular food or the way it is being prepared and eaten—often marks
the boundary between the collective self and the other. Food has many
meanings: it may have a social, cultural, or symbolic meaning, and even
an emotional function. Obviously, food also has a biological function and
a nutritional value. But do people know what is good for them when it
comes to food? Alexander Kaplan, in 1925, was not too sure: "Everyone
knows that if catching a cold, you might get a lung infection, and if you
work too hard you could get heart disease, but seldom do people know
what one is allowed to eat and what food could be harmful to them."[1]

After World War I, many changes took place in food production and
consumption habits in Europe and the United States. The industrialization of farming, and thus of the food supply itself, allowed greater
variety in people's diets, and the quantity and the quality of their nutrition
improved.[2] These new developments led to changes in the way people

got foods, ate them, and perceived them. This period also witnessed new scientific discoveries related to nutrition, which, again, affected people's understanding of food and its consumption.

The early twentieth century also marked other unprecedented changes, which transformed the face of Eastern European Jewry. Jewish persecution and economic difficulties provided the impetus for mass emigration and the blossoming of new political movements, ranging from the secular socialists' Bund to Zionism, as well as the strengthening of competing religious ideologies.[3] The "Jewish question," namely, the existence of a Jewish minority within a society composed of a Christian majority, brought about not only the need for "Jewish history," in Simon Dubnow's formulation, but also the need for "Jewish science," dedicated to the study of specifically Jewish health issues and offering cures for "Jewish diseases." The desire to remold the attitude and practices of the Jews regarding health and hygiene was motivated by both altruistic and self-serving goals: to improve the health of the Jewish people, but also to improve their image and status within modern society in order to render them worthy of acceptance as equals in the eyes of the other peoples.[4] Thus, health became an important lever for promoting Jewish political rights as a minority people and as a tool for the potential development of the Jewish people as a nation.[5]

Popular medical periodicals in Yiddish were a central means to disseminate medical knowledge and science to the public. A few medical publications, such as *Der Yidisher Hoyz-Doktor* (The Jewish house physician), *Der Doktor* (The physician), and *Folksgezunt* (People's health) appeared in Eastern Europe before the outbreak of World War II, aiming to promote modern concepts of health and healthcare among the Jewish population in its native tongue.

This essay analyzes the food- and nutrition-related articles published between 1923 and 1940 in the Yiddish magazine *Folksgezunt: Ilustrirter Populer Visenshaftlikher Journal fur Higyene un Meditsin*, an illustrated, popular scientific journal of hygiene and medicine published in Vilna, Lithuania, by Obsgcgestvo Zdravookhraneniia Evreev (OZE), the Organization for the Preservation of Jewish Health. Founded in St. Petersburg in 1912 by Jewish physicians, the OZE's goal was to address the health problems of Russian Jews.[6] After World War I and during the Russian civil war, the OZE expanded its activities into other Eastern European countries by opening hospitals, maternal and children's clinics, a network of stations (called A Drop of Milk) for supplying milk to children, and tuberculosis sanatoriums.[7]

Folksgezunt (People's health) was the first bulletin of the Vilna branch of the OZE, published under the editorship of the political activist and physician Tsemakh Shabad.[8] It was a magazine for hygiene and medicine that aimed at educating the Jewish masses on topics of health and hygiene by publishing articles by physicians writing in Yiddish for a general audience and usually accompanied by illustrations.[9] The didactic nature of the periodical included a few strategies to reach the average reader: the titles of the articles were often formed as questions with a practical purpose; some of the texts were presented in the form of "responsa," that is, short questions and answers on daily life issues, which was a common method in Judaism for communicating and disseminating customs and rules; and publishing articles as if they were the Ten Commandments.[10]

This bimonthly magazine was circulated among Yiddish readers throughout Eastern Europe and Germany. The magazine was created to serve several different goals. First, the OZE aimed to produce its books and periodicals for mass consumption in Eastern Europe. Second, it responded to the wish of Jewish activists from both Western and Eastern Europe to reform and transform the life of poor, uneducated Jews in Eastern Europe, as far as health and hygiene were concerned, by introducing them to Western ideals of science. Third, it joined in the usage of Yiddish—an inferior jargon that Eastern European Jews used in everyday interaction—along with other newspapers, journals, pamphlets, and books, which were dedicated to translating and distributing scientific knowledge among lay people.[11]

Between 1923 and 1940, around ninety articles on food and nutrition reflecting contemporary scientific knowledge were published in the *Folksgezunt*. Some of the articles, due to their length, were split over a few issues, which meant that in almost every issue of *Folksgezunt* an article dedicated to food and nutrition appeared. Some of the articles included recipes, and readers could also write in questions to the editors about nutrition and other material published on the theme. Some of the articles were original articles written especially by the OZE's physicians for *Folksgezunt*, while others were reprints and translations of articles published in scientific journals from abroad and in other languages. The articles on these subjects were typically located at the end of the magazine, suggesting that, in relation to other health issues, food and nutrition placed low in the information hierarchy.[12]

Since food has a social meaning and function in historical transformation as well, I use the articles from the *Folksgezunt* to understand the reality of Jews in Eastern Europe in the interwar period, as reflected in their food consumption and eating habits, as well as ideas and concepts they held related to food.[13] More specifically, I answer questions such as: What were Eastern Jews eating in the interwar period? What new foods were they introduced to and consuming after World War I? What were Jews supposed to eat and how were they expected by Jewish physicians to treat their nutrition and health? I argue that the post–World War I era was a transitional period for East European Jews, not only in politics and society, as many studies have shown, but also in the field of food and nutrition.[14] Eastern European Jews got access to new food products and they were exposed to new eating habits, which also influenced their health. According to the *Folksgezunt*, the increased variety of food and relative prosperity of the Jewish people had both positive and negative impacts on their health, which became a topic of discussion and concern among the physicians of the OZE.

JEWS AND FOOD

Throughout history, food, and especially the Jewish dietary laws, served as a way of making distinctions between Jews and their non-Jewish neighbors.[15] Food was also connected to religious rituals such as the Shabbat dinner and meals at the Jewish holidays and was viewed as a source of both physical and spiritual nourishment.[16] The food of Eastern European Jews was in many cases a byproduct of poverty and scarcity. However, despite their poverty, Eastern European Jewish social life fostered culinary cosmopolitanism as they were exposed to different types of food through peddlers, relatives who came from other regions and countries, internal migration due to economic needs or marriage, urbanization, and communication.[17]

Although industrialization and urbanization did take root, nutritional conditions for the East European population, gentile and Jewish alike, in the late nineteenth and early twentieth century were still bad.[18] From a study conducted in 1907 on the nutrition and food hygiene of Jews who lived in small towns in the kingdoms of Poland and Galicia, we can learn that Jews consumed a lot of flour, potatoes, legumes, buckwheat, barley, and oats. In contrast, they consumed very little dairy, vegetables, or fruits.[19] In comparison to the non-Jewish population in these areas, they consumed too little protein and fat. World War I and later the civil war in Russia in 1921–23 led to horrible famine, which caused many deaths and hunger-related diseases, especially among infants and children—many of them Jewish refugees who were caught up between the lines. Although the population was helped by the Red Cross as well as other international organizations, the famine left its mark on the collective memory of both Jews and non-Jews.

THE EMERGENCE OF FOOD SCIENCE

At the end of the nineteenth century, research in the field of food and nutrition can be divided into two types. The first provided information about the quality and quantity of food needed in order to maintain good health based on an average quantity of nutrients and the energy value of food intake per day in relation to age, sex, and other characteristics. The second type of research focused on the detrimental effects of certain foods on human health.[20] It was, however, only after World

War I that contemporary medical views on food began to spread among the uninitiated. This included information and knowledge on what people should eat, alongside cooking instructions and education. In this period, we witness the popularization of nutritional information, especially for the lower classes.

The interest of scientists in food and nutrition among Jews had traditionally two aspects. The first was an old fascination among both scientists and theologians: the examination of Jewish dietary laws, hygiene, and especially Jewish animal slaughter, as well as the separation between meat and milk and the aversion to pork, according to new scientific discoveries on nutrition, hygiene, and the digestive system.[21] For some Jewish physicians, the Jewish dietary laws were one of the important proofs of ethical and scientifically intuitive civilization created and adopted by the Jewish people through the ages. However, those who strove to reform Judaism argued that avoiding pork was no longer necessary because they could avoid the reason for the taboo in the first place by properly cooking the pork.

The other aspect of scientific interest in Jewish dietary habits and practices evolved in the middle of the nineteenth century. Both gentile and Jewish physicians noted that Jews in Germany suffered six times more than did gentiles from diabetes. Diabetes even received the name *Judenkrakheit*, the Jews' disease.[22] Although some physicians explained it by the seemingly racial attributes of the Jews, the majority related it to certain lifestyle features. It was argued that with the assimilation of German Jews into gentile society, many of them joined the wealthier class in the urban centers.[23] Assimilated German Jews were trying to emulate their gentile neighbors with their eating and drinking habits and, therefore, suffered from diabetes. Physicians recommended a strict diet and individually designed nutrition programs for these wealthy German Jews. The "heftiness," which was part of the culture of scarcity and had once symbolized the poverty of the Jews in Europe, had now to be replaced by "healthiness."

In this respect, the articles published in the *Folksgezunt* went well beyond "traditional" scientific interests in Jews and food. The magazine dealt with a wide range of topics in nutrition and health, from poor appetites among children and adults to the impact of warm and cold drinks on the stomach and the principles of vegetarianism. Many articles were accompanied by illustrations. Their themes can be divided into a few main categories: nutrition and health; food and Jewish dietary laws; historical and cultural articles on food and nations around the world; food hygiene, which included how and when certain food should be eaten; and nutritional concerns for certain groups such as infants and children, pregnant women, and sick people.

As an introduction to the new series on nutrition for the winter issue of 1923, the editors of *Folksgezunt* explained to the readers:

We are printing this article which was sent by a dignified author as a beginning of a series of articles about nutrition that we selected for our journal. It has to be mentioned that during the horrible World War, when people starved, a row of new studies on the physiological impact of certain foods on health were conducted. Another point is that today in developed countries, many people are suffering because they do not have enough to eat, but some are getting sick because they eat too much, or eat whatever they like.[24]

The first article in the series, by Julius Laypuner, discussed vegetarianism. Laypuner presented the benefits of a vegetarian diet according to its supporters: it is ethical, cheap, and a more feasible solution for world hunger than a carnivorous diet.[25] Nevertheless, he explained that science did not validate most of the vegetarians' central arguments for not eating meat, showing instead that an average working individual needed 118 grams of protein per day, which could be found in meat and eggs. In any case, Laypuner clarified to readers that an exclusively vegetarian or carnivorous diet was not good for the human organism. The best combination was an omnivorous, balanced diet.[26]

Laypuner did not hint at the social meanings of consuming meat among the Jews. Meat was the most desirable food possible because it symbolized abundance and was a status symbol.[27] In some areas of Eastern Europe, kosher meat cost twice the price of meat eaten by the rest of the population because of the kosher meat tax that was paid directly by consumers. However, in big cities like Warsaw meat was cheaper and very popular among Jews. Through the nineteenth century, more poor families began to eat all kinds of affordable meat, ceasing to eat kosher meat.[28] In any case, at the beginning of the twentieth century, even the poorest Jews consumed meat a few times during the week, mainly poultry, beef, and veal, while rich Jews would eat meat a few times a day.[29]

Within the framework of the nation-state, the emergence of the science of nutrition was also connected to political and economic questions, such as the "social question" of what to do with the urban poor. A connection between nutrition, national efficiency, competitiveness, identity, and the survival of the nation were also part of this agenda.[30] Laypuner's closing statement focused on the importance of meat as a nutritional necessity for the working class and its high price, an issue that went well beyond the medical sphere. Based on studies published in the *Berliner Klinischer Wochenschrift*, which determined that meat as part of protein consumption is essential for the laborer, Laypuner ended his article by saying, "The working person, in general, must have enough meat to eat, and must, therefore, earn a high enough wage in order to be able to buy it."[31]

A large part of the articles in *Folksgezunt* were dedicated to obesity, as the magazine asked the question, Are we eating too much? The insistence on this topic hinted at the fact that Jews in Eastern Europe suffered in this period from obesity and from health problems related to it. From a nutritional point of view, Jewish physicians like Arnold Puld, Avraham Neustaedter, and others pointed to the war years: "The war brought misfortune but had also an advantage: diabetes disappeared and the rate of heart attacks declined. Why? Because everyone ate less." With the end of the war and the normalization of daily life, alongside greater access to food, it was claimed by Jewish doctors that Jewish adults ate too much and were too sedentary.[32]

Between 1924 and 1925 Vilna physician Alexander Kaplan published a series of articles on food hygiene.[33] His articles reflected two contemporary scientific landmarks: the notion of preventive medicine and the discovery of vitamins. Preventive medicine, which emerged at the beginning of the twentieth century as part of the scientific revolution, argued that common diseases have their roots in lifestyle, social factors, and the environment, and that the promotion of health depended on the implementation of preventive means such as vaccinations and hygienic norms. The OZE adopted and propagated preventive medicine, partly by educating the Jewish masses in Eastern Europe about hygiene and health, hoping to reduce contentious diseases such as tuberculosis, ringworm, and trachoma, which were related to poverty and stigmatized as "Jewish diseases."[34] In addressing nutrition, the OZE opened kitchens in Jewish kindergartens and schools that would supply breakfast for poor and hungry pupils, but it also taught the masses what to eat, how to avoid faulty food, and how to keep and cook food products through lectures, movies, and articles like those of Kaplan's in the *Folksgezunt*.

The second scientific concept reflected in Kaplan's series of articles was the new and gradual discovery of vitamins. Whereas the nineteenth century had been the century of the discovery of proteins, carbohydrates, fats, and calories, the twentieth century was characterized by an obsession with vitamins. As a consequence, the consumption of vegetables received scientific legitimacy for the first time.[35] During the 1920s and 1930s, the discovery of vitamins was popularized by scientists and became accessible as popular knowledge.[36] Articles that presented scientific clarifications about vitamins A, B, and C, as well as noting which foods contained them, were widespread and also included recipes for dishes with vegetables. Articles titled "How Should One Eat to Stay Healthy?," "Why Vegetables and Fruits Are Important for the Organism," "Consume More Vegetables!," "Do You Know What You Are Eating?,"

"The Meaning of Fresh Vegetables to Our Health," and so on, aimed to educate the readership and to familiarize them with vegetables in order to change the eating habits of Jews in Eastern Europe, which almost totally lacked vegetables and fruits.[37]

Kaplan explained that whereas primitive man had used his instincts while searching for food, the modern and civilized man enjoyed variety and had to rely on science to choose his food according to his age and needs.[38] In his articles about food, Kaplan criticized urbanization and modern life. Jews in the city tended to have their main meals in the second part of the day, causing harm to the digestive system.[39] They were inclined to eat too much deep-fried food: "fried meat, fried fish, fried herring, fried dough (blini and latkes), fried onions, potatoes, eggs, etc.—all unhealthy fats! Up to a certain extent, deep-fried food is good because it awakens the appetite, but this stimulating property means that it should be consumed with moderation." Kaplan connected the search for stimulating substances such as fried and spicy food to hectic urban life. Food hygiene was not only about what we eat but also how we eat it. "Today, when 'time is money,' people are eating too fast, they are chewing badly, and the food spends too little time in the mouth, with the saliva and food entering the stomach still needing to be thoroughly digested." He also warned readers about the impact of alcohol and nicotine consumption on the digestive organs.[40]

Instead, Kaplan emphasized, one has to consume natural, healthy stimulants and keep away from harmful ones that first awaken the person but later make him tired and sick.[41] "One has to find a balance between happiness and being morally contained versus gambling or other unhealthy pleasures such as ether, cocaine, alcohol and other poisons." Kaplan also discussed food preparation. He warned about overcooked food that reduced vitamins, too much water that drained out salts, and too much sugar. In his opinion, the worst food possible was to be found in canned goods like sardines, sprats, herrings, and sausages, which might contain bacterial poisons. The new industrial production of canned food made it popular, accessible, and cheaper than the same food product in its fresh state. However, because poisoning could still occur prior to the mechanized canning process, physicians still considered canned food unsafe.[42]

A special group of articles was aimed at mothers and focused on instructions about how to feed babies and children. This was part of the OZE's goal to raise a healthy young generation of Jewish children and its special focus on mother-child care within which A Drop of Milk stations and mother-child clinics were opened and home visits by nurses to instruct mothers on how to take care of their children were carried out. In their articles Jewish physicians discussed issues like overfeeding children or mothers complaining to the doctor that their child did not eat enough food: "Some mothers believe that to make their child happy, they should always give more food to their baby: one more egg, one more glass of milk or chocolate. This is absolutely wrong. Mothers must educate their children to eat moderately from their early months."[43] In a 1928 article Dr. Shults warned that mothers fed their children too many eggs—a special-occasion food for Jews in Eastern Europe until the turn of the twentieth century.[44] "Eggs are an ideal food, especially for children from the age of two. But life teaches us that every coin has its flip side. This is also the case with eggs. Mothers who feed their children five to six eggs a day actually do not do them any good."[45] Children might get a rash, have problems sleeping, and suffer from asthma as a consequence. Shults and others recommended that children who are healthy should eat no more than one to two eggs a day.

Many articles dealt with preparing and consuming foodstuffs that before the war were hardly accessible to Jews in Eastern Europe. The revolution in agriculture and transportation brought new food products to market and made other foods cheaper. Thus, new tastes were introduced to the Jewish table and the role of the physicians in the *Folksgezunt* was to help these new tastes be socially accepted, if considered healthy and good.[46] This was the case with fresh milk and dairy products that were consumed before pasteurization, mainly by people who lived next to a farm, and in any case were considered to be good only for infants and children.[47] In the 1920s, as urban Jews consumed more and more milk, articles began to appear on topics like "Why Milk Is White?," "About Milk for Children," "Kefir and Yogurt," as well as on consuming milk and meat together in light of both Jewish dietary laws and scientific findings. Other newly introduced products, like certain types of wheat and grains, slowly became affordable and sometimes replaced potatoes, the main source of survival for the poorest East European Jews throughout the nineteenth century. Doctors published articles on how to eat wheat and how to prepare various kinds of grains as a recommended food in order to convince readers to consume them.

Jewish physicians in the 1920s and 1930s also dealt with questions of body fat, the cure for obesity, and the appropriate diet for women. In *Folksgezunt's* second issue of 1933, the opening article was on "Appetite and Hunger." Written by the magazine's editor, Tsemach Shabad, the article dealt with the hunger instinct and the conditions under which a healthy appetite is developed.[48] In the same issue, Professor Wisozki warned female readership about the dangers of dieting. "Today's fashion requires a skinny figure. Women are using all kinds of tricks to become skinny. The existing artificial means mostly have a bad impact on health, and the 'overly thin' (*Oysgeschlankte*) women must, poor them, recover for a long period to get healthy again."[49] Hunger, Wisozki explained, weakens the organism. Women who want to lose weight should consume less sugar, bread, and pastries. Fasting should be done only under medical supervision. "Everyone, and, in particular, women, should keep in mind that to be healthy means also to be pretty. If you want to be pretty you have first to take care for your health."[50]

The last series of articles dealt with food and Jewish dietary laws. Only three articles were published in this category, which might hint at the fact that Jewish dietary laws were of less interest to the physicians who wrote on food and nutrition, as well as to their readers, in the interwar period. One article referred to the scientific evidence for waiting at least six hours between eating meat and milk, based on the experiments Ivan Pavlov had conducted on dogs' digestive systems. The other articles explained scientifically why pork is one of the unhealthiest meats and how the wisdom of Judaism realized it a thousand years ago.

Only one article talked about a contemporary issue: the openly antisemitic attempt brought about in 1923 by some Polish members of parliament to outlaw the Jewish shehitah (the kosher slaughtering of animals). The effort to stop Jewish kosher animal slaughtering in Poland, which reached its peak in the mid-1930s, amplified the tension between Jewish communities in Poland and the government.[51] In this article, author S. Lockerman highlighted the positive effects on health of Jewish animal slaughtering as well as the liberal laws regulating it in other European countries.[52]

The articles on food and nutrition in the *Folksgezunt* avoided discussing hunger and food scarcity. Hunger was still common among Jews in Eastern Europe in the interwar period, as we know from the available data and from the OZE's own efforts to open public kitchens to feed undernourished Jewish children. The absence of articles on hunger and scarcity can be explained differently: first, the readership of the magazine generally did not suffer from hunger; second, since hunger among Jews in Eastern Europe was not a new phenomenon, it did not have to be explained and scientifically explored; finally, Jewish physicians' primary concern was East European Jews' access to a new, unprecedented quantity and variety of food which thus became the focus of their publications.

One can learn about the reactions of their readership to these publications on nutrition and food in the *Folksgezunt* by examining the correspondence in the *Brifkasten* (mailbox) section of the magazine, which began to appear in the second issue, in 1923. Letters from readers became an integral part of the periodical and were very popular among those who were interested in a range of topics coming from many social and ideological backgrounds.[53]

Questions about food and nutrition became very popular. In 1924 eight letters about these topics were published with a reply from the editor.[54] The most common questions focused on egg and milk consumption and the danger of bacteria, as well as the correct dietary norms to be followed for babies and children. Other readers' questions focused on beer consumption, appetite loss, and on the Talmud as a source of scientific knowledge.[55] The growing correspondence between readers and the magazine's editors showed that readers had been internalizing the new discourses on food, nutrition, bacteria, and hygiene as these issues had been articulated by the *Folksgezunt* doctors in their articles.

Anthropologist Emiko Ohnuki-Tierney has argued that for a particular food to function as a metaphor of the "self," each member of the social group must consume that food, and the food is to be eaten together.[56] If we adopt this argument, what can we say about food consumption and nutrition among Eastern European Jews between the two world wars, as reflected in the articles of *Folksgezunt* magazine between 1923 and 1940?

The more than ninety articles on food and nutrition that were published from 1923 to 1940 in *Folksgezunt* suggest the importance of the topic for Jewish physicians in Eastern Europe during the interwar years. This was a period when food and nutrition were understood as a significant component in the individual's health and as part of preventive medicine—a concept which was central to medical professionals and became popularized through journals and magazines. The number of articles on these topics also suggests that it was the physicians' role to be the main teaching authority for the Jewish public about nutrition and health. Finally, *Folksgezunt's* insistence on food and nutrition issues shows that there was a significant demand from its audience for valuable information about nutrition and how to prepare healthier food. At least in the 1920s, some Jewish communities in Eastern Europe and Germany enjoyed relative prosperity, which allowed them to experiment with new foods and dishes, bringing more diversity to the table. In this period, East European Jews could choose what to eat as well as how to feed their children.

Another question is whether the articles published in *Folksgezunt* on nutrition indeed reflected existing reality: did articles focusing on the perils of eating too much and unhealthily echo a real problem for East European Jewry? If read against the backdrop of articles about other health issues published in the magazine, the articles on fat and overeating reveal that it was in fact an emerging problem; a number of Jews in Eastern Europe suffered from obesity. In fact, Jews' exposure to new and more abundant food began earlier than World War I. The Great War and the famine that followed interrupted the process and turned back the clock; when in 1923 *Folksgezunt* writers took notice, they were reacting to an issue that had already been emerging years before.

Finally, *Folksgezunt* articles also indicate that Jewish dietary laws were not a sufficient framework for East European Jews in dealing with new dietary and nutritional conditions. Owing to the processes of secularization and urbanization confronting Eastern European Jews at the time, the rabbi was not the only authority to be believed concerning what one should eat, because Jewish dietary laws were no longer the single prism through which food was to be evaluated. To be sure, the spread of new ideas on food and nutrition in popular magazines was not a phenomenon unique to Jewish audiences. Since the early twentieth century, most populations in Europe and North America listened to scientists to choose what kinds of food to put into their bodies. Within this overarching question, *Folksgezunt* included some review of Jewish dietary laws in light of new scientific evidence. The many articles on the perils of obesity, the importance of vitamins, and the recommended consumption of vegetables appearing in *Folksgezunt* not only indicated a change in the food habits of Eastern European Jews, but suggested the amplitude of their growing urbanization, secularization, and integration within Christian society.

NOTES

1. Alexander Kaplan, "Higyene fun Shpayz [Vos, vi un vendarf men esn]," *Folksgezunt* no. 5 (1925): 142.
2. Amy Bentley, "Introduction," in *A Cultural History of Food*. Vol. 6: *A Cultural History of Food in the Modern Age (1920–2000)*, ed. Amy Bentley (New York:

Berg, 2011), 5; Annemarie de Knecht-van Eakelen, Anneke H. van Otterloo, "'What the Body Needs': Developments in Medical Advice, Nutritional Science and Industrial Production in the Twentieth Century," in *Order and Disorder: The Health Implications of Eating and Drinking in the Nineteenth and Twentieth Centuries*, ed. Alexander Fenton (East Linton UK: Tuckwell, 2000), 112–44.

3. Benjamin Nathans, *Beyond the Pale: The Jewish Encounter with Late Imperial Russia* (Berkeley: University of California Press, 2002); Ezra Mendelsohn, *Class Struggle in the Pale: The Formative Years of the Jewish Workers' Movement in Tsarist Russia* (New York: Cambridge University Press, 1970); Ezra Mendelsohn, *Zionism in Poland: The Formative Years, 1915–1926* (New Haven: Yale University Press, 1981).

4. Mitchell B. Hart, *Social Science and the Politics of Modern Jewish Identity* (Stanford CA: Stanford University Press, 2000); John M. Efron, *Defenders of the Race: Jewish Doctors and Race Science in Fin-de-siècle Europe* (New Haven: Yale University Press, 1994).

5. Marek Tuszewicki, "Giving *Tshuve* to the Sick: Correspondence Columns of the Yiddish Medical Press in Poland," *Science in Context* (forthcoming).

6. On the history of OZE and its activities, see Nadav Davidovitch and Rakefet Zalashik, "'Air, Sun, Water': Ideology and Activities of OZE (Society for the Preservation of the Health of the Jewish Population) during the Interwar Period," *Dynamis* no. 28 (2008): 127–49; Rakefet Zalashik and Nadav Davidovitch, "Taking and Giving: The Case of the JDC and OZE in Lithuania, 1919–26," *East European Jewish Affairs* 39, no. 1 (2009): 57–68; Rakefet Zalashik, "Expansion et functionnement de l'OZE-OSE," in *L'Oeuvre de Secours aux Enfants et les Populations Juives au XX Siècle*, ed. Nathias Gardet, Laura Hobson Faure, Katy Hazan, Catherine Nicault (Paris, Armand Colin, 2014), 112–26.

7. L. Gourevitch, *Twenty-Five Years of OSE (1912–1937)* (Paris: OSE, 1937); Leon L. Wulmann, ed., *In the Fight for Health of the Jewish People (50 Years of OZE)* (New York, 1968).

8. Yulian Rafes, *Doctor Tsemakh Shabad: A Great Citizen of the Jewish Diaspora* (Baltimore MD: VIA Press, 1999).

9. "Unzere Oyfgabebikhlaliz nit tsuheylnkrankhayten, neyertzeytsuferhiten, un das volenmirtunnurdurkhoyflkerendembraytenolam, vi azoy un fun venen di krankhaytenkomen," *Folksgezunt* no. 11 (1923): 28.

10. Tuszewicki, *Science in Context*.

11. On Yiddish as the daily language of Eastern European Jews, see Stephen Corrsin, "Literacy Rates and Questions of Language: Faith and Ethnic Identity

in Population Censuses in the Partitioned Polish Lands and Interwar Poland (1880s-1930s)," *Polish Review* 43, no. 2 (1998): 131–60; Gennady Estraikh, *Soviet Yiddish: Language Planning and Linguistic Development* (Oxford: Clarendon Press, 1999). There were other popular magazines in the field that were published in Yiddish besides *Folksgezunt*: *Zay Gezunt*, a youth magazine on hygiene and physical education; *Toz Yedies*; *Kalender Higyene*; and *Di Sotsiale Meditsin*. Commission on European Jewish Cultural Reconstruction, "Supplement: Tentative List of Jewish Periodicals in Axis-Occupied Countries," *Jewish Social Studies* no. 3 (1947): 1–44. See also the case of the distribution of knowledge about cancer to the Yiddish readership: Nathan Cohen, "What Did East European Yiddish Readers Know About Cancer (1902–1939)?" *Modern Judaism* 32, no. 2 (2012): 216–41. There are no available data on the scope and type of the *Folksgezunt* readership, but in general it targeted working-class and lower-middle-class urban Jews.

12. Pieter Jacobus Fourie, ed., *Media Studies*. Vol. 2: *Content, Audiences, and Production* (Cape Town, South Africa: Juta Academic, 2001).

13. Deborah Valenze, "The Cultural History of Food," in *Routledge International Handbook of Food Studies*, ed. Ken Albala (New York: Routledge, 2012), 101.

14. See, for example, Ezra Mendelsohn, *The Jews of East Central Europe between the World Wars* (Bloomington: Indiana University Press, 1987); Joseph Marcus, *Social and Political history of the Jews in Poland, 1919-1939* (Berlin: Walter de Gruyter, 1983); Celia Stopnicka Heller, *On the Edge of Destruction: Jews of Poland between the Two World Wars* (Detroit MI: Wayne State University Press, 1993).

15. On pork and Jews in ancient times, see Jordan Rosenblum, "'Why Do You Refuse to Eat Pork?' Jews, Food and Identity in Roman Palestine," *Jewish Quarterly Review* 100, no. 1 (2010): 95–110.

16. Gil Marks, *Encyclopedia of Jewish Food* (New York: Wiley, 2010), ix–x.

17. Hasia R. Diner, *Hungering for America: Italian, Irish, and Jewish Foodways in the Age of Migration* (Cambridge MA: Harvard University Press, 2009), 149. On the impact of urbanization on nutrition and food consumption, see Hans Juergen Teutenberg, "Urbanization and Nutrition: Historical Research Reconsidered," in *Food and the City in Europe*, ed. Peter J. Atkins, Peter Lummel, and Derek J. Oddy (Aldershot UK: Ashgate, 2007), 15–20.

18. On Poland, see Katarzyna Cwiertka, "Propagation of Nutritional Knowledge in Poland, 1863-1939," in *Order and Disorder: The Health Implications of Eating and Drinking in the Nineteenth and Twentieth Centuries: Proceedings of the Fifth*

*Symposium of the International Commission for Research into European Food History,
Aberdeen 1997*, ed. Alexander Fenton (Edinburgh UK: Tuckwell, 2000), 97–98.

19. BronisłavKoskowski, "Warunki higieniczne w małych osadach I sposób żywie-
nia się ich mieszkańców głównie Żydów," *Zdrowie* 10–11 (1908): 677–79.

20. Annemarie de Knecht-van Eakelen and Anneke H. van Otterloo, "'What the Body
Needs': Developments in Medical Advice, Nutritional Science and Industrial
Production in the Twentieth Century," in *Order and Disorder*, ed. Fenton, 114.

21. On the question of Kosher slaughtering, see Shai Lavi, "Animal Laws and
the Politics of Life: Slaughterhouse Regulation in Germany, 1870–1917," *The-
oretical Inquiries in Law* 8, no. 1 (2007): 221–50; Robin Judd, *Contested Rituals:
Circumcision, Kosher Butchering, and Jewish Political Life in Germany, 1843–1933*
(Ithaca NY: Cornell University Press, 2007).

22. John Efron, *Medicine and the German Jews* (New Haven: Yale University Press,
2001), 132–33; Lena Gorelik, *Die Pathologisierung von Judenimausgehenden 19.
und Anfang des 20. Jahrhunderts* (Munich, Germany: GRIN Verlag, 2005). On
American Jews, see Arleen Marcia Tuchman, "Diabetes and Race: A Historical
Perspective," *American Journal of Public Health* 101, no. 1 (2011): 24.

23. Marion A. Kaplan, *The Making of the Jewish Middle Class: Women, Family, and
Identity in Imperial Germany* (New York: Oxford University Press, 1991); David
Blackbourn and Richard J. Evans, *The German Bourgeoisie: Essays on the Social
History of the German Middle Class from the Late Eighteenth to the Early Twentieth
Century* (New York: Routledge, 2014); Mirjam Triendl-Zadoff, *Nächstes Jahr
in Marienbad: Gegenwelten Jüdischer Kulturen der Moderne* (Göttingen: Vanden-
hoeckund Ruprecht, 2007).

24. Y. Laypuner, "Vegetarianism," *Folksgezunt* nos. 2–3 (1923): 35.

25. Laypuner, "Vegetarianism," 37.

26. Laypuner, "Vegetarianism," 38. On the history of vegetarianism, see Stuart
Tristram, *The Bloodless Revolution: A Cultural History of Vegetarianism from 1600
to Modern Times* (New York: W. W. Norton, 2007).

27. Diner, *Hungering for America*, 164.

28. John Cooper, *Eat and be Satisfied: A Social History of Jewish Food* (New York:
Jason Aronson, 1993), 168–69.

29. David Kraemer, *Jewish Eating and Identity Through the Ages* (New York: Routledge,
2007), 138; Koskowski, "Warunki Hygieniczne," 678. On Judaism and vegetarianism, see Daniel Breslaur, "The Vegetarian Alternative: Biblical Adumbrations,
Modern Reverberations," in *Food and Judaism*, ed. Leonard Greenspoon, Ron-
land Simkins, Gerald Shapiro (Omaha NE: Creighton University Press, 2005),

92–93. On Jewish physicians in the 1920s who supported vegetarianism, see Barbara Kirshenblatt-Gimblett, "Cookbooks," in *The Yivo Encyclopedia of Jews in Eastern Europe*, http://www.yivoencyclopedia.org/article.aspx/Cookbooks.

30. On politics, economy, and the science of nutrition within the German context, see Corinna Treitel, "Food Science/Food Politics: Max Rubner and 'Rational Nutrition' in Fin-de-siècle Berlin," in *Food and the City in Europe*, ed. Atkins, Lummel, and Oddy, 52–60.

31. Laypuner, "Vegetarianism," 40.

32. Neustater, "Tsiesnmirtsufil?" *Folksgezunt* no. 8 (1925): 258.

33. Alexander Kaplan, "Vas Darf Man Esen un Trinken Kedei Tsu Zayn Gezunt? [Velkhe Shpayz Enthalten Vitaminen]," *Folksgezung* no. 8 (1924); Kaplan, "Higyene fun Shpayz."

34. Rakefet Zalashik, "The Anti-Favis Campaign in Poland: Jewish Social Medicine," *Polin* 27 (2015): 369–84; Nadav Davidovitch and Rakefet Zalashik, "'Air, sun, water': Ideology and Activities of OZE (Society for the Preservation of the Health of the Jewish Population) during the Interwar Period," *Dynamis* 28 (2008): 127–49.

35. Hans Teuteberg, "The Discovery of Vitamins: Laboratory Research, Reception, Industrial Production," in *Order and Disorder*, ed. Fenton, 226.

36. Teuteberg, "The Discovery of Vitamins," 264. On the popularization of vitamins, see Harmke Kamminga, "'Axes to Grind': Popularizing the Science of Vitamins, 1920s and 1930s," in *Food, Science, Policy and Regulation in the Twentieth Century: International and Comparative Perspectives*, ed. David Smith and Jom Phillips (New York: Routledge, 2000), 86–91.

37. Tsemakh Shabad, "Vegen Grinsnals Shpayz un vegenvitaminen," *Folksgezunt* nos. 11, 12, 13 (1931); "Higyenishe Klelim fun Esn," *Folksgezunt* no. 17 (1931): 135; "Vi darf man zikhderneren: Zat, gezunt un volful," *Folksgezunt* no. 13 (1932): 98; Anonymous, "Vi darf man zikhderneren: Tsu vas nuzendemkorper di bezonderedernershtofen un vi fil darferzain," *Folksgezunt* no. 14, (1932): 106–7; "Vi darf man zikhderneren: Zat, gezunt un volful, *Folksgezunt* no. 15 (1932): 115–17; Sulima Samoilo, "Gebroikht vas merer Grinsen," *Folksgezunt* no. 6 (1933): 42.

In the study from 1908 on the nutrition of Jews in small towns in Poland and Galicia, it was found that Jews hardly consumed vegetables and that it was mainly women and children who ate fruits during the summer. Koskowski, "Warunki Hygieniczne," 678.

38. Kaplan, "Vas Darf Man Esen": 195–98. This new variety has intensified what the sociologist Claude Fischer calls the Omnivore's Paradox: the human need

for a diverse nutrition and its inclination to innovation on the one hand, and the potential danger in new food on the other. Claude Fischer, "Food, Self, and Identity," *Social Science Information* 27, no. 2 (1988): 275–93.

39. Kaplan, "Higyene fun Shpayz," 142.

40. Kaplan, "Higyene fun Shpayz," 145–46.

41. Kaplan, "Higyene fun Shpayz," 143.

42. Bentley, "Introduction," *A Cultural History of Food*, 5.

43. Saul Pergament, "Di Tsuzamenshtel fun unzere spaiz," *Folksgezunt*, no. 5–6 (1923): 13.

44. Cooper, *Eat and Be Satisfied*, 159.

45. Z. Shults, "Vegenayer in dernerung fun kind," *Folksgezunt* no. 12 (1928): 221.

46. On the social construction of taste, see Pierre Bourdieu, *Distinction: A Social Critique of the Judgement of Taste* (Cambridge MA: Harvard University Press, 1984).

47. Koskowski, "Warunki Hygieniczne," 677.

48. Tsemakh Shabbad, "Hunger un Apetit," *Folksgezunt* no. 2 (1933): 9–11.

49. Wisozki, "Vi azoi kan a froi haben a shlanke figur?" *Folksgezunt* no. 2 (1933): 14.

50. Wisozki, "Vi azoikan a froihaben a shlankefigur?" 14.

51. Szymon Rudnicki, "Anti-Jewish Legislation in Interwar Poland," in *Antisemitism and Its Opponents in Modern Poland*, ed. Robert Blobaum (Ithaca NY: Cornell University Press, 2005), 158; Eva Plach, "Ritual Slaughter and Animal Welfare in Interwar Poland," *East European Jewish Affairs* 45, no. 1 (2015): 1–25.

52. On *shechita* (animal Jewish slaughtering), see S. Lockerman, *Folksgezunt* no. 7–8 (1923): 25–26.

53. On readers' letters in *Folksgezunt* and other Jewish medical periodicals in Eastern Europe, see Tuszewicki, *Science in Context*.

54. For the whole list, see "Inhalt fun *Folksgezunt* furnyar 1924," *Folksgezunt* no. 1 (1924).

55. "Brifkasten," *Folksgezunt* nos. 5–6 (1923): 34; "Brifkasten," *Folksgezunt* no. 12 (1923): 24; "Brifkasten," *Folksgezunt* no. 5 (1924): 122; "Brifkasten," *Folksgezunt* no. 6 (1924): 154; "Brifkasten," *Folksgezunt* no. 2 (1925): 61.

56. Emiko Ohnuki-Tierney, *Rice as Self: Japanese Identities through Time* (Princeton NJ: Princeton University Press, 1993), 129–30. From Roman times, not eating pork marked a practice-based Jewish identity. Jordan Rosenblum, "'Why Do You Refuse to Eat Pork?' Jews, Food and Identity in Roman Palestine," *Jewish Quarterly Review* 100, no. 1 (2010): 95–110.

8

The Battle against Guefilte Fish

Asserting Sephardi Culinary Repertoires among Argentine
Jews in the Second Half of the Twentieth Century

....

ADRIANA BRODSKY

This chapter examines Argentine and Jewish Argentine cookbooks in
addition to personal recollections of food, dishes, and eating, to chart
the conversations through which Sephardim, Ashkenazim, and Argentines were connected *and* separated throughout the twentieth century.
Looking at what women cooked, what they served, when and where the
served it, how they called what they prepared, how they defined their
culinary traditions, and their intentions in all these different activities
provides a window into the process through which ethnic identities
were constructed and maintained. The variety of sources that I bring
together in this chapter allows me to shed light on how, as a minority
seeking to establish and maintain their cultural identity, Sephardi women
negotiated on three fronts: with the constantly evolving Argentine culture, with the dominant Ashkenazi culture, and with the heterogeneous
regional identities of their places of origin (Moroccan, Ottoman, Syrian,
etc.). Situating food within a broader set of cultural and social practices, I trace the specific place that the production, consumption, and

commemoration of particular foods and dishes had in the making and subsistence of a Sephardi identity in Argentina.

Previous scholarly approaches to cookbooks have tended to focus on the role that these texts played in the construction of national cuisines that were crafted deliberately from a variety of regional culinary traditions.[1] Studies of Jewish food, in particular, have been especially interested in how kashrut regulations were maintained, adapted, or dropped, and in the ways in which the local realities encountered by Jews in the places where they settled presented eaters with new food choices.[2] These national and diasporic approaches have therefore allowed us to learn about the battles waged by elites over food in their efforts to disseminate their own view of the nation, and about Jews' flexibility (or lack thereof) in adapting to their surroundings *and* in keeping their traditions (and identity) alive. In this chapter, I place these two types of cookbooks (national and diasporic) in conversation with each other with the aim of characterizing the position of Jewish Argentine cookbooks in relation to two processes: on the one hand, I examine how these cookbooks were connected to the practices of Argentine elite projects that defined the country as a modern nation and offered people the chance to claim belonging to the nation and to the social class that was espousing these ideals. Throughout, I also trace the evolution of the diasporic dimension of Jewish identity, analyzing how Jewish Argentine cookbooks were sites of conflict for various battles over the very meaning (and borders) of diasporic identities, whether in struggle for the coexistence of Ashkenazi and Sephardi culinary traditions or in the successive definitions of Sephardi cuisines vis-à-vis the various cultural identities that contribute to the Sephardi repertoire.

How can we define the place and function of cookbooks and cooking in relation to the broader process of formation and maintenance of Sephardi ethnic identity in Argentina? While one can point to multiple endeavors and initiatives that the Sephardi community undertook in Argentina to consolidate their presence, the cookbooks and oral history interviews I conducted also illuminate how, in the later second half of the twentieth century, Sephardim engaged in unplanned, uncoordinated, unnoticeable, and sometimes unintended actions aimed at asserting their right to be a visible part of Jewish Argentine culture. Food was one of the many fronts on which Sephardim fought against the hegemony that Ashkenazim enjoyed in Argentina, where the Jewish community was unmistakably majority Ashkenazi. A minority group in Argentina, Sephardim never accounted for more than 10 percent of the Jewish Argentine community. Originally expelled from Spain in 1492, Sephardim then settled in Ottoman lands and North African regions and subsequently moved across the ocean to Argentina and other places across the globe, in the late nineteenth and twentieth century. Once in Argentina, these Sephardi groups, which included Jews from Morocco, present-day Turkey, Aleppo, and Damascus, initially maintained their particular (local) identities by each organizing their own immigrant associations (mutual aid societies, religious schools, synagogues, butchers, cemeteries, etc.) and settling in distinct Buenos Aires neighborhoods, rarely crossing paths. Beginning in the late 1920s, these Sephardi groups in Argentina attempted to create "collective" Sephardi organizations, even if most were short-lived. They founded a Sephardi Rabbinical Consistory, a Sephardi Anti-Tuberculosis League, a Sephardi Jewish Confederation—an umbrella organization that gathered all Sephardi institutions, the Union of Sephardi Jewish Associations of the Argentine Republic, two Sephardi Zionist centers (the second of which continued to operate well into the 1960s), Sephardi branches of the Jewish National Fund, and even a Sephardi Sports Club. Sephardi efforts to claim belonging in Jewish Argentine culture through food emerged in the second half of the twentieth century, and although these attempts were part of larger demographic changes, they nonetheless attest to the Sephardim's struggle, as a minority, to remain an integral part of Jewish Argentine life, and how, in this process, they crafted a new meaning for their Sephardi identity.

Focusing both on concerted efforts and on everyday practices, this chapter, then, examines how Sephardim, in particular women and their organizations, related to both "their" past and present "Argentine" culinary practices before the 1950s, and how that changed in the second half of the twentieth century. Sephardi women, I will show, began the century cooking their (Moroccan, Aleppoan, Izmirli) dishes for their families (even when, out of necessity, these were adapted to the ingredients found in the new land), and consuming Argentine/French recipes when their organizations organized public events; they later incorporated new concerns about health and modernity and more fully embraced "Argentine" culinary options, but continued to cook their "traditional" dishes on special occasions. I also examine how, as part of this shift, Sephardi women also began to publish cookbooks, attempting to insert Sephardi culinary practices into the (Ashkenazi) Jewish Argentine repertoire. In their attempt to assert the distinctiveness of Sephardi culture in comparison with Ashkenazi practices, these initial publications did not recognize regional differences between Sephardi cuisines. Later cookbooks would depart from this homogenization by offering a vision of Sephardi traditional food that understood these dishes as coming from distinct cultural contexts. By reconstituting the story of Sephardi food in Argentina through different strands, this chapter sheds light on how this story is defined by conversations and exchanges between and among Jews, Argentines, and various non-Ashkenazi groups. In the end, these nonviolent, subtle, and uncoordinated attempts proved to be more successful than the "organizational" efforts in which Sephardim had engaged in the early part of the twentieth century to become visible among the Jewish Argentine community.

At home and at community events, the immigrant generation of Sephardi women attempted, whenever possible, to continue to prepare for their families what they had learned to cook prior to their migration to Argentina. Estela Levy, a Jew from Istanbul, recalled how her mother prepared special dishes to bring in a basket to Sunday outings in the parks of Palermo, in the city of Buenos Aires. These dishes included *burecas* (stuffed phyllo pastries), *huevos jaminados* (slow-cooked hard-boiled eggs), and *bulemas* (cheese pastries).[3] Even when the lack of specific ingredients needed to prepare these recipes may have posed a challenge, women still continued to cook these foods. Bulisa, for example, remembered that her mother, who was born and raised in Smyrna and used to prepare and sell *boios* (pastries usually filled with spinach) when she was in Turkey, did not want to do without *bamias* (okra) in order to make the stew that was very traditional in the Ottoman Empire. To maintain this cultural tradition, Bulisa's mother went to the extreme of planting her own okra garden, as she could not find this key ingredient in the markets of the town of Concordia in the province of Entre Ríos.[4] These women's insistence on continuing to prepare these specialties reveals the extent to which they felt that these dishes defined them, their families, and culinary culture.

These dishes were part of Sephardi tables during the initial years of immigration. All of the Sephardi women who participated in an oral history workshop that I organized in the late 1990s remembered their mothers (the immigrant generation) as makers, almost exclusively, of what are now called "traditional" Sephardi dishes. Nevertheless, it also became clear in the workshop sessions that these foods were associated with a specific "origin." That is to say, people did not prepare "Sephardi" food, but *"platos marroquíes, sirios, o turcos"* (Moroccan, Syrian, or Turkish dishes). "My food," claimed an interviewee of Syrian origin speaking to a mostly Ottoman Jewish group of ladies, "has nothing to do with yours."[5] "Sephardi" food did not yet exist, and it would take a little longer for it to enter into the imagination and practice of Argentine Jews.

Growing up in Argentina understandably placed these immigrants in contact with Argentines, other immigrants, and their (evolving) food traditions. Those who arrived in Argentina at a very young age, or the generation that was born there and attended free public schools, learned from those around them. Buenos Aires and smaller towns in the Argentine interior never saw the development of de facto ghettos that were characteristic of other contexts of the Jewish diaspora. Rather, immigrants lived in true "mixed" neighborhoods, although those arriving from the same city or town tended to congregate in the same areas. This dynamic generated multiple opportunities for immigrants to gain exposure to other traditions. This is the case of Esther Acrich, a woman whose parents were born in Morocco but arrived in Argentina when they were very young and settled in a very small town in the province of Córdoba, and who recalled that her mother "rarely made Moroccan food." Instead, her mother had adopted *criollo* (Argentine) recipes and made them for the family: "pasta, stews, roasts."[6] Marcos Levy remembered his weekly Sunday lunch meal of *ravioles con estofado de lomo* (raviolis with tomato and meat sauce) entirely prepared by his immigrant father who had learned how to make pasta (from scratch!) from his Italian peers.[7] Estela Levy, the Ottoman Jew who lived among Jews from Syria in the neighborhood of La Boca, recalled how her mother exchanged recipes of "typical foods from their countries of origin" with a native of Damascus who worked at her husband's store.[8]

Important local (Argentine) developments in cooking also impacted the extent to which immigrants learned about other ways of eating and preparing food. From the 1920s through to the 1930s, corporations began to appeal to and celebrate women consumers (this was, of course, part of a worldwide phenomenon) and increasingly used home economics to sell their products. Primitiva, for example, a British gas company that sold products in Argentina, utilized a dual strategy based both on advertising campaigns aimed at showing the "time, money, and happiness" that its gas stoves would bring women and their families, and on free cooking demonstrations led by *"ecónomas,"* women trained in the "science" of homemaking. One such *ecónoma* was Doña Petrona C. de Gandulfo, the author of the now iconic cookbook *El Libro de Doña Petrona*. Doña Petrona's book was first published in 1934 and is now in its 103rd printing.[9] She would launch her career as a cooking demonstrator for Primitiva and move on to host very popular cooking shows on the radio and then on television, also writing columns for women's magazines.[10]

El Libro de Doña Petrona was mostly likely the first cookbook that many (Sephardi) women purchased in Argentina. But it offered more than a mere collection of recipes. It acquainted its readers with the proper etiquette for the order in which food should be served, gave suggestions for how to set the table, rules about what the butler or maid should wear, a list of which pieces of furniture should be part of a dining room, and even included a list of cocktails that aided women's complexions. The recipes themselves were organized according to categories (appetizers, soups, pastas, sauces, etc.) and the book included several weekly menus from which women could choose to prepare for their families and social events.

The new technology of gas stoves and the French cooking techniques presented in the pages of Doña Petrona's book and through her radio shows were initially aimed at well-off women (and their cooks). Yet, in the following decades, the success of Petrona C. de Gandulfo and her empire took a new direction: she took the upper-class ideal that she embodied in the vision of domesticity that defined good and proper women as full-time homemakers and turned it into a model for the middle class to follow. Similarly, immigrant women wished to emulate the exemplary housewife portrayed in the pages of Doña Petrona's book, precisely because that housewife initially belonged to a social class that most immigrants had not yet become a part of.

The imitation, I believe, was not evidence of lack of imagination, but the result of a conscious, even strategic, decision on the part of immigrant and middle-class women. Historian Ezequiel Adamovsky maintains that, prior to the emergence of a middle class in Argentina, Argentines wished to consume that which had become synonymous with the upper class. "The services and goods offered," he states, "became symbols of social status."[11] "Thus," he continues, "through the supply of products and advertising, the market contributed to 'classify' the population according to their ability to recognize and acquire the necessary accoutrements of those with 'distinction' and 'good taste.'"[12] This strategic consumption of specific products was practiced by women who belonged to Sephardi organizations when planning social events intended to raise funds for their charitable activities.

On September 26, 1937, for example, a *té danzante* was held at the Alvear Palace Hotel, a very famous and expensive Argentine hotel in a rich neighborhood of Buenos Aires. The party was organized by the Sociedad de Damas de Beneficencia "La Unión," a group created in 1922 by Sephardi women from the Balkan community. An account in the magazine *La Luz* described that the event took place in "one of the most luxurious salons of the house," which was "lit '*a giorno*' (flood-lit) [and] prepared with exquisite taste for this dance." The article took note of how "the efficient attention paid to all the guests by the untiring ladies of the organizing commission of this group merits mentioning. With exquisite delicacy, the impressive turnout was served [tea and pastries] in small separate tables giving way to cordiality and friendship. The famous orchestra of René Cospito with its singer Fernando Torres was in charge of the music." "The success of the party," the story ended, "was in every sense the worthy outcome of the organizers' unceasing activity."[13]

The "organizers' unceasing activity" was strategically directed. Jewish women's organizations in general *chose* to hold most of their money-raising events in the same theaters or dance halls where elite Argentine women held theirs. The choices that Jewish women made in planning their parties all point to a desire to emulate a culture of upper-class Argentine philanthropy that had been in existence for several years—a desire shared by other groups.[14] These choices are reflected in a bevy of details ranging from the type of events held, the venues selected, the language used to advertise and later describe the events in newspapers and magazines, the orchestras hired to play in them, the singers heard, and, of course, the food consumed. While the Jewish organizers of the events had no intention of being diverted from their money-raising endeavors, these practices turned them into zealous guardians of these Argentine class ideals. These women's groups capitalized on the customs of the Argentine philanthropic organizations and on the spaces in which the upper crust of Buenos Aires paraded their social status. They legitimized their events by consuming goods that were recognized as symbols of distinction. By signaling their role as members of a class, and as participants of respected philanthropic organizations in the eyes of Jews and Argentines alike, these groups sought to guarantee the success of the events they organized.

But more importantly, the decision to mimic upper-class Argentine culture was not, as one might imagine, solely driven by these women's desire to fit in, nor did the adoption of these practices entail the loss of ethnic identity. The strategic dimension that guided this choice becomes clear when we consider how the consumption and use of the proper Argentine upper-class style, in fact, ensured the continuity of the Jewish community in the new land. It was by adopting Argentine norms and customs, including food (for example, by clearly selecting special recipes over other options), that Jews preserved their own identity as Jews in the new nation. After all, the events organized by these women's groups were aimed at supporting Jewish institutions in the new land. The money raised in these events helped Jewish orphans (both boys and girls) and the elderly, provided treatment for Jewish tuberculosis patients, and aimed to fund a Jewish tuberculosis hospice, keep a Jewish hospital running, protect Jewish immigrants, and raise money for Eretz Israel. In a context in which most of the charity for those in need in Argentina was administered within Catholic organizations headed by pious Catholic women, Jewish institutions provided a safe environment in which Jews who needed help could in fact remain within Jewish networks.[15] By "consuming" Argentine cultural goods in their events, these Jewish philanthropic organizations raised sufficient money to enable Jews to continue being Jewish.

REINSCRIBING JEWISH AND SEPHARDI CUISINES: BETWEEN MODERNIZATION AND TRADITION

The success of Doña Petrona's book rested in part on its ability to provide women with a manual from which they could learn about the "proper" behavior, products, and food practices that would define them as (aspirant) members of a certain class. The book's countless editions speak, as well, to its successful adaptation to the changing realities and conditions that shaped Argentine women's daily lives. Subsequent printings would include, for example, sections on what to do when there wasn't a sleep-in maid (or butler) at home, or when there was no service at all (this was a clear indication that those buying the books were likely not upper-class women, but middle class). Doña Petrona published new books addressing people's concern over calories and fat, and, in later decades, published magazine columns stressing the need to adapt recipes (and indeed homemaking itself) to the high prices and inflation that plagued Argentina from the late 1960s onward.

In what could likely be the first Jewish Argentine cookbook, *Especialidades de la cocina judía* (Jewish cooking specialties), published in 1955, we can also see some of the same concerns that had guided both the publication of Doña Petrona's original book and the concerns that resulted from women's desires to adapt to changing realities.[16] Erna Schlesinger, the author and wife of Rabbi Guillermo Schlesinger, who led the Libertad Street Temple (the oldest congregation in Buenos Aires), stated in her introduction that the book was meant for "Jewish housewives to discover (finally!) the secrets of those typical dishes they tasted when they were young, those old and traditional dishes that their mothers made."[17] From the first pages, then, it is clear that the book's intended audience was Jewish daughters who had tasted traditional Jewish food made by their mothers but had never really learned how to make those dishes. One of the book's objectives was to make sure that culinary traditions that seemed to be on the verge of disappearance did not get lost once the "older" generation was gone. In function of this imperative, the book features nine recipes for *cholent* (meat, potato, beans, and barley stew), seven versions for borsch (beet soup), twelve versions for *kneidlej* (matzo balls), five versions for *latkes* (potato pancakes), five versions for *tsimes* (sweet stew with or without meat), and nine versions of strudel.

The inclusion of a glossary of foreign terms also strongly suggests that readers were imagined to be unfamiliar with certain key terms related to both Jewish food (like *guefilte fish*) and Jewish laws and festivities (like *brit milá*). These readers were likely daughters born in Argentina and/

FIG. 8-1. Cover of Erna Schlesinger's *Especialidades de la cocina judía* (Buenos Aires: Biblioteca de Mucho Gusto, 1955). Courtesy of IWO–Buenos Aires.

or perhaps domestic (non-Jewish) servants. In an effort to explain what *kreplej* were, the author compared them to *capeletti*, an Italian stuffed pasta dish that would have been recognized by most people living in Argentina at the time.[18] The book also contains a full section on kashrut, for example, that even described a quick homemade solution to prepare kosher meat at home. It also explained in detail which dishes were traditionally served for each Jewish religious celebration.

But the book also aimed to acquaint young Jewish women with ingredients associated with "Jewish foods" with which they may have been less familiar. The author wished for readers to "learn how to prepare and make up *new* [my italics] recipes using as base these wonderful favorite ingredients: ground fish, smoked fish, brie, poppy seeds, etc."[19] "Modern" women would likely have found the idea of re-creating taste more appealing than simply continuing to make "traditional" dishes. The author hoped that tradition could become a space of transformation and innovation.

A new Jewish Argentine cookbook published in the early 1960s continued to stress the idea of innovation and change within tradition. *La cocina judía moderna: de acuerdo a las normas tradicionales* (Modern Jewish cooking: according to traditional standards) was also unmistakably geared toward young women, but the intended reader differed from the housewife that Petrona C. de Gandulfo had imagined in the early decades of the twentieth century.[20] The readers were imagined to be first- or second-generation Argentines, already fully immersed in Argentine culinary traditions. The authors explained that they had included "not only typical Jewish recipes from the countries in the old continent and Israel," but hoped, rather, to create a "complete casher [*sic*] cookbook... including regional dishes from Argentina, attentive, as well, to the latest advances of nutritional sciences."[21] Also echoing Doña Petrona C. de Gandulfo's concerns, the authors stated that they had every intention of contemplating "each household's budget by including, in many cases, similar recipes with cheaper ingredients, so the housewife could choose according to her taste and budget."[22]

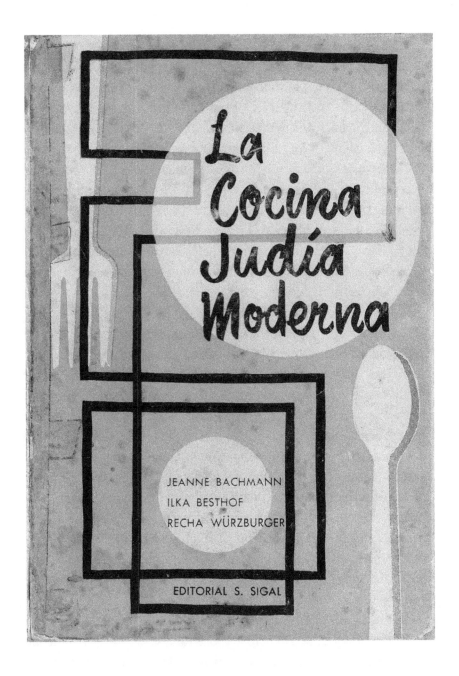

FIG. 8-2. Cover of Jeanne Bachmann et al., *La cocina judía moderna: de acuerdo a las normas tradicionales* (Buenos Aires: Editorial Sigal, 1961). Courtesy of IWO–Buenos Aires.

Some of the recipes included in the book, then, are criollo staples like *asado* (grilled meat), *chimichurri* sauce (to accompany the asado), a variety of *empanadas* (savory individual pies), *mazamorra* (sweet white-corn porridge), *locro* (squash, meat and hominy stew), along with originally Italian and Spanish dishes that had become part of the Argentine food repertoire: ravioles, *tuco con carne* (tomato and meat sauce), risotto, and *tortilla de papas* (Spanish potato omelet), among others. This book, and therefore these authors, understood Jewish food in modern times as including not exclusively traditional European Jewish dishes, but also those from the local repertoire prepared following simple kashrut (and dietary) laws. By observing these simple laws to prepare asado and tortilla de papas and serving her family in Argentina, a housewife could be both Jewish and modern.

The concerns over calories consumed and the availability of time for busier housewives that guided Doña Petrona's changes to her original book, and influenced the choice of recipes in *La cocina judía moderna*, were clearly part of what Sephardi women remember as reasons for abandoning the daily preparation of "traditional" dishes. When I asked Bulisa if she continued to tend to her mother's okra garden in order to prepare *bamia* stews, she claimed that she did not, as she had "moved to Buenos Aires and lived in an apartment building," but more importantly, because "it was too much work."[23] Bulisa also added during that meeting that because her husband suffered from a heart condition, cooking the "old way" was to be avoided, as it had been prohibited for medical reasons. Echoing these health concerns, Luna, another informant, explained that "our food was too greasy and oily. . . . We can't eat those foods now."[24] Traditional dishes were exiled from the daily table and reserved for special occasions.

In her analysis of the culinary practices of the French Jewry, Joëlle Bahloul argues that the type of food cooked and served varied in function as to whether the recipient of food was the family/community or the French/outside — a characterization which applies to some extent to the Sephardim culinary choices discussed in the previous section — however second-generation Argentines do not follow this pattern.[25] In the private space of the dinner table at home, or among coreligionists, Sephardi as well as Ashkenazi women began to cook dishes that they considered to be less greasy, less complicated to make, and more readily available, thus making them part of a repertoire that now included other traditions. For example, a youth group from the Moroccan social club organized to celebrate the "national flag day" on June 22 and decided to prepare an *asado criollo* (grilled meat) with *chinchulines y chorizos* (sausage and intestines).[26] And for the celebration of the May Revolution, they settled on *chocolate con buñuelos* (hot chocolate and fried pastries), the typical food used in celebrating this national Argentine holiday.[27] It should be noted that they settled on *buñuelos* (which also have Sephardi roots, even if they are a typical staple in criollo-Argentine cuisine), a compromise made after rejecting the suggestion to prepare *fiyuelas*, a typical Moroccan fried pastry which, while delicious, involves painstaking attention and time-consuming preparation.

Despite their embrace of Argentine contemporary dishes, young Sephardi women could not yet find a book that put into writing the traditional dishes *their* mothers and grandmothers had likely cooked on a daily basis. Both of the aforementioned Jewish cookbooks only included a few non-Ashkenazi recipes. Schlesinger's cookbook contained four unmistakably Sephardi dishes from each of the Sephardi groups that had settled in Argentina: shish kebabs (pieces of meat grilled on a skewer), *cuscusú* (couscous), *borecas de queso* (cheese-filled phyllo pies), and *dolmas de pazi* (stuffed chard leaves). But none of the dishes suggested for Shabbat meals and for other religious festivities had a connection to the Sephardi world. *La cocina judía moderna*, as well, listed some dishes that could have Sephardi origin, but they were not signaled as such, as the dishes' traditional names or geographic origins were omitted.

Patricia Finzi, the descendant of Italian Jews who moved to Brazil escaping persecution during the 1940s, was the first author to put together a true "Jewish Argentine cookbook" that incorporated both

FIG. 8-3. Cover of *La cocina judía: tradición y variaciones*, 1984. Personal collection of the author.

Platos apropiados para Rosh Hashaná y Yom Kipur

Pasta de huevos y nueces	**ENTRADAS**
Paté de hígado a la Dina	
Pasta de hígado	
Ikre	
Babaghanouj	
Paté de berenjenas	
Berenjenas con mayonesa	
Pescado escabechado al coñac	
Cogote de pollo relleno	
Kibbe Senya	
Kibbe neye	
Sesos a la mayonesa	
Ensalada de carne	

Caldo de gallina	**SOPAS**
Caldo de carne	
Caldo de cordero	
Kappará	
Borsht a la rusa 1	
Borsht con crema	
Caldo con bollitas de huevo	
Chlof	
Beda b'lemune	
Kneidlej (todas las recetas se adaptan)	
Matza mandlej	
Farfel tostado de matzá	
Kreplaj de pollo	

Gefilte fish 1	**PESCADOS**
Gefilte fish 2	
Gefilte fish 3	
Gefilte fish 4	
Gefilte fish 5	
Gefilte fish 6	
Gefilte fish 7	
Gefilte fish al horno	
Gefilte fish al horno 2	
Gefilte fish al horno 4	
Carpa o trucha a la oriental	
Pescado frito	

Pollo con hierbas	**AVES**
Gallina al horno con miel	
Pollo al horno israelí	
Pollo con paprika y limón	
Pollo con cebolla y ciruelas	
Pollo relleno con salsa de naranja	
Pollo relleno con damascos	
Pollo con especias, cebolla y almendras	
Pavo a la polaca	
Pollo con frutas desecadas	

Asado de ternera	**CARNES**
Ternerita asada con tahine	
Carne con membrillo	
Higos con carne	
Albóndigas agridulces	
Hígado de ternera con manzanas	
Alcahuciles con carne	
Costilla de cordero a la cacerola	
Asado de cordero con uvas	

Pastel de fideos con pollo y seso	**PASTAS**
Lahmagine	
Masitas de cebolla	
Arrollado de cebolla	
Arrollado de repollo	

Niños envueltos	**GUARNICIONES**
Repollo marrón	
Repollo colorado con manzanas	

25

FIG. 8-4. Menus for Rosh Hashanah from *La cocina judía: tradición y variaciones*, 1984. Personal collection of the author.

Ashkenazi and Sephardi culinary traditions into one comprehensive tome.[28] The book was suggestively titled: *La cocina judía: tradición y variaciones* (Jewish cooking: tradition and variations). Did this title hint at the existence of a "single tradition"—as suggested by the use of "tradición" in the singular—upon which several variations existed? Did it refer to tradition as Ashkenazi and to its variations as Sephardi? As with previous Jewish cookbooks, *La cocina judía* also opened with a description of the main Jewish religious holidays, kashrut laws, and other introductory essays that discussed food and memory, as well as sections of literary works that discussed food. A big difference, however, was that the suggested menus included both Ashkenazi and Sephardi options, hinting at a readership that was both or either.[29] One section titled "Some Traditions from the Judeo-Spanish World" summarized Sephardi traditions and practices.[30] In the section that listed appropriate traditional dishes for Jewish holidays, for example, one finds, borsch and kneidelej, together with *lahmagine* (small sweet meat-topped pizza bites) and *kibbe* (meatballs cooked or raw meat with cracked wheat).

Patricia Finzi's decision to include both Ashkenazi and Sephardi traditions was a response to the changing realities of the Argentine community. By the last decades of the twentieth century, the Jewish Argentine community was undergoing important changes. The divide between Ashkenazim and Sephardim, once so clearly drawn, particularly by the existence of separate institutions, separate residential patterns, and intracommunity marriages, was becoming blurred. By the 1960s, marriages between Sephardim and Ashkenazim were very common, and indicative that the common shared "Argentine" culture of the bride and groom had taken precedence over the distinct traditions of their parents. As *La cocina judía: tradición y variaciones* merged these two culinary repertoires, the book would be very appealing to the many households who wished to own a single Jewish cookbook: both mothers *and* mothers-in-law could be impressed with the culinary abilities of their host.

This cookbook was not, however, overly nostalgic. The book reads more like a compendium, a tome that described what Jewish Argentines were likely to be cooking (or wishing to cook) then. But while the book made reference to the past, and claimed that "food was and is a link between yesterday and the new generations," its matter-of-fact attitude was contrary to the tone of *Especialidades de la cocina judía*. The past was gone, Patricia Finzi claimed, and Jewish housewives now "have modern ovens, freezers, [and] clean vegetables," that made their dishes clean and healthy. The book suggested, subtly but clearly, that the Jewish community of Argentina had changed: Jewish (food) now resulted from the blending of these groups' traditions as well as the incorporation of modern comforts.

But the nostalgic call to save "Sephardi" culture *was* voiced elsewhere (just as it had been among Ashkenazim in previous decades), in a venue that was contemporary to *La cocina judía*'s combination of traditions. In 1994 Las Amigas Sefaradíes de Na'amat (previously called Comité Femenino Sefaradí 'Amigos de la Histadrut'), a group of women whose philanthropic activities supported the federation of trade unions in Israel published *Cocinando al estilo sefaradí* (Cooking Sephardi style). The book indicated the existence of a Jewish community that included both Ashkenazi and Sephardi traditions, while ensuring the preservation of the legacies of the Sephardi immigrant generation.[31] "We want to share our favorite recipes with you," they announced in their short introduction, adding that "most [of the dishes] are Sephardi."[32] These women had clearly learned dishes not only from their own mothers and grandmothers, but also from friends, extended families, and neighbors. The recipes are organized according to the types of dishes (salads, fish, meat, etc.), and a few sections toward the end of the book include general cooking and freezing tips, observations on the uses of herbs and seeds, as well as what dishes are appropriate for Passover and Shavuot. Each recipe bears the name of the woman who contributed it to the project, and this information suggests that women came from the Arabic-speaking communities, as well as from the Ottoman and Moroccan communities.[33]

While most of the dishes clearly originated from the Sephardi world, no distinction was made between dishes from one community and those from others. This book therefore used "Sephardi" as an umbrella term to refer to diverse culinary traditions that constituted a "whole" that stood in opposition to Ashkenazi food culture. Yet, interestingly, the book included recipes for guefilte fish, *jrein* (horseradish/beet sauce), *kreplaj* (small dumplings served with soup), and *leicaj* (honey cake). What's more, the recipes for these Ashkenazi dishes had not been contributed by Ashkenazi women: the one for guefilte fish, for example, had been submitted by Sofía Setton Hasse.[34] The recipe for *acelga con kibbe* (chard and kibbe), on the other hand, had been provided by Elisabeth Frumanski.[35] In this sense, this collection suggests, much like *Cocina judía moderna*, that the Jewish Argentine community was no longer neatly divided into groups of origin. Yet, unlike the authors of *Cocina judía moderna*, the collection *Cocinando al estilo sefaradí* did not suggest that Jewish food could be(come) something other than traditional dishes from the *viejo continente* (Old World). The collection is a mere reflection of the multiethnic Jewish Argentine community.

Cocina sefaradí was another cookbook published in Argentina that, in its first edition, also stemmed from a collective project taken on by Sephardi Zionist women, and that took root in a nostalgic longing for the almost lost traditions but celebrated the desire that these traditions continue to exist.[36] The Sephardi section of the Women's International Zionist Organization compiled various recipes as remembered by those who had made them, and the collection was "published" in 1978 for the members of the group (unfortunately, no copy of the book remains from this initial printing). In 1980, Estela Levy, one of the compilers of the "first edition" updated the collection by including new sections on "affordable dishes" (again, echoing what other cookbooks had done), "useful tips," and "important tips." The author, who was herself of *turco* (Turkish) origin but had married into a Jewish-Arab family learning the two (culinary) traditions, introduced the revised version by explaining to the reader that "a cookbook is memories that do not want to die, [memories] that are written on the skin; a cookbook shows changes that had to be incorporated as a result of the wandering, but also the desire to keep traditions alive."[37] After the expulsion from Spain, the author asserted, Sephardi culinary culture suffered "modifications" depending on the "contexts and climate in which [people] lived their lives."

As with the book *Cocinando al estilo sefaradí*, very few recipes clearly state their origin, again suggesting an understanding of Sephardi traditions as homogenous. The prologue, for example, contains a few sentences describing Sephardi culinary tradition as "appetizing and light . . . with no creams or heavy sauces, [full of dishes that use a lot of] lemon, and no [big] cakes, but individual sweets."[38] The prologue closed by reminding readers that this genuine cuisine [Sephardi food] was intimately linked to *canticas y romanzas* (songs and stories) that our ancestors would break into after their meals."[39]

The nostalgic longing and the association of food with other aspects of culture (namely language, sayings, and songs) were important features of the book *Sabores y misterios de la cocina sefaradí* (Tastes and mysteries of Sephardi food).[40] Written by Patricia Finzi, who authored *La cocina judía* referenced above, this 1993 publication shared some of the characteristics of previous Jewish Argentine cookbooks. One the one hand, it echoes the urgent call to keep Sephardi tradition alive, but it is also attentive to "modern" concerns: "We see the significance of Sephardi food: its historical and sentimental importance with regards to the past, and its social importance in Israel's present. It's up to us to continue it in the future, choosing—with this book in hand—what is more attuned to our current taste, trying and trying again those recipes inherited from our mothers until we make them our own: if not, we'll lose them forever." Survival is imagined as adapting tradition to current sensibilities and realities, but it is also made clear that the Sephardi "present" is in Israel and not in Argentina: in Israel, Sephardi food is everywhere and central to Israeli culture.

What is new in this Sephardi cookbook is an understanding of Sephardi culture as multivocal. Patricia Finzi tells us that "I did not wish to limit the book to a segment of Sephardi cooking, but to provide [the reader] with a panoramic view that included the simplicity of Sephardi *turca*, Italian, Bulgarian and Greek food, the exotic dishes of Yemen, Morocco and Syria, without leaving aside Israel and the Latin American contributions." Each recipe, then, states which tradition the dish follows, including, when necessary, the name of the dish in the language of origin. The recipes come from Yemen, Bulgaria, Turkey, Egypt, Israel, Syria, Rhodes, Spain, Morocco, Italy, Greece, Persia, Lebanon, and Iran. For the first time, it is explicitly stated that Sephardim belong to a variety of different groups.

But while attentive to the complexity of Sephardi culture, the book also essentialized Sephardim and claimed the existence of a single tradition (even if it is never spelled out). For example, we read that "Sephardi cooking is, although diasporic, absolutely original," and that what characterizes Sephardi food "is that Jews impregnated sweetness to traditional Arabic and Turkish [*turca*] food."[41] In another section, written by Matilda Koén-Sarano, we learn that "Sephardi food is deeply Jewish, not only because all dishes follow kashrut, but also because the food is linked to Shabat [sic] and Jewish festivities."[42] The desire to show the richness and diversity of Sephardi cultures while also retaining a singularity based on (some) common experiences and traditions—a discursive move that was also attempted by other Argentine Sephardi institutions and individuals—suggests that food (through these recipe books) was another arena in which community was created and re-created. And similarly to the way these other attempts stressed diversity (linguistic, geographic, and cultural), the authors unquestionably designated Ladino culture (as it developed in Turkey) as the essential element of the Sephardi cultural past. The book contains popular Ladino sayings that are associated with cooking and food (*La mansana el mal sana; Ken kome solo, muere solo; Por la boka se keinta el orno; Los pichkados grandes se komen a los tchikos*, etc.), and each recipe section is introduced by a related *refrán* (popular saying). But the book includes no such references to Judeo-Arabic sayings, or to *ḥaketia* (vernacular Jewish-Moroccan language).

I close this chapter with one, perhaps the clearest, example of the "fight" to rescue Sephardi cooking, food, and culture from invisibility. This battle, however, was not waged through any publication, but in person. Lucha F., a woman born in Paso de los Libres, in the province of Misiones, prepared traditional sweets at her home (the same ones she had enjoyed as a child with her grandmother for Rosh Hashana) and "smuggled" them into the United States for her grandson's bar mitzvah. Her son, married to an Ashkenazi Jew, had immigrated to Miami several years before the event. When I asked her why she went to such lengths, she responded with a matter-of-fact shrug: "There was only going to be "Russian" [Ashkenazi] food (at the party); that [was] not right."[43]

I have shown that "Sephardi food" in Argentina traveled a sinuous path: from the period following immigration in which *turco* (Turkish), *marroquí* (Moroccan), and *sirio* (Syrian) dishes were served at home for all meals, to contemporary times in which these dishes were reserved for religious/family occasions; it went from it being a mere footnote, or being entirely neglected in Jewish Argentine cookbooks, to meriting books entirely devoted to Sephardi dishes; from "Sephardim" being an essentialized entity, to being a collective that included geographical and cultural diversity. But the fact that, in October 2003, a major Argentine (non-Jewish) newspaper would exclusively feature Sephardi recipes in a special section on "Jewish food for the New Year" might very well mean that the Sephardi struggle (even if nonviolent, unorganized, and uncoordinated) for a space among Argentine culinary traditions has been successful, despite the greasiness of their dishes, their hard-to-find ingredients, and the Ashkenazi majority.

NOTES

I wish to thank Irene Munster, Liliana Benveniste, Malena Chinski, Celia Rabinowitz, Hilde Muchow, and the librarians at IWO–Buenos Aires for their help with locating and scanning much of the material I used for this essay. I also wish to thank the organizers and participants of the International Conference on "The Global History of Jewish Food," which took place in Pollenzo, Italy, June 9–10, 2014. The wonderful conversations during those two days shaped the essay into its current form.

1. The list is long indeed. See, for example, Arjun Appadurai, "How to Make a National Cuisine: Cookbooks in Contemporary India," *Comparative Studies in Society and History* 30, no. 1 (1988); Jeffrey M. Pilcher, "Recipes for Patria: Cuisine, Gender, and Nation in Nineteenth-Century Mexico," in *Recipes for Reading: Community, Cookbooks, Stories, Histories*, ed. Anne L. Bower (Amherst: University of Massachusetts Press, 1997); Hasia R. Diner, *Hungering for America: Italian, Irish, and Jewish Foodways in the Age of Migration* (Cambridge MA: Harvard University Press, 2001); Lara Anderson, *Cooking Up the Nation: Spanish Culinary Texts and Culinary Nationalization in the Late Nineteenth and Early Twentieth Century* (Woodbridge UK: Tamesis, 2013).

2. Sue Fishkoff, *Kosher Nation* (New York: Schocken Books, 2010); David M. Freidenreich, *Foreigners and Their Food: Constructing Otherness in Jewish, Christian, and Islamic Law* (Berkeley: University of California Press, 2011); Leonard J. Greenspoon, Ronald Simkins, and Gerald Shapiro, *Food and Judaism* (Omaha NE: Creighton University Press, 2005).

3. Estela Levy, *Crónica de una familia sefaradí* (Buenos Aires: Carcos, 1983), 41. Unless otherwise noted, I have maintained the spelling of food used by authors, even if they don't follow transliteration rules.

4. Interview with Bulisa, August 18, 1998.

5. Workshops held at the Círculo Israelita Social, Buenos Aires, August 27, 1998.

6. Interview with Esther Acrich, May 19, 1997.

7. Marcos Levy and Ricardo Reinoso, *La vida, según Marcos Levy: biografía de un inmigrante de origen sefardí*, unpublished manuscript, 2002, 109. Marcos Levy's father owned a vegetable store in the main market in Tucumán, where "most other stall owners were Italians or Spanish."

8. Levy and Reinoso, *La vida, según Marcos Levy*, 55.

9. I own a copy of the 35th edition. Petrona C. de Gandulfo, *El libro de Doña Petrona: recetas de arte culinario* (Buenos Aires, 1950). The book has sold more than three million copies.

10. Rebekah E. Pite, *Creating a Common Table in Twentieth-Century Argentina: Doña Petrona, Women, and Food* (Chapel Hill: University of North Carolina Press, 2013).

11. Ezequiel Adamovsky, *Historia de la clase media Argentina: apogeo y decadencia de una ilusión, 1919–2003* (Buenos Aires: Planeta, 2009), 69.

12. Adamovsky, *Historia de la clase media Argentina*, 72.

13. *La Luz* (October 8, 1937): 436–37.

14. Other ethnicity-based philanthropic organizations also used the same places to host similar events. The Syrio-Lebanese Patronage Circle, for example, "offered tea and dance at the *Alvear Palace*." See *La Prensa*, July 18, 1937.

15. The "Sociedad de Damas Israelitas" expressed their fears regarding the presence of Jewish orphans in both Catholic and state institutions. See Donna Guy, "Women's Organizations and Jewish Orphanages in Buenos Aires, 1918–1955," *Jewish History* 18, no. 1 (2004): 79–80.

16. Erna C. Schlesinger, *Especialidades de la cocina judía* (Buenos Aires: Biblioteca de Mucho Gusto, 1955).

17. Schlesinger, *Especialidades de la cocina judía*, 1.

18. Schlesinger, *Especialidades de la cocina judía*, 16.

19. Schlesinger, *Especialidades de la cocina judía*, 1.

20. I have not been able to find out when the first edition of this book was published. Jeanne Bachmann, Ilka Besthof, Recha Würzburger, *La cocina judía moderna: de acuerdo a las normas tradicionales*, 2nd ed. (Buenos Aires: Editorial S. Sigal, 1961). Jeanne Bachmann worked for the Argentine German newspaper *Argentinisches Tageblatt*, and in the 1940s she published selected recipes sent to the newspaper by German-speaking readers, translating them into Spanish. I thank Irene Munster for sharing this information with me.

21. Bachmann, Besthof, Würzburger, *La cocina judía moderna*, 9–10.

22. Bachmann, Besthof, Würzburger, *La cocina judía moderna*, 10.

23. Bulisa and I met three different times in July 1998 to discuss her experiences in Concordia (province of Entre Ríos) and Buenos Aires.

24. Oral History workshop, August 20, 1998.

25. Joëlle Bahloul, "Food Practices Among Sephardic Immigrants in Contemporary France: Dietary Laws in Urban Society," *Journal of the American Academy of Religion* 63, no. 3 (1995): 485–96.

26. Club Social Alianza, Minute Books, Youth Department, June 1, 1958.

27. Club Social Alianza, Minute Books, Youth Department, May 12, 1958.

28. Patricia Finzi, *La cocina judía: tradición y variaciones* (São Paulo, Brazil: Editora Shalom, 1984).

29. The inclusion of sections that "explained" Jewish festivities hints at the hope that these books could also attract non-Jewish readers.

30. Finzi, *La cocina judía*, 20.

31. Amigas Sefaradíes de Na'amat, ed., *Cocinando al estilo sefaradí: Berajá y salú: Comidicas y dulzurias al estilo de nuestras madres y abuelas* (Buenos Aires: Amigas Sefaradíes de Na'amat, 1994).

32. Na'amat, *Cocinando al estilo sefaradí*, 3.

33. But note that they decided to use Ladino in the subtitle of the book.

34. Na'amat, *Cocinando al estilo sefaradí*, 69.

35. Na'amat, *Cocinando al estilo sefaradí*, 31.

36. Estela Levy, *Cocina sefaradí*, unpublished manuscript, 1980.

37. Levy, *Cocina sefaradí*, 3.

38. Levy, *Cocina sefaradí*, 4–5.

39. Levy, *Cocina sefaradí*, 5.

40. Patricia Finzi and Viviana Gorbato, *Sabores y misterios de la cocina sefaradí* (Buenos Aires: Grupo Editorial Shalom, 1993).

41. Finzi and Gorbato, *Sabores y misterios de la cocina sefaradí*, 8.

42. Finzi and Gorbato, *Sabores y misterios de la cocina sefaradí*, 11.

43. By "Russian" she meant "Ashkenazi." Interview with Lucha Funes, June 21, 1997.

9

Still Life

Performing National Identity in Israel and
Palestine at the Intersection of Food and Art

....

YAEL RAVIV

Ran Morin's *Orange Suspendu* (1993) hangs in the old city of Jaffa in Israel. An orange tree bursts out of an oversize metal orange sculpture, hanging a few feet above the ground (see figure 9-1). The piece, like several other Morin works, speaks to questions of rootedness (or lack thereof), inverting the relationship between tree and fruit, disconnecting the tree from the soil. Using an orange, and situating the piece in the Arab-Israeli city of Jaffa, inevitably brings to mind the Jaffa orange brand and the orange's complex meaning for both Israelis and Palestinians. These choices transform the piece from a comment on universal rootlessness in an age of globalization to a specific, localized investigation of a relationship to land and place. Many artists use food products in their work as a device for exploring national identities and identifications, harnessing food's central role in our perception of "home" and identity. This chapter aims to bring together two of my main research areas over the years: food and nationalism in Israel, and food and art. I study the changing use of food products as both subject and medium in Israeli and Palestinian artists' work as a window to multifaceted, constantly

FIG. 9-1. Ran Morin, *Orange Suspendu*, 1993.

changing, national identities. Beginning with early Zionist work and its role in shaping Jewish-Israeli national identity and comparing it to more recent Palestinian work, the chapter examines changes in food-centered artwork over the past few decades and its implications. I argue that the artwork both reflects changing perceptions and representations of the nation and helps to shape it. I explore it as a site for the performance of national identity, a living entity, constantly in the process of becoming.

The current political situation, with recurring eruptions of violence in the region, and particularly the boycott of joint Israeli-Palestinian projects as promoting a "normalization" of the current situation, is a constant reminder of the complexities inherent in the subject of this chapter. Although both food and art are often held up as tools for bridging differences and forging peaceful bonds, they are both, in fact, inexorably linked to identity (personal, communal, and national) as well as to politics, economics, and religion, thus becoming more effective tools for articulating differences than of erasing them.[1]

WHY FOOD?

The foods we grow, buy, cook, and eat are everyday performances of affiliation with a greater community (or communities). However, food is not only an instrument of nostalgia and of remembering a homeland, it can be a tool for creating and shaping one, for negotiating old and new affiliations and identities. Food products are a common device for representing national identity like rice in Japan or steak and chips and wine in France (as eloquently articulated by Emiko Ohnuki-Tierney and Roland Barthes, respectively). These products and dishes are used to perform a national affiliation for members of the community as well as a sign for outsiders (tourists, neighboring nations), a reiteration of national unity in everyday life. These dishes and products have been examined by scholars and used as windows to a deeper understanding of nations, ethnic communities, and cultures. The unique case of both Zionism and Palestinian nationalism is their relatively new point of origin, allowing us to distinguish and trace these products' manipulation and change over time.

Historically, Jewish nationalism used food to remake the Jewish figure, to aid in the construction of an identity that is as different from the diasporic Jewish image as it is from the local population of the land— using it, among other tools, as a way to make the abstract idea of a Jewish nation into a concrete reality. This device was not only used in the fields and markets, but was reflected in artists and designers' work in posters, paintings, and book illustrations from the period. The unique case of Jewish nationalism, physically transplanting a people from a variety of other countries of origin and fusing them to each other and to the land, while simultaneously disconnecting them from two thousand years of existence in the diaspora, required the development of new, secular, cultural devices establishing a common national bond beyond Jewish religion. Food products and agricultural labor offered effective tools on both the conceptual and the material level.

In the case of Palestinian nationalism, we have a somewhat inverted process, a nation that has come into being in the midst of a process of dispersal and separation. Palestinian nationalism has to perform both its steadfast connection to its land of origin and to a common culture, uniting several groups currently living under different governments and conditions. The physical land and Palestinian rootedness are central tropes, encoring Palestinian national discourse. Agriculture work and certain food products like citrus, olives, and prickly pears, became important markers of this essential link.

Carol Bardenstein's insightful exploration of the notion of rootedness in both Israeli and Palestinian imagery presents the use of trees, oranges, and the prickly pear as instruments for demonstrating/forging a close relationship to the physical land. Bardenstein contrasts the early Zionists' anxiety over their tenuous connection to their new homeland and their lack of rootedness with the Palestinian sense of uprootedness and loss.[2] Artists of both nations used food products and agriculture to tell these contrasting national stories.

In her discussion of collective memory and national tradition in Israel, Yael Zerubavel asserts that "the power of collective memory does not lie in its accurate ... mapping of the past, but in establishing basic images that articulate and reinforce a particular ideological stance."[3] This claim can be applied to both early Zionist artwork and to some Palestinian artwork, both reflecting an idealized image of a pastoral agricultural existence that is not necessarily a reflection of an actual, experienced past or present, but of a performance of the national image. The changing use of food products, themselves mutable and performative in Israeli and Palestinian artwork, highlights these qualities and the performative nature of nationalism, supporting Homi Bhabha's view of nation as ambivalent and temporal.[4]

As sites of performance, I distinguish between artists who use food as their subject and artists who use food as a medium, experimenting with everyday, time-based materials. The second group allows a more straightforward discussion of performance in that its artists are grounded in process and change (disintegration, consumption). The medium in these artworks is integral to the message. The first group, creating art in more traditional visual media, is still pertinent to the discussion, since their art "performs" identity, presenting a specific image of the nation and its place in the world. In both cases the use of food creates a meaningful, tangible connection between art and everyday life, between private and public representations. I review both types of work here not in the context of art history, but as sites of material culture and as reflections of the ongoing negotiation of nation, place, and identity.

FOOD ICONS

Basic food products are common and powerful devices in both Israeli and Palestinian iconography because of the prominent place of agriculture in both cultures' past and mythology and the centrality of the concept of creating/maintaining literal links to the physical land. These products are particularly useful as sites for the performance of the nation in pre-statehood time, offering images of unity and a common culture when a flag, a currency, or any other tool of an independent state is not yet available. They speak not only to the very existence of the nation by presenting a single symbol, but also to the story the nation tells of itself—Who is it? Where is it located? What does it stand for?

Certain food products become as familiar and as layered with meanings and associations as any flag, and as such, become powerful symbols that can be appropriated by artists and reshaped. Their appearance in a work of art alludes to a wealth of meanings and enables both direct and ironic messages with a simple, recognizable object. In this case, images of agricultural labor appear in several contexts in both cultures and several products, mostly prickly pear cactus (*tsabar, sabir*), oranges, olives, and olive trees, have taken on iconic significance and appear repeatedly in artists' work. They are employed in different way in both cultures to present alternative national narratives.

EARLY ZIONIST ART

For the early Zionist immigrants to Palestine, growing food meant strength and self-reliance in the present and the future as well as a bond with the physical land both by working its soil and by consuming its fruit. Food products were particularly important in Zionist propaganda since they were able to convey both a link to history and a new Jewish persona—seemingly contradictory concepts. Presenting certain food products or dishes as originally and continually belonging to the nation strengthens its claim for authenticity, communal origins in antiquity, and historical persistence.[5] Foodstuffs of biblical origin, like wheat, dates, and olives, were presented on Zionist commemorative postcards and on fundraising posters.[6] Export products—such as grapes and wine, olives and olive oil, as well as figs, dates, and pomegranates—"sold" Zionist ideology abroad. These foods, as well as certain agricultural tools, can be traced back to biblical times, and thus evoke the sense of historical continuity and enforce the claim of an inherent bond between the Jewish people and their ancient land—a necessary condition for Jewish nationhood.[7] On the other hand, agricultural innovations and new, successful food products advertised a modern Jewish existence in Palestine, an existence which sustained a link to biblical times, but

FIG. 9-2. "Land of wheat and barley, of vines and figs and pomegranates, a land of olive trees and honey." Deuteronomy 8. Illustration from the 1940s. From the Zionist Archive poster collection Central Zionist Archives, Jerusalem.

was divorced from two thousand years of "spiritual" existence in exile. Agricultural work and its products "performed" a vital existence, sustained by a direct bond with the land as well as the authenticity of Jewish nationhood through historical ties to an ancient past.

Zionist imagery often included the biblical seven "minim" (species) that the land of Israel was blessed with: wheat, barley, grapes, figs, pomegranates, olives, and honey. These images were popular in Jewish tradition since, unlike the human figure, there was no religious prohibition on the depiction of plants and fruit.[8] The Zionists embraced the image of the seven species as signifying biblical-time glory reclaimed by new Jewish settlers, forging a direct link between the modern settlers and ancient times. Significantly, the images often presented the land in modern times as empty and desolate, waiting for Jewish settlers to "save" and revitalize it through their agricultural work. As figure 9-2 shows, the bounty of fruit and grains seems to result from new agricultural intervention in an otherwise empty desert landscape.[9]

By presenting the land as "empty" and emphasizing Jewish agricultural labor, early Jewish settlers could view themselves not as colonizers oppressing a native population, but as pioneers and direct descendants of their biblical forefathers. "Working the land" was a most fundamental stage in the Zionist national project, a performance of Zionist ideology in the sense of "execution," "doing": connecting to the land of Israel in the most literal way and establishing an independent economic foundation. The idea of self-labor or Hebrew-labor, particularly agricultural labor, is cited as one of the central contributions of the immigrants of the First Aliya (immigration wave), who arrived in Palestine between 1882 and 1904, right around the First Zionist Congress in 1897.[10] Images contrasting older Jewish figures in attitudes of prayer in Europe with young and vital figures engaged in agricultural labor appeared often in Zionist propaganda, linking agricultural labor to a new, dynamic, and independent Jewish existence in the land of Israel. E. M. Lilien's postcard for the Fifth Zionist Congress (figure 9-3) inverts the traditional representation of Adam and Eve's banishment from heaven, by portraying

FIG. 9-3. E. M. Lilien, Fifth Zionist Congress, 1901.

the angel sending the old, hunched, traditional Jewish figure out of the thorns of diaspora and into a golden future of freedom and the promise of a vital new life redeemed by agricultural labor in the land of Israel.[11]

During the 1920s and '30s, Jewish artists often depicted the new and vital figure of the Jewish pioneer (*halutz*) in their work: a completely new Jewish persona, linked to the land and to physical agricultural labor. Artist Reuven Rubin *First Fruit* triptych's central panel titled *Fruit of the Land* (1923) shows the figure of the halutz as large, powerful and dark-skinned (evidence of his work out in the fields), carrying a bounty of fruit. The figure has a sturdy physical presence, and, like the female figure next to it, her breasts exposed, carrying an orange, speak to fertility, vitality, and passion.[12] This work too, shows the Jewish pioneer figure carrying agricultural products and cultivating the land, while in the background the country's landscape is an empty desert, reaffirming the Zionist narrative of revitalizing a desolate land.

Another common image in Zionist visual language is that of an oversized bunch of grapes. Grapes star in the biblical story of the spies sent

FIG. 9-4. E. M. Lilien, Cover for *Altneuland*, 1904.

to explore the Promised Land, bringing, upon their return, a large bunch of grapes as evidence of the land's bounty. These images create a visual association between ancient biblical times and modern Jewish agricultural success through concrete objects, rather than through abstract arguments. E. M. Lilien's illustration of the subject graces the cover of Theodor Herzl's novel *Altneuland*, which lays out Herzl's utopian vision for a new Jewish settlement in the land of Israel. The image of the spies bearing a large bunch of grapes (figure 9-4) was later adapted to many different contexts including the logo for Israel's Ministry of Tourism.

The early Jewish settlers arriving during the First Aliya made a serious effort at vine cultivation inspired by these images and the associated mythology, as well as by practical considerations and encouragement by the Baron Rothschild and his local advisers, but they soon realized that the time, expertise, and financial investment required for developing the infrastructure for a serious wine industry was beyond their capabilities. They turned their attention to citrus growing, a branch requiring no additional processing of exportable products and very well suited to the climate—as attested by the successful Palestinian citriculture. As a result, grapes were soon replaced by oranges as symbols of the Jewish nation in the land of Israel, representing its agricultural success and a literal "setting roots" in the land.

Over a period of about six years following the First World War, the area of Jewish citrus groves tripled. The orange became associated with successful Jewish agricultural labor in Israel. Despite the fact that citrus growing in the region began as a product of Arab labor, its growing success as an export product was tied to Jewish labor and initiative. The Jaffa orange brand in particular became a recognizable symbol of Israel and used to advertise the Zionist project and later the Israeli state abroad. The orange even inspired the design of El-Al (the national airline) stewardess' uniforms at the time (1970s).[13] The orange indicated certain characteristics that the state wished to promote as part of its image; it painted a specific national portrait of self-sufficiency and rootedness in the land.

Oranges appear in artists' work from the 1920s and '30s, signifying Jewish agricultural success, as in Reuven Rubin's *Fruit of the Land* (1923) triptych or in Mane Katz's *Am Israel Hai* (the Israeli nation lives) (1938), where a halutz carrying a full basket of oranges occupies the center of the painting. Even though in recent times the citrus industry (and agriculture in general) has been replaced as an important economic branch in Israeli economy, the orange retains some of its iconic power. Today the Jaffa brand can be purchased by other countries (if their product passes the requirements of an Israeli board) and is as likely to come from Spain or South Africa as from Israel, but the layers of meaning it acquired over time made it into a powerful vehicle for reflecting and commenting on the Zionist project and the Israeli state. Israeli artists use it as a device for critique or ironic comment, as in Ran Morin's work *Orange Suspendu*. This change in the representation of the orange in artists' work reflects a change in the perception of the nation: from idealized utopian images to critique and questioning of Zionist ideology.

PALESTINIAN IMAGERY

The orange and the orange grove are powerful Palestinian icons as well. Some Palestinian artists use them as a nostalgic emblem, presenting a longed-for rural existence, exemplifying both an idealized past and a utopian future. Even though it appears Palestinian society had been away from subsistence agriculture, even prior to Israeli independence, developing citrus as a moving export industry more than as a local commodity, citrus groves and fruit remain powerful reminders of an intimate connection to the land.[14] Sliman Mansour, one of the most prominent Palestinian artists from the post-1948 generation, created several paintings during the 1970s and '80s depicting Palestinian farmers in traditional dress, carrying or picking a bounty of oranges, bathed in golden light. They are sometimes presented with a backdrop of vast citrus groves, reaching to the horizon. According to Mansour, his work "imagines how life would be without the occupation."[15] Through these seemingly pastoral images, Mansour reaffirms and strengthens the Palestinian connection to the land and to traditional cultural roots. As stated earlier, the images are not meant to represent necessarily an actual past, but rather an imagined, mythical, yet no less powerful one. Their power lies in the portrait of the nation that they paint: proud and grounded, and in the future they imagine for it.

The power and wealth of associated meanings allow the use of citrus as a marker of political struggle and resistance. The resistance in Mansour's images might be relatively subtle but is very direct in Abnan Zbeidi's work *Squeezing the Life/Juice Out of the Palestinian Jaffa Orange*, showing a fist crushing a whole orange and squeezing its juice into a Star of David mold (1987). A more recent interpretation of the subject is presented in Jumana Abboud's video work, *Smuggling Lemons* (2006). In the film, the camera follows Abboud as she collects lemons in a garden in Galilee, places them in a special belt resembling a rig for carrying grenades, and travels with them through Jerusalem and across the border to Ramallah where she deposits them on a bare and dusty patch of earth. The lemons are presented as actual characters in Abboud's film: held so they can "view" the changing scenery on the bus ride to the border, waiting patiently in line to cross the border. The lush green garden where Abboud collects the lemons and begins her journey stands in stark contrast to the arid land where she deposits them. The absurdity of these treeless/rootless lemons speak to Abboud's view of the absurdity of the Palestinian situation, their longing for the green garden, their rootless current state.

The notion of Palestinian rootedness and connection to the land is perhaps most commonly invoked through the image of an olive tree. Olive picking, like the citrus industry, appears as both a romanticized image of a pastoral past and as a comment on the Palestinian condition, their dispersal and dislocation on the one hand, and their steadfast connection to the land they were separated from on the other. Often both interpretations are present in the same image as in Sliman Mansour's *Olive Picking Triptych* (1989), showing a Palestinian man (a *fallah*—farmer) climbing and standing within the branches of an olive tree, both working among the branches and linked to them.

Walid Abu Shakra's etchings and drawings return often to the olive tree as a central subject, their titles describing specific places like *Olive Tree in Ein Jarrar* (1980) or *Olive Tree in Al-Baten* (1980). The trees' fragile, stark look combined with the particular knowledge of place represented in the titles speaks to an intimate connection to the land and to a sense of sadness and loss.[16] Kalil Rabah's work *Grafting* (1995) comprised transplanted olive trees from the artist's home in Ramallah to Geneva, where they were replanted (their newness marked with piles of soil, standing out on the green lawn) and wrapped in colorful embroidery strings. The artist's later video and photography work (2001) shows Rabah shaping his body to emulate the shape of the trunks of olive trees.[17] The identification between artist/Palestinian and tree is self-evident. Rabah identifies as a Palestinian through his choice of the olive tree as both medium and subject, yet he speaks to a complex relationship between (home)land and exile, tradition and globalization.

Larrisa Sansour's *Olive Tree* (2011) is a large-scale photograph, part of the *Nation Estate* project that depicts a futuristic Palestinian state housed in separate floors of a high-rise building.[18] The olive tree is planted indoors, in a large, bare room, its roots cracking the cement floor. Through the window, unreachable, is a view of the city of Jerusalem. The olive tree, like the Palestinian figure, signifies a natural connection to the land and the absurdity of the expectation of it taking root in concrete, detached from its native soil. Raafat Hattab's *Bidun Unwaan* (literally Untitled, or without mailing address) (2009) is somewhat similar in its approach. The video piece shows a man carefully watering and lovingly tending an ancient olive tree. As the camera pans out, however, the viewer realizes the tree is growing in a small plot in the center of Rabin Square in Tel-Aviv. The man is drawing the water for the tree from the square's fountain, near Tel-Aviv city hall. The video's musical score is by a Lebanese singer; sung in Arabic with no subtitles, it speaks of longing for a faraway place, repeating the phrase "I left a place."[19] Much like Sansour's work, the absurdity of the piece positions the olive tree as a marker of rootedness in a foreign context. Its connection to the soil is clear, but the landscape around it has changed, the urban environment and the prominent Holocaust memorial sharing the square space raise new questions on longing and belonging.

Vera Tamari's *Tale of a Tree* (1999) combines a large black-and-white image of an olive tree hanging in back of a grove of small, pastel-colored olive trees made of clay. Tamari's work in clay adds a layer of meaning to the piece that is as powerful as its subject. The clay is a literal use of earth within the piece, strengthening the trees' association with the physical land. The black-and-white photograph of the olive tree on the wall stands in contrast to the forest of small, artificial-looking trees that are made of "real," tangible earth.

THE MEDIUM IS THE MESSAGE

Mansour's more recent mud sculptures, shaped from earth to resemble bread, are another example of work whose medium (earth) is as important as its subject. The two elements are linked, particularly since the bread Mansour depicts is shaped like a traditional *fallah* (farmer) loaf. These objects speak to a Palestinian connection to the land, but the inedible loaf and the dry, cracked earth it is fashioned from combine to present a bleak picture. This work stands in contrast to Mansour's earlier *Still Life* painting (1981) concerned with a similar subject: loaves of the same bread are shown together with tomatoes, olives, and an onion, comprising a simple farmer's meal. Though both works present a portrait of Palestinian identity as tied to the land and farming life, their different mediums reflect a different outlook, with the more recent work painting a much darker and pessimistic picture.[20]

Another version of "medium as message" appears in Mona Hatoum's use of everyday objects. Hatoum incorporates metal kitchen utensils in her work with a dark edge or twist, like the oversized, sharp-edged kitchen tools in *La Grande Broyeuse (Mouli-Julienne x17)* (1999); in *Grater Divide* (2002), an oversized metal grater standing like a folding screen; a metal serving spoon embellished with short spikes, rendering it useless in *No Way* (1996); or an installation of an "electrified" kitchen setting in *Home* (1999). Galit Ankori views Hatoum's use of these household products as a reflection of her heritage as a "daughter of exiles, a second-generation survivor of the Nakba." By using these kitchen tools, yet rendering them useless and even potentially violent, Hatoum evokes a sense of disorientation and alienation.[21] Hatoum uses household settings and instruments in an unsettling manner to explore the idea of "home" in exile, reflecting a nomadic identity and a complex relationship to something most of us take for granted and view as a safe haven: home. Kitchen implements are particularly useful in this context as the kitchen often stands for the entire home in our collective imagination, representing a warm, safe, inviting space. Hatoum's work can be seen as a cautionary tale, as a representation of the threat to Palestinian sense of identity with exile. Without the rootedness to the specific soil, the elements most evocative of home and belonging are rendered powerless and ineffectual.

Like Hatoum, Rana Bishara's work uses everyday objects and products in a new, unsettling context. Bishara often uses food products as a medium. Spices, flour, cactus leaves (fresh and dried), chocolate, and pita bread are some of the materials of her sculptural and installation works. Bishara transforms these everyday materials, manipulating them with visible interventions that gain their power from the unexpected use of these seemingly benign objects. Some of Bishara's earlier work like *Home* (1995), dried cactus leaves sewn together and draped over a wooden window frame, or *The Fragrance of the East* (1996), spices and leaves arranged in beautiful circular patterns on the floor, rely on personal products (the window frame from her childhood home, spices from her mother's kitchen).[22] They present Palestinian female traditions in new ways, reflecting a more personal exploration of a sense of identity in a greater cultural context. Her later work, however, is more focused on the national level and more overtly political. In *Bread for Palestine* (2006), for example, a pita bread round is studded with metal pins rendering it inedible and dangerous, or in a more extended performance piece with the same title, Bishara stuffed pita bread rounds with cotton wads and sewed them shut, again, rendering them inedible.[23] Using actual food products in her work emphasizes the break with everyday life, since they are always rendered inedible.

Israeli artist Micha Laury created a series of soldiers in military gear, carrying rifles in different positions, and cast them in chocolate in *Don't Be a Chocolate Soldier* (1969–94). The piece was a reaction, shared by several other Israeli artists, to the euphoria in the aftermath of the 1967 Six-Day War and the enthusiasm for the military that spread through

Israeli society at the time.[24] The sense of security and economic prosperity that followed the war allowed artists, writers, and activists to overtly critique the prevailing Zionist agenda and methods. Laury's work emerged at a time of greater political awareness and self-appraisal in the Israeli art scene. Reacting to similar movements in Europe and the United States in the 1970s, Israeli artists began experimenting with blurring the boundaries between art and life, while replacing former attitudes of idealization, reverence, and support for the national project with a more cynical, mature, and critical approach. Laury's invitation to his audience to break apart and eat the chocolate soldiers is a significant departure from the hallowed approach that characterized the young Israel's attitude toward the military up to 1967. In this case, the edible, time-based, everyday material serves to solidify the irreverent treatment of the subject. If the soldiers were cast in bronze or carved in stone the entire story of the piece would change; the message, in this case, is firmly embedded in the medium.

Other more recent Israeli artwork employed food as a device for straightforward political commentary. Shachar Marcus, who uses food often in his performance and video work, created *Golda* (2013), a video project presenting the artist costumed as former Israeli prime minister Golda Meir. Meir's character is baking a cake in her home kitchen while making a speech about Israeli-Arab relationships (based on an actual 1969 speech). The juxtaposition of the two spheres (kitchen and political arena) creates a jarring, disorienting feeling, causing the viewer to doubt and question both parts of the work (the politics on the one hand, and the baking, as it relates to gender roles, on the other). Artist Hanoch Piven re-created Meir's figure as well. Piven creates collage portraits of famous figures by using everyday materials and objects. On several occasions he uses foodstuffs, not simply for their visual qualities but also for the meaning they impart. Meir's portrait, for example, is constructed around a piece of boiled chicken (1999), whereas former prime minister Ariel Sharon (1997) is shaped out of raw ground beef.

MANUFACTURED TERROIR

Most discussions about the relationship between place, food, and identity focus on locally grown food or traditional dishes, on products with traceable histories that can be followed back to their origins. Terroir, or *goût du terroir*, is a French expression most commonly used to describe a wine's relationship to its geographical environment. More recently the concept has been expanded to describe other products, such as coffee and cheese, whose flavor and aroma can be affected by environmental conditions. Amy Trubek developed the concept of terroir, or "the taste of place," as her book on the subject is titled, to include cultural influences and to expand the range of products and practices it covers and the way we think about the influence of place on taste in a global society.[25] Trubek finds the sites of local production, islands of intimate connection between place and taste, even within the industrial, commercial American landscape, illustrating a way of expanding the concept of terroir in an age of globalization. The concept could be used to shed new light on processed foods—factory-made, globally distributed products that are linked to a particular place/land and invoke their "taste." These products (candy, condiments, specific brand names, etc.) make up a large part of childhood experiences and landscapes and are sought out by immigrants to faraway countries since they have the power to evoke the memory of home.[26]

Ilana Godberg's short documentary film *Makolet* (2000) shows the community of immigrants gathered around a Brooklyn grocery store that carries a variety of "Israeli" products. One of the products that resonated most with many of the shoppers was Krembo, a sweet confection with a chocolate-covered fluffy egg cream filling. This product is factory made, and always has been, but is instantly recognized by any Israeli, evoking a very particular time and place. Similar items such as Bamba (a peanut-flavored snack), lemon-flavored popsicles, and soup croutons (*shkedey marak*) not only evoke nostalgia for a lost childhood, but also play a powerful role in constructing a "taste" of Israel. They are shared products, familiar to everyone who grew up in Israel in the past several decades. Like falafel, they are unaffiliated with any one particular ethnic group and serve as markers of affiliation with a greater community.

Artist Naama Orbach's piece *Every Woman and Girl Lights Shabbat Candles* (2004) shows a familiar simplified image of a woman covering her face, engaged in a blessing over the Shabbat candles standing lit in their candlesticks before her.[27] The unique element in Orbach's image is that it is constructed entirely out of soup croutons: yellow, uniform squares known as *shkedey marak*. The image, created on a well-worn, wooden cutting board, uses the croutons as representatives of a modern, secular Israeli identity. In this simple gesture, replacing traditional art materials with a recognizable food item, Orbach illustrates the dilemma of secular Jewish nationalism: the attempt to fashion a secular cultural identity within the Jewish state.

SHIFTING AFFILIATIONS

A recent short article in the Israeli daily *Haaretz* followed the use and representation of the watermelon in Israeli art, referring mostly to an earlier exhibit on the subject at Beit Reuven in Tel-Aviv (2009).[28] The article quotes the exhibit curator, Shira Naftali, saying that the presence of watermelon in Israeli art can be divided into two main periods: in the earlier period, starting in the 1920s, watermelons were mostly characterized as an Arab local product, while during the later period, starting in the 1990s, watermelons begin to appear as "Israeli," and to convey more complex meanings.[29] The early pioneers embraced the watermelon as a local product, a sign of their affiliation with the East. Reuven Rubin's *First Fruit*, mentioned earlier, includes a watermelon as one of the "native" fruits of the land, embraced by the new pioneers. Nahum Gutman's *Afternoon Rest* (1926) and the later *Watermelon Salesman* (1965) both portray the watermelon as an Arab product, alongside local Arab figures. In the 1920s the Zionist movement began employing food products as instruments of unification and encouraged their purchase as a demonstration of direct support for the national project and the future of the nation. The campaign for *tozeret haaretz* (product of the land) involved the tagging of certain food products with a label distinguishing them as "Hebrew," meaning produced or grown specifically by Jewish labor. This mark was necessary since, in fact, both Hebrew and Arab labor products were "products of the land," and the designation as "Hebrew" was the only way to distinguish the two. In 1936 the Union for Tozeret Haaretz was established, and the "Hebrew" watermelon graced posters encouraging shoppers to pay attention to their food products' origin and labor and to support Jewish labor and products over Arab ones. Thus the watermelon began to morph from a local Arab product into a marked Hebrew product. By the 1980s, it was already recognized as simply Israeli and came to signify Israeliness as a locally grounded identification.

By the turn of this century, watermelon's status as an Israeli cultural product was already taken for granted. Both Sharon Glazberg and Sigalit Landau created video works that explored the juxtaposition of salty and sweet by staging a watermelon-related project at the Dead Sea. In *Black Moon, Dead Sea* (2004) Glazberg turns watermelons into bowling balls (with the aid of an apple corer) and sends them rolling toward the Dead Sea far below. In *Dead Sea* (2005), Landau floats a chain of watermelons on the salty water, curling into a spiral, with the artist's body inserted into the watermelon chain. The watermelons mostly float intact, but a few have been broken open, their red interiors exposed. Both projects play with watermelon's colors, exposing the red interiors strategically, in what seems a violent, intrusive gesture. The juxtaposition of salty and sweet, interior and exterior speaks to the complex nature of the relationship between Israeli culture and place. Both artists also insert more personal explorations of women's bodies into their work, linking the personal and the national. Once the watermelon has been embraced as "Israeli" it can be explored and utilized as any other unmarked product to reflect a variety of universal connotations.

Perhaps the most recognized and contested shifting affiliation in the area of food products is that of hummus and falafel. Both dishes originated in the Arab kitchen but have been embraced by Israelis to the extent of taking on the mantle of national icons, replacing the orange and other agricultural products in that role. As the importance of agriculture as an economic branch declined, and as ethnic groups of Middle Eastern and North African origin became more influential within Israeli society, replacing the orange with falafel seemed a natural step. In order to facilitate the adoption of hummus and falafel by the Israeli kitchen, they needed to go through a process of naturalization. The Arab origin of these popular street foods was erased early on, and their presence in Israel attributed to Jewish ethnic groups from Middle Eastern countries. They became national markers of unity, popular with all socioeconomic and ethnic groups. Their power to unite perhaps derived from the fact they did not belong to any one group within Israeli society and so could be embraced freely by all.[30] Both falafel and hummus began to appear in formal state dinners, representing Israel abroad in culinary competitions, on tourist brochures, and as markers of affiliation with Israel at Jewish events abroad (particularly those geared toward a younger crowd).

In recent years, these dishes' status as markers of Israeliness has solidified to such an extent that their origin in the Arab kitchen is readily acknowledged again. Israelis are not necessarily claiming the invention of hummus or falafel but are certainly asserting their right to use them as a reflection of their location in the Middle East. As I have noted elsewhere, choosing falafel as a national icon reinforces Israel's assertion that it belongs in the Middle East, distinct from Jewish existence in the Diaspora, and that the various ethnic immigrant groups that make up its population share certain secular cultural products.[31] The reason falafel and hummus were so readily adopted by the Israeli state was that they contributed to the performance of the Israeli nation as located in the Middle East and as visibly unified. It is important to note here that the fact that both hummus and falafel are considered low-status street foods supported the acknowledgment of their Arab roots, since they do not dispute the original Zionist narrative of the local Arab community as cultureless and antiquated.

As hummus and falafel's status as Israeli national icons solidified, their

FIG. 9-5. Dorit Maya-Gur, *Falafelman*, 2006.

FIG. 9-6. Dorit Maya-Gur, *Falafelman*, 2006.

visibility in Israeli artists' work grew correspondingly, particularly in the past two decades: falafel and hummus appear in a variety of projects, from comic books to art installations, reflecting their current status as icons of Israeli national identity. Despite their popularity with Jewish communities abroad and their prevalence as markers of Israel toward the outside world, Israelis have a more ambivalent relationship to these dishes: they are ubiquitous and popular, yet their representations in art are often ironic. Their origins and the contention around them support their use in art contexts to critique the current political situation and to reflect on notions of Israeliness.

Dorit Maya-Gur's *Falafelman* comic book (2006) offers one example of this ambivalent attitude. The artist presents the figure of a new and powerful Israeli superhero (figures 9-5 and 9-6), his newfound powers a result of an experiment gone wrong and an unintentional cross between man and falafel ball. However, the mild-mannered alter ego is portrayed as a lazy, underachieving, vulgar slob.

Micha Laury, whose *Chocolate Soldier* was discussed above, created in 2005–6 sculptural pieces titled *Falafel Towers*. The towers, comprised of several layers of "pita rounds" and "falafel balls," are stacked precariously on top of each other; made of resin and paint, they are distinctly inedible. The transition of these everyday subjects into the gallery space speaks of their important cultural role, while their precarious, fragile structure intimates vulnerability and uncertainty in their status as markers of identity. Eli Petel's *Hummus Plate* (2002) reflects a similar method and subtext: the "hummus" in the piece is made of oil paint that resembles hummus in its color and texture and is presented on a plate that hangs on the wall, sagging in this unnatural position. The combination of hummus and the vertical china plate, reminiscent of the collection of decorative plates popular in certain old-fashioned Ashkenazi households, can be read as a comment on the absurdity of this "union" and speaks to the artist's reaction to the Israeli appropriation of the product.[32]

Several Palestinian artists reflect on the appropriation of these foods by Israel—they rarely use these products to signify Palestinian or Arab identity, but rather to comment on the relationship between Israel and the Palestinians. Sharif Waked's *Khumus* (2008) is one example: the artist set up a table and two chairs on the sharply sloping pathway leading up to the Palestinian restaurant Al-Bayt in the village of Ayn Hawd. To balance the furniture on the sharp slope he extended the legs on one side of the table and on one of the chairs, addressing the imbalance, but also calling attention to it. The table includes two inset bowls filled with cooked chickpeas, beginning to sprout. The setting, outdoors on the sloping path, near a Palestinian restaurant popular with Israelis searching for "authentic" fare, and the use of cooked chickpeas, speak to the tenuous relationship and the imbalance of power between Israelis and Palestinians.[33]

Falafel Road is the title of a Palestinian-Israeli collaboration that took place in London in 2010. The artists, Larissa Sansour and Oreet Ashery, created a series of falafel-centered meals in a variety of locations in London and documented them on film and as a web blog. They were investigating the ownership of falafel as a way to discuss cultural appropriation. The artists used the preparation and consumption of falafel as a way of allowing new voices into a conversation about the relationship between Israel and Palestine, linking it to exile and immigration.[34]

COMPLEX DISHES, COMPLEX IDENTITIES

Relatively few Palestinian artists use complex dishes in their work—Sansour is one of the exceptions. Prior to *Falafel Road* she created a video project titled *Soup Over Bethlehem — Mloukhieh* (2006), showing a family gathered around a table for a meal of *mloukhieh* soup and conversation. The artist describes this soup as the "national dish." The project resembles a documentary film, yet devices such as the use of color (black-and-white film with just a couple of vibrant yellow objects on the table) remind us it is a staged art project. Mloukhieh is common in a variety of Middle Eastern and North African cuisines (known as Jew's Mallow in English). It can be gathered in the wild in Israel among other regions. Significantly, Israelis have not adopted Palestinian dishes such as mloukhieh, particularly not ones based on gathered native plants. Though in recent years they are making more frequent appearances, they seem to be located in the realm of "nature" rather than "culture," and for a long time were seen by Israelis as only appropriate for times of shortage and crisis. Liora Gvion, in her discussion of the complex relationship between Israeli Palestinians and Jews around food, suggests that Palestinians tend to keep their home cooking in the home. They do not share it with Israelis in restaurants or through cookbooks — among other reasons, for fear it would be appropriated and compromised.[35] This results, however, with a lack of familiarity with more complex Palestinian dishes outside the Palestinian community. Significantly, Jewish Israelis from Egyptian descent see mloukhieh as their own, a traditional ethnic food made by their mothers and grandmothers. Mloukhieh appears as a device in film and theater work by Jewish Israelis signifying a link with home, family, and ethnic heritage, as in Assaf Lapid's short film *Muluḥiyah* (mloukhieh) (2008) and Nissim Zohar's autobiographical book and one-man play, *Mother's Mloukhieh* (2006).

It is important to note that when accusations of appropriation of Palestinian foods are raised against Israel, they are generally aimed at the Ashkenazi (European descendant) population, but Jewish Israeli society has a significant population whose origins are in Middle Eastern and North African countries, and whose cuisine was similar to that of their Muslim and Christian neighbors. These ethnic groups have gone through a process of acculturation in the Israeli state's early years, trying to rid them of their traditional culture, equated with the culture of the "enemy," and to teach them unified (read: Western/European) eating habits. This process has been mostly abandoned since the 1970s, slowly allowing more room for non-European cultural expression (though it still has far to go).

Several Israeli artists use food to explore questions of ethnic identity and affiliation within a greater Jewish nation. Boaz Arad's *Gefiltefish* (2005) shows the artist's mother's hands as she prepares a traditional gefiltefish dish, instructing her son in its making and answering his questions about her views of ethnicity in Israel. This particular dish clearly locates the artist in an Eastern European (Ashkenazi) ethnic group. We never see his mother's face, only the artist's as he parrots her words. The video invokes a popular cooking television segment, yet disrupts it through certain interventions, which highlight its distance from this everyday, familiar context and transforms it into a commentary on these seemingly innocuous, everyday acts. Shachar Marcus uses an exaggerated version of *sabich*, a popular Israeli street food and a kind of sandwich of Iraqi origins, to comment on the work of art and its relationship to everyday life in Israel. In *Sabich* (2006) Marcus lays an oversized, loosely formed round of dough on the floor to form the foundation of the sandwich and proceeds to cover it with a variety of traditional toppings such as eggplant, hard-boiled eggs, and hot sauce. He does this in an imitation of Jackson Pollock's famous painting style, marking the raw food ingredients as "art materials" and his creation as "art." Again, this particular food, like gefiltefish or mloukhieh, has a clearly identifiable ethnic origin, which adds a layer of meaning to the piece. Unlike early Zionist work that focused on finding and articulating a unified national identity and symbols, more recent Israeli artwork functions in a more confident nation and can investigate more subtle, complex multilayered identities.

A recent Israeli project (2013) helmed by young artists Yael Ravid and Goore Somer, titled *Kitchen Talks*, brings together instructors from African migrant communities with Israeli diners in teaching workshops. African refugees and illegal workers comprise the most recent wave of emigration to Israel and remain suspect and separated from mainstream Israeli society, concentrated mostly in the south of Tel-Aviv. The workshops allow the instructors (from Ivory Coast, Eritrea, Nigeria, and Darfur) a position of power and authority, creating a setting for an intimate meeting and exchange.[36] The meal and the entire event are framed as an art experience, an ongoing, participatory project that aims at affecting social change. *Kitchen Talks* presents a new approach to thinking through Israeli identity, since this particular group of immigrants is obviously not Jewish. It points to the possibility of new ways of thinking about Israeli nationalism and identity.

LOOKING AHEAD

The art projects described here perform the nation and national affiliation; they reflect socioeconomic and demographic changes, as well as changing attitudes. The two themes that seem to run through many of these works are homeland and exile, within and without. The tension between these two concepts shapes representations of both nations.

Early Zionist art was concerned with representing the new Jewish persona as separated from two thousand years of living in the Diaspora, while simultaneously forging links with the land of Israel. Palestinian artists reaffirm in their work a steadfast connection to their homeland despite separation and dispersal, and they question the concept of "home" in exile. More recent Israeli art investigates the relationships between the different groups of immigrants and ethnic populations (both Jewish and not), exploring the essence of the nation, defining it through the myriad outside influences that have shaped it. The artists described here use food-related products to explore these questions.

Food is intimate and personal—what could be more intimate than accepting something into the body, making it part of yourself? Yet it also functions in the public sphere through its production, retail sales, and consumption in restaurants and at public events. It separates "us" from "others" through religious prohibitions and different cooking methods and eating customs. Therefore, food is a perfect medium for exploring the tension between inside and outside, here and away, home and exile. Food products as subjects for artwork facilitate an exploration of these tensions. Food as a medium for artwork provides a concrete, tangible link to life. It serves as a reminder that art can be connected to everyday life, that it can be affective and influential. Early Zionist art, depicting biblical products and agricultural work, was recruited to perform the (re)new(ed) Jewish nation and help mold it. Can the more recent performances described in this chapter be recruited to affect change as well? Can reimagining the nation to encompass other groups, be they refugees from Darfur or Palestinians, through concrete actions and tangible materials, trickle up to change perceptions and affiliations?

NOTES

1. I found it difficult to receive permission for publishing Palestinian artists' work in this chapter, partially due to the boycott. I urge the reader to search out visual representations of their work online and in other sources.
2. Carol Bardenstein, "Discourses of Rootedness," *Edebiyat* 8 (1998): 1–36.

3. Yael Zerubavel, *Recovered Roots: Collective Memory and the Making of Israeli National Tradition* (Chicago: University of Chicago Press, 1995), 8.

4. See Barbara Kirshenblatt-Gimblett, "Playing to the Senses: Food as a Performance Medium," *Performance Research* 4, no. 1 (1999): 1–30; Homi K. Bhabha, *The Location of Culture* (New York: Routledge, 1994).

5. Sami Zubaida, "National, Communal, and Global Dimensions in Middle Eastern Food Cultures," in *Culinary Cultures of the Middle East* (New York: I. B. Tauris, 1994), 39–41.

6. Michael Berkowitz, *Zionist Culture and West European Jewry before the First World War* (Chapel Hill: University of North Carolina Press, 1996).

7. Ben-Yehuda, *The Masada Myth* (Madison: University of Wisconsin Press, 1995); Zerubavel, *Recovered Roots*, 1995.

8. Alec Mishori, *Shuru, Habitu, uReu, Ikonot uSmalim Hazutiyim Zioniyim baTarbut haIsraelit* [Lo and behold, visual aspects of Zionist myths in Israeli culture] (Tel Aviv: Am Oved Publishing, 2000).

9. Art historian Alec Mishori describes an additional interpretation that emerged in early holiday celebrations in Israel: bringing together of the seven species symbolized the "ingathering of exiles," merging different ethnic groups into a single nation.

10. See Israel Bar-Tal, "Al HaRishoniyut: Zman uMakom BaAliya HaRishona [Of primacy: time and place in the First Aliya]," in *Lesoheah Tarbut im HaAliya HaRishona*, ed. Yafa Berlovitch and Yosaf Lang (Tel Aviv: HaKibbutz HaMeuchad, 2010), 15–24, on the origin of this ideology in Eastern and Central European thinkers in the late eighteen hundreds, who viewed agricultural labor and craft as essential to a country's economic prosperity (unlike commerce and trade).

11. Bar-Tal, "Al HaRishoniyut."

12. Yigal Zalmona, *A Century of Israeli Art* (Jerusalem: Israel Museum, 2010), 48–49.

13. Carol B. Bardenstein, "Trees, Forests, and the Shaping of Palestinian and Israeli Collective Memory," in *Acts of Memory: Cultural Recall in the Present*, ed. Mieke Bal, Jonathan Crewe, and Leo Spitzer (Hanover NH: University Press of New England, 1999), 148–70.

14. See Salīm Tamārī, *Mountain Against the Sea: Essays on Palestinian Society and Culture* (Berkeley: University of California Press, 2009).

15. Silman Mansour, "Art under Occupation," *Emel.com* no. 87 (2011), http://www.emel.com/article?id=92&a_id=2608.

16. Tal Ben-Zvi, *Sabra: Representations of the Nakba in Palestinian Art Created in Israel* (Tel Aviv: Resling, 2014), 125.

17. Ganit Ankori, *Palestinian Art* (New York: Reaktion Books, 2006), 156–58.

18. http://www.larissasansour.com/nation_estate.

19. Ben-Zvi, *Sabra*, 207.

20. Ankori, *Palestinian Art*, 89.

21. Ankori, *Palestinian Art*, 142.

22. Ankori, *Palestinian Art*, 212–13.

23. See also Bishara and Alan Schechner's collaboration in *Dialog of Equals* (2003) described in Alessandro Imperato, "The Dialogics of Chocolate: A Silent Dialog on Israeli-Palestinian Politics," in *Global and Local Art Histories*, eds. Celina Jeffery and Gregory Minissale (Newcastle UK: Cambridge Scholars Publishing, 2007). The use of chocolate in this work brings to mind Karen Finley's performance *We Keep Our Victims Ready* (1989), and Janine Antoni's *Lick and Lather* (1993) sculptures. The more universal food product paradoxically places Bishara's piece into a more personal context, away from the overtly national symbols specific to Palestinian life.

24. Zalmona, *A Century of Israeli Art*, 262–63.

25. Amy B. Trubek, *The Taste of Place: A Cultural Journey into Terroir* (Berkley: University of California Press, 2008).

26. My thanks to Dorothy Chansky for her inspiring paper "The Terroir of Matzha," presented at Doing Things with Food(s), ASTR Conference, November 2014, and her insightful comments.

27. Naama Orbach, *Eich Ossa Yalda* [What a girl does], (Jerusalem: Shoken, 2004).

28. Shani Litman, "Omanut al haSakin," *Haaretz*, August 8, 2014, 12.

29. Litman, "Omanut al haSakin," 12.

30. For an extended discussion of the evolution of falafel as an Israeli national icon, see Yael Raviv, "Falafel: A National Icon," *Gastronomica* 3, no. 3 (2003): 20–25; Yael Raviv, *Falafel Nation: Cuisine and the Making of National Identity in Israel* (Lincoln: University of Nebraska Press, 2015).

31. Raviv, "Falafel: A National Icon."

32. Saguy Green, "Soul Food," *Haaretz*, May 11, 2005.

33. My thanks to Dafna Hirsch for bringing this work to my attention.

34. http://www.falafelroad.blogspot.com.

35. Liora Gvion, *Beyond Hummus and Falafel: Social and Political Aspects of Palestinian Food in Israel* (Berkeley: University of California Press, 2012).

36. Dafna Arad, "African Migrants Help Israelis Acquire a Taste for Their Neighbors," *Haaretz*, June 12, 2013.

PART 4

The Food of the Diaspora

The Global Identity, Memory, and History of Jewish Food

10

From the Comfort of Home to Exile

German Jews and Their Foodways

....

MARION KAPLAN

A little gray metal file box sat in my closet for years. I recognized it from my childhood as my mother's trove of recipes. As she aged, she could no longer cook, and I had no time to inspect her culinary history. But last year, upon her death, the box beckoned. What I saw in her handwriting—an embrace of novelty and a longing for the familiar—concurred with my own discoveries about Jewish food cultures. I had found that in Germany, and as German-Jewish refugees moved to temporary and new homes abroad, most continued certain food traditions while also adapting to new cuisines and customs. Using cookbooks, memoirs, and my mother's recipe box, this essay asks how Jews adapted to new food challenges while attempting to retain food customs. It examines German-Jewish foodways from the Imperial era (1871–1918) through the Nazi period (1933–45) as well as the varied food experiences refugees encountered as they sojourned in Portugal en route to safer havens. It will then consider food habits in a tiny refugee settlement in Sosúa in the Dominican Republic, to see how Central European Jews adapted to tropical foods. Finally, it explores, through the use of one recipe box, one refugee's cooking experience in the United States.

These uneven numbers and sources present methodological problems with which historians must grapple. First, sources vary from a broad variety to one small recipe box. Plentiful sources exist for the food cultures of about 500,000 Jews in Imperial and Nazi Germany, ranging over newspapers, memoirs, archival materials, cookbooks, and anthropological studies. For tens of thousands of refugees in Lisbon, the sources narrow: memoirs and letters identify the kinds of foods Jews ate and the milieus in which they ate them. Memoirs play the most important role describing the Dominican refugee kitchen of about seven hundred settlers. Becoming even narrower, one set of recipes from one German-Jewish refugee woman provides a peephole into how she revisioned her culinary expectations, evoking the choices she made among German Jewish, German, American Jewish, and American traditions.

Second, memoirs, as has been noted often enough, offer a view colored by hindsight. Frequently written for children or grandchildren, they may also place excessive weight on the family, understating the extent to which Jews interacted with other Jews outside the family and with non-Jews. Also, memoirs nostalgically depict families solving problems—rather than creating them. Self-representations color these documents as well, attempting to display the attributes of the well-mannered bourgeoisie. And yet, they remain indispensable if one seriously hopes to portray lives within the family circle.[1] Cookbooks and recipes printed separately, whether in newspapers or handwritten and stored in recipe boxes, tantalize and disappoint as well. No one knows whether housewives (or, in some cases, servants) actually used the recipes. As gifts, they may have remained on the shelves. Recipes in newspapers, solicited by male editors for the "women's pages," may or may not have come to fruition. Further, no one can state with confidence that Jews who cooked or ate these foods understood them as "Jewish" or "German" or even "German Jewish." What seems certain, however, is that some cookbooks went through many editions. In addition, memoirs report on Sabbath and festival meals, often with joy in the details. And, finally, one can assume women's carefully clipped and saved recipes more generally, and the well-worn cards in my mother's recipe box in particular, tell a genuine tale. For women carefully collected and organized those recipes that they hoped to bake or cook. Whether they succeeded or not, they probably intended to produce a dish or a dessert. And on a microlevel, as "witness," this historian can testify that the well-worn cards in my mother's recipe box repeatedly found their way to family dinners. In sum, cookbooks, memoirs, and recipes must be used with care as sources on Jewish family history, Jewish identities, and even Jewish food habits, but they must be used. They shed light on areas otherwise unapproachable and provide details of daily life that would otherwise remain in obscurity.

In nineteenth-century Germany, known as the era of Jewish emancipation, Jews sought both to integrate but also to retain their ethnic or religious identity. They desired to acculturate to German middle-class habits and politics, acquiring and displaying appropriate manners, educations, and attitudes in order to prove to a reluctant German polity that Jews could be and should be treated as citizens. Jewish men achieved legal and civic equality with the founding of the German Empire, although Jewish women, and all other women, had to wait until 1919 when the Weimar Republic granted them the vote. Socially, Jews reached out to non-Jewish society, happily joining non-Jewish circles in increasing numbers. At work, Jews met non-Jewish business contacts that sometimes led to social contacts. They shared some leisure time, from a weekly beer to a professional organization that offered evening lectures and annual excursions. Some made lasting friendships, including marriages. Indeed, historians now suggest that the era around 1900 saw the high point of Jewish social integration.[2]

Jews nonetheless navigated two worlds. Notwithstanding their successful acculturation and their ongoing integration into the public worlds of education, business, and the professions, a lively Jewish social life flourished. Jews maintained strong communal ties, religious and philanthropic. They maintained friendship circles, as well as single-sex and mixed social clubs. Activities ranged from private coffee visits to dinner parties and dance classes. Jewish associations, like nonsectarian organizations more generally, burgeoned on the local and national levels in late nineteenth-century Germany.

Most commonly, however, for Jews in Imperial Germany, leisure time meant family time. Indeed, Catholics and Protestants assumed the same. Daily and weekly family gatherings, special family celebrations for life cycle events such as marriages, family observance of the religious holidays, and family visits during summer vacations meant that Jews spent most of their leisure time with immediate and extended family. Jewish families provided more than sociability, however. In a society plagued by endemic social and religious antisemitism as well as public and political outbreaks of antisemitism, families offered social and psychological support, a safe haven from outside prejudices or discriminations. Also, in a society on the move—Jews migrated from small towns and villages to larger cities at rates far exceeding those of other Germans—families sustained social and economic safety nets as bonds stretched over distances.

These family moments occurred most frequently at the table. Food culture played a significant part in the maintenance of family cohesiveness around Jewish traditions. Indeed, the two were inseparable. Certain food customs and, in particular, family gatherings at Sabbath and holiday meals, indicated Jewish aspiration to both enact community and retain aspects of their Jewish identities. Still, German bourgeois table manners and food recipes seeped into these meals, creating a *German* Jewish relationship to food. Later, during Nazi persecution and while fleeing for their lives (1933–45), Jews maintained a similar course, keeping elements of their old foodways while adapting first to severe food shortages in Germany and later to new food customs in countries of temporary and, later, permanent refuge.

Jewish cookbooks from the Imperial era illustrate that many German Jews—eagerly attaining middle-class status—performed their Germanness by aspiring to German middle-class norms.[3]

FIG. 10-1. Title page from Witwe Marie Kauders, *Vollständigesisraelitisches Kochbuch* (Breslau: Jakob B. Brandeis, 1903).

These cookbooks (see figure 10-1, for an example) focused on the types of foods to serve to guests, even the ways to fold cloth napkins attractively, for example into a swan. Earlier cookbooks offered "thrifty" meals and later ones provided both traditional recipes and also "finer" dishes and international fare such as "English plum pudding" or "French almond cake."

Some of these cookbooks explained the rules for keeping a Jewish kitchen, explaining to presumably modern women that science and religion could coexist ("Wissenschaft und Religion ruhig nebeneinander bestehen können") and reminded them that koshering meat had "sanitary (healthful)" reasons, too. Frequently, these cookbooks included recipes for Easter (*Oster*) or the "Easter kitchen" (*Osterküche*), although upon closer inspection these turned out to be traditional foods meant for Passover. In fact, in some, the Hebrew letters for Passover appeared in parentheses after the word "Easter," and the recipes included matzos. This confusion resulted from linguistic acculturation: "Easter" even appeared in books with kosher recipes and even with prayers (in Hebrew) to be spoken on the Sabbath and holidays.[4]

Jewish customs, such as the traditional Saturday dish, called *Schalet* in Germany (and *cholent* in Eastern Europe), appear regularly in these cookbooks. Writers offer many varieties of these stews, with meat, potatoes, noodles, beans, or grains depending on the region. Slow overnight cooking, or baking in a nearby baker's oven, allowed the meal to be ready for midday without any actual preparation on the Sabbath. Indeed, the schalet grew so beloved that Heinrich Heine, the German Jewish poet who converted to Christianity, immortalized the schalet in a parody of Schiller's *Ode to Joy*, the text sung in Beethoven's Ninth Symphony:

> Schalet, wondrous sparkle of the gods,
> Daughter of Elysium!
> That's how Schiller's Ode would have sounded,
> Had he ever tasted Schalet
>
> . . . .
> Schalet is the true God's
> Kosher Ambrosia.[5]

As Jews acculturated and modernized, they remained loyal to this dish, if not to the way Jewish food regulations required its preparation. Instead of the sixteen-to-twenty-hour schalet that avoided work on the Sabbath, they made a one-hour Sabbath schalet. They could break the rules of Sabbath rest and still provide a traditional dish—at least with regard to ingredients.

Memoirs describe unusual food and ritual combinations; for example a German Jewish woman could write in her memoirs about Christmas pudding and special Sabbath meals without exhibiting any sense of contradiction.[6] Walking a tightrope between acceptance of German pork-centered cuisine and Jewish prohibitions against pork, many Jews rejected pork on "aesthetic" grounds but ate other nonkosher meat.

Others refused to have dairy with meat dishes because "they didn't taste good together."[7] These instances display a de facto allegiance to traditional Jewish foodways even as most Jews observed them in the breach.

In villages, where Jews remained observant with regard to kosher rules and Sabbath rest, much longer than in cities, Jews cooked German regional and national variations and non-Jews picked up some Jewish recipes. For example, in Württemberg, village peasant women baked *Bubele* (plum cake), a southern Jewish recipe. In Hesse, the peasants enjoyed a bean stew/soup (probably a form of the Sabbath schalet) and would say, "Today I'm a Jew." Swabian Jews, on the other hand, enjoyed the local specialty, dumplings (*spätzle*), and prided themselves on cooking them as well as other Swabians. But they ate them on workdays, not on Sabbath, whereas their neighbors ate them on Sundays. Jews could not cook on the Sabbath and these dumplings had to be prepared fresh. By the 1920s, the Jewish midday Saturday meal often resembled the middle-class Swabian Sunday dinner, with the exception of Jewish bread, or challah (*Berches*). Conversely, German non-Jews noticed that Jews ate certain foods in, for them, unusual combinations, because of rules against combining milk with meat.

In cities, Jews had many more food options. The family of chief rabbi Joseph Carlebach in Hamburg, for example, maintained kosher standards, eating "half a la Berlin-Prussian cuisine and half a la North Sea fish," but dined on traditional dumplings for the Jewish holiday of Sukkot. Urban life also introduced Jews to tropical fruits, only recently available from German colonies. Toni Ehrlich's mother, who had fifty-two cousins in Breslau alone, held regular "cousins' cafés" at which she served tropical delicacies such as dates, figs, raisins, and almonds.[8] By the turn of the century the majority of urban Jews no longer obeyed most laws of kashrut but a form of gastronomic Judaism persisted, often to appease the older generation, to ease their own consciences, or from tradition.[9] Most commonly, they seem to have agreed about what they would eat "inside" in private and "outside" in public, the latter offering more nonkosher options. These compromises could bring strange contradictions: one memoirist noted that with regard to his mother's kitchen "I would set the word kosher in quotation marks. Although my father refused to eat pork, he ate ham."[10]

Nowhere do we see the adoption of food habits more clearly than in the German Jewish adherence to the German ritual of the coffee and cake hour. Coffee hour grew to one of the main forms of social activity among German-speaking Jews (as among other Germans) in the late nineteenth century. When the extended family of a Berlin woman got together, they frequently visited cafés on Berlin's famous Unter den Linden boulevard where they would sit over their coffee and cream cakes "for as long as three hours."[11] For such a coffee and cake gathering, one Jewish cookbook recommended four to five pies and two platters of assorted baked goods for twenty-four women! Indeed, in the Complete Israelite Cookbook of 1903 (*Vollständiges israelitisches Kochbuch*) the author lists 208 meat, vegetable, and salad recipes (102 meats, 42 vegetables, 25 salads, and 39 chicken recipes) compared to 368 cake and dessert recipes(!) comprised of 200 cake and 98 tart recipes—not to mention 70 sweet dishes containing flour (*Mehlspeisen*).[12] It is no wonder then that a recent researcher found the majority of orally transmitted recipes in her grandmother's cookbook to be cookies, cakes, and *Torten*.[13]

In general, Jews continued to enjoy traditional meals and to observe some dietary rules disguised as preferences. They aspired toward a German and international menu to testify to their embourgeoisement. Their cookbooks saw no contradiction in a "French pudding" with the warning that this was a "milk product."[14] Yet food alone would not have sufficed to maintain a connection with Judaism. The family meal remained a central focus for the expression of Jewish feeling and commitment.[15] Women made special arrangements for the holidays, with most rural and observant women taking special care for the weekly Sabbath. The Sabbath entailed a white tablecloth, candles, special clothing, and, importantly, family gatherings (see figure 10.2 for a photograph of the Naumann family at table, for example). Particular foods and rituals

FIG. 10-2. The Naumann family at Sabbath meal. Courtesy of Leo Baeck Institute, New York, AR25459.

combined religious and familial celebrations. The two elements reinforced each other, impossible to disentangle.

For example, even lower-middle-class, relatively modest families made Sabbath meals into minor banquets. A letter from newlywed Sigmund Hirsch to his wife, Rosa, in 1895, described the Sabbath he spent with her family in the tiny village of Pflaumloch (Swabia). She was one of seven children whose father ran a small cigar manufacturing and retail business from home. Hence the meals reflect the income of a man of middling means, whose wife may have added a few more courses for her new son-in-law. Hirsch wrote that on Friday evening they had a meal of soup, beef, asparagus, bean salad, chicken ragout, roasted capon, a meat roll with chicken sauce, salad, and a variety of desserts. On Saturday, synagogue started at 8:00 a.m. Thereafter, the family took a short walk before the main Sabbath meal, then ate dumpling soup with soup meat;

asparagus, celery and carrots, cucumbers and horseradish, five types of preserved pike, tongue with peas, roast goose, salad with hard-boiled eggs, cherry pie, fruit, and coffee. Hirsch decided that he would not eat an evening meal or he would get sick.[16]

The meal served as a connection to family and Jewishness, if not always to religious observance. One woman wrote of the 1880s in Berlin: "Besides the ceremony of Friday nights, there was a strict rule of family togetherness." When certain situations made it impossible for all her siblings to appear on the Sabbath, her father recited the blessing over bread for those children present and for those absent. The sharing of cooked food emphasized being part of a close and interdependent group. The holidays and Sabbath provided occasions for Jews to reaffirm the family and the group.

Jewish food customs in the Imperial era offer an insight into Jewish bourgeois standards of consumption and the performance of Germanness in creative tension with the maintenance of Jewishness. Anti-Jewish persecutions of the Nazi era caused dramatic shifts as families shrank, as incomes dropped, and later as the government rationed food. The Nazis disrupted family gatherings, which grew smaller and more infrequent as individuals escaped from Germany any way they could. The Jewish extended family that celebrated holidays together ceased to exist. Particularly, older generations—grandparents—remained behind as the young fled. Thus, the Nazis had brutally replaced voluntary "Jewishness," whether defined in terms of food traditions or family holidays, with racial repression, squeezing the remaining Jews together in "Jew houses" (1939–40) to make further persecution swift and efficient.

The major food issues in these years focused on finding nutritious alternatives for restricted foods. Aware of the Nazi ban against kosher meat slaughtering (April 1933), Jewish newspapers tried to give nutrition tips, with one coining the slogan "Fish is also meat."[17] Advice columns suggested that housewives consider vegetarian menus because they were cheaper and healthier. Although meat might be easier and more time-efficient to prepare, columnists asserted that "good will [was]

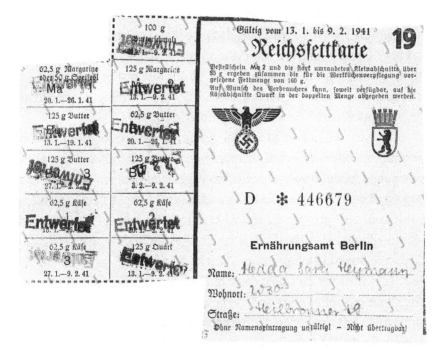

FIG. 10-3. Ration card, 1941. Courtesy of Leo Baeck Institute, New York, AR1253.

an important assistant in a vegetarian kitchen," and papers printed vegetarian menus and recipes.[18] The League of Jewish Women, the organization of the Jewish feminist movement in Germany, published its own cookbook in 1933, including the use of nuts as a meat replacement. It went through four editions by 1934. By November 1937, the league's winter menus placed a heavy emphasis on apples, potatoes, and cabbage. A typical menu included breakfast oatmeal; cabbage stuffed with rice and steamed apples for the main meal; and salad, a hard-boiled egg, and cooked plums for the lighter one.[19] As Jews faced further economic decline and, later, impoverishment, the issue turned on what could they buy and what could they eat at all.

More serious limitations on shopping began in September 1939, ten days after the start of the war. The government restricted Jews to particular stores. Some cities then set up "Jew shopping locations" in districts with a large Jewish population. In addition, the malicious combination of assigning Jews to shops a long distance from their homes and the ban on Jews using public transportation meant that, as of mid-1941, Jews faced hour-long "shopping marches."[20] It grew time-consuming and enervating to obtain even trivial items.[21] Severe rationing also restricted consumption for all Germans, but more so for Jews.

As of 1940–41, Jews could no longer purchase rice, legumes, canned vegetables, coffee, tea, cocoa, artificial honey, sweets, fruit, poultry, game, or smoked foods. They could only buy vegetables such as rutabagas, cabbage, and beets.[22] In 1942 the Nazis added more banned items, including meat and meat products, eggs, wheat products, whole milk, and even skimmed milk. Also, the times at which Jews could shop, usually limited to one or one-and-a-half hours a day at closing time, meant that non-Jews had already purchased most of the necessary foods. To aggravate the situation, police raids on "Jew houses," the apartments or buildings into which Jews had been crammed, sought out "forbidden" foods and arrested people if these foods appeared on their shelves. Additionally, neighbors and other shoppers harassed Jews if they appeared to shop earlier than the regulated times. In addition to ostracism, fear, and cold, Jews left in Germany faced serious hunger.

Those lucky enough to flee Germany left persecution and subjugation behind, but faced nagging uncertainty in places of refuge. In many cases, they did not know how long it would take to move on or whether they could stay in their new refuge. Two examples that I have studied—refugees in Portugal and in the Dominican Republic—can show the tenacity of food cultures as well as the adaptability of the refugees. In both cases, large families rarely functioned as engines of cultural continuity, since only the rare family managed to get all members out. In those small, nuclear families lucky enough to escape, women took on the challenge of creating meals out of new products while attempting to retain some old familial culinary favorites.

In Lisbon, Portugal, for example, refugees from Germany waited until their visas and ship passages to the United States, Latin America, or

Britain came through. Some stayed months or years. Sometimes these refugees had no idea about Portugal, besides its foods, and just tried to get as far away from Nazi Germany as possible: For example, the Arons family of four "didn't know anything about Portugal, just Port wine, cork and sardines."[23] Those who remained only a few weeks or months made daily visits to cafés similar to those they had frequented in Germany or Austria. Sharing angst and empathy, they bonded quickly over a cheap cup of strong coffee, creating a temporary solidarity among themselves. The writer Hermann Kesten endowed the café with symbolic meaning: "In exile, the café becomes home and homeland. . . . The café becomes the only site of continuity. I sat in cafés in a dozen lands of exile and it was always the same café. . . . I only have to sit in a café and I feel at home."[24]

Jan Lustig described the cafés more practically: "The emigrants sit in cafes with hollow cheeks . . . stick their heads together and talk, talk. Day and night, day and night. One says with a sigh: ". . . visa . . ." Another smiles ironically and bitterly: ". . . visa . . ." The third gives a long, excited speech, but one understands only: "visa . . . visa . . . visa . . ."[25]

Stretching their cups of coffee for many hours, women and men found solace among people in the same situation. Many café patrons faced the same "psychic hell," worrying about family and friends left behind, exchanging information and inferences from the letters they received.[26] Mourning their losses, they dreaded the process of starting all over again in a new place with a new language and new rules. These table partners deeply understood each other's grief.

At dinnertime, they generally ate in their rooms or boarding houses, finding the cheapest foods available, sardines, dry fish, and green beans. One woman noted that the Portuguese prepared "everything" with oil, instead of the German staple, butter.[27] Others, having undergone rationing and hunger at the beginning of the war, as well as food lines in France as they headed toward Portugal, found themselves overwhelmed by the varieties of fruits, vegetables, and breads available in neutral Portugal. Refugees felt heartened by the adequate, even plentiful food available to them. Most had taken food for granted in their previous lives. With rationing, little money, and scarcity, food had evolved into a high priority physically and emotionally. If food had previously caused pleasure, its absence caused anxiety and hunger pangs. Portugal provided relief. For some, this started when they boarded a Portuguese train at the Spanish-Portuguese border. One man still smiled in 1999 when he remembered the smell of fresh rolls on that train, since he and his family had experienced hunger the previous year during their escape from Austria.[28] Alfred Döblin noted a "fantastic amount of food: thick, nutritious soup, fish, meat, and fruit, three times the quantity of a French meal. . . . We were so hungry that in the beginning that was all we cared about."[29] Similarly, Paul Krebs, whose family had run out of food on their journey, appreciated the simple "three meals a day" in Lisbon.[30]

Food and Portuguese generosity went hand in hand. In the village of Goveia, en route to Lisbon, the Rony family stopped to feed their baby. They only had a banana, but within minutes villagers showed up with bread, eggs, butter, cheese, and milk. When George Rony took out some Portuguese money, "they would have none of it." Others "beamed with pride at being able to receive a weary group of refugees."[31] These refugees and many others, fleeing for their lives, gratefully imbibed Portuguese foods and hospitality in the same gulp. The Portuguese Jewish community, too, provided about 250 meals a day at its soup kitchen (Cozinha Económica, est. 1899).[32]

An interesting mixture of German and Portuguese food customs resulted among those who stayed longer. Irene Shomberg, whose parents had immigrated and settled there, remembered that the Portuguese cooked with tomatoes, a rarity in Germany, and that she "loved that cooking." Furthermore, her family got used to the salted dried cod, *bacalhao*, a staple of the Portuguese cuisine and its most popular food. Her mother would cut a piece from a large dried cod fish, soak it for two days, changing the water often due to its saltiness. Then she could boil it and add potatoes, tomatoes, onions, fish, and sauté the mix. One could also include hard-boiled eggs and make many different varieties. The

Portuguese, Shomberg recalled, believed "you [could] make a different version every day of the year."

Every Friday, the Portuguese Jewish Community (which consisted of a fairly large group of German and Dutch and Portuguese Jews who had lived there before the refugee influx) had a *bacalhao* lunch. Yet the German element remained: "They had beautiful cakes from "strictly German" recipes," such as: (1) *Rahmtorte* (cream cake): pastry tart, milk, eggs, vanilla (sort of a cheese cake); (2) *Bienenstich* (their version had no cream filling): dough plus sweetened almonds, sugar, and butter; and (3) *Mürbeteig* (cookie or pastry tart with rich, crumbly texture) with fruits. Indeed, German pastries even acquired some popularity among the Portuguese. For example, the Davidsohn family earned money with the mother's homemade baked goods, peddled by her children.[33] Another Jewish woman began to sell her baked goods, such as the Berliner donut.[34] Jewish vendors also sold these donuts door to door.[35] The German donuts, renamed *bolas de Berlin*, grew popular in cafés in Estoril and Lisbon. (Today, Portuguese bakeries offer *bolas* as standard fare.)[36] Hungarian pastries, too, appeared in Lisbon cafés.[37]

Pastries, of course, did not comprise the whole menu. Friday night dinners at home consisted of the traditional German-Jewish chicken soup and chicken, "a Jewish meal, not Portuguese." Passover, too, had a German touch: with jellied carp (but the whole fish with bone) and noodle soup or Schwaemmchen (made of matzoh meal, fat, egg, parsley, not as stiff as a matzoh ball. Cut into little pieces, it floated in the soup.) Matzoh balls made with matzoh served as a side dish, basically a form of potato dumpling (*Kartoffel Klösse*) turned into matzoh dumplings (*Klösse*). Ultimately, those who just passed through Portugal retained some of their German foods and adapted to their new lands' cuisines, maintaining little of the Portuguese flavor. But those few who stayed and married in Portugal adapted Portuguese cuisine but continued to enjoy German baking traditions. And food memories persisted. Having spent her entire adult life in Portugal, Ruth Arons, at age ninety, "can still smell and taste the dishes" that her grandmother cooked for her over eighty years ago.[38]

Similarly, in the Dominican Republic, where refugee Jews lived on a collective farm in Sosúa, the Central European Jews preferred to mix their traditional foods and Dominican specialties. Settlers appreciated the profusion of tropical fruits and vegetables, most of which they had never seen before. Miriam Sondheimer, for example, scrutinized "all kinds of tropical fruits" she did not recognize and bought her first plantain in Puerto Rico, en route to Sosúa. Because they looked like "big bananas," she tried to peel and bite into it. "We learned better later," she recalled.[39]

The dining hall, built and run by the American Jewish Joint Distribution Committee and the settlers themselves, provided breakfast and dinner. Breakfast consisted of bread, cheese, and marmalade, similar to what refugees had eaten in Europe, but also oranges, limes, bananas, eggs, sausages, and "excellent Dominican coffee." Dinners included beef and chicken as the main proteins, with only the first a European staple.[40] Pork appeared regularly, since the settlers also raised pigs. Dominican rice and beans, yucca, plantains, bread, sweet potatoes, corn, and seasonal items such as pineapples, mangoes, or avocados made up the side dishes.[41]

Familiar with heavy Austrian and German foods, the refugees took a while to grow accustomed to Dominican fare. As sociologist Pierre Bourdieu has reminded us, food "reflects directly back to the oldest and deepest experiences."[42] Thus, the older refugees clung to traditional foods even though the tropical climate worked against them. For example, these formerly middle-class Germans required meat, something working-class Germans had not eaten every day. Yet with almost no refrigeration available, one had to cook meat on the same day the animals were slaughtered. This could cause major inconveniences, but these Europeans, amidst their meat-eating Dominican neighbors, did not switch to fish. In addition, the tropical climate prevented the cultivation of potatoes, the Central European staple with which they had grown up, and the local equivalent, yucca, had to serve instead. While some, especially younger people, adjusted well to the variety of ways yucca could be served, older settlers found that whether "squashed, fried, ground, baked or broiled . . . they always came out tasting like soap."[43]

Ernest Weinberg, ten years old when he arrived in Sosúa, liked "rice and beans . . . fried meats (beef, goat), yellow and green plantains." His younger brother enjoyed them too, but his parents expressed shock, having expected European food, potatoes, meat, and sauce: "Everything appeared strange (fremd) to them."[44] Weinberg's mother never learned to cook Dominican foods and continued to prepare meals the "German way," that is, in heavy fats, as she had done back home in northern Germany. The food "coagulated on the palette," according to her son. His father was more adaptable, but the eating customs of most of the older generation remained European, and in some cases, specifically Austrian. The younger people ate more of the Dominican foods. In Weinberg's case, he truly enjoyed "[his] rice and beans and . . . plátanos."[45]

In December 1942, American doctors working at the Hebrew University visited the settlers and noted that those who used the dining hall, rather than cooking on their own homesteads, still ate "more or less as they [had] in Vienna." The visitors, aware of similar food preferences among refugees in Palestine, expressed concern that the settlers' meat consumption, three times the normal requirement for protein, could be "harmful in a tropical climate." Thus they recommended a "radical reorganization of the kitchen and menu," with more milk and cheese and less pork and other—to their palate?—"greasy and indigestible foods."[46] Finally, the doctors observed an "inordinately high" rate of sugar consumption in the settlement, not related to the canning and preserve industry.[47] Two local cafés established by refugees continued to delight settlers with their sweet European indulgences and remind them of their European roots. Also, housewives continued to bake Central European pastries at home. (In addition, we should consider that recent medical studies have hypothesized a link between depression and a craving for sugar.[48] Perhaps some refugees attempted to drown their sadness in coffee and cake.)

Eventually, the homesteaders learned to substitute yucca, plantains, sweet potatoes, and rice for European bread and potatoes.[49] They even adapted recipes brought by the older generation to create interesting mixtures. Observers noticed them "prepar[ing] the novel and unaccustomed foods in the traditional native way but . . . adapt[ing] them to familiar recipes brought along from the homeland. Thus the Dominican visitor is delighted to find instead of his familiar boiled yucca, appetizing yucca pancakes, green mangoes substitute for the familiar applesauce, and green papaya . . . put up as sweet and pungent pickle."[50]

In Sosúa, as in many sites of refuge, settlers began to establish and, in some cases, reestablish their family units, but their stay in the Dominican Republic proved too short to draw conclusions as to the power of family food customs. Whereas only about a dozen settlers retained kashrut, there is some evidence that homesteading families did not serve pork at home as compared to the dining hall that did. For those few who remained in the Dominican Republic for their lifetimes, they and their children gradually adopted Dominican foods, but Passover remained an important community holiday.

German Jewish foodways in permanent exile, for example in the United States, requires much more research. Returning to my mother's little gray metal box stuffed with folded newspaper clippings and three-by-five-inch index cards, I can observe how one young German Jewish woman, arriving in 1936 at the age of twenty-two, attempted to integrate American foods as well as Jewish-American foods (of Eastern European heritage) into her Central European repertoire. I can do this by analyzing what she collected in that box as well as the change over time in her use of English rather than German and the names of the friends (European and American-Jewish) whose recipes she copied. She did not keep recipes of her most frequently cooked meals, the meat and potatoes of the German (but also the American) palate, since she

Bounce a Buffet.

Serve a Celery Nut Circle.

2 packages (3 oz. each) or
  1 package (6 oz.)
  JELL-O®
  Brand Lime
  Flavor Gelatin
½ teaspoon salt

2 cups boiling water
1½ cups cold water
1 tablespoon vinegar
½ cup sour cream
1 cup chopped celery
½ cup chopped nuts

Dissolve gelatin and salt in boiling water. Add cold water and vinegar and chill until slightly thickened. Spoon half the gelatin into 5-cup ring mold and chill until set but not firm, about 10 minutes. Blend sour cream into remaining gelatin; then fold in celery and nuts. Spoon over clear layer in mold. Chill until firm, about 4 hours. Unmold. Serve with assorted diced fresh fruits and garnish with crisp celery leaves, if desired. Makes 5 cups or 10 servings.

FIG. 10-4. Green Jell-O. Unknown magazine. Personal collection of the author.

knew them by heart. Nor did she note the timing of meals, which due to American work schedules, changed radically, from the heavy German midday meal to the main meal at the end of the day. Indeed, even the German daily "coffee hour" from 4:00 to 5:00 p.m. suffered drastic modifications, occurring only on weekends.

Central European dishes, mostly desserts, show up in the recipe box, especially at the beginning of her married life, at age thirty, and because her husband preferred this cuisine. Still using German, she detailed a "*Gemüsering*-mixed Veget," using canned vegetables and adding sour cream. She wrote the recipe for "Zitronencreme" (lemon cream), for example, in English and German and gave German titles to *Mürbe* cookies, Austrian crescent-shaped cookies (*Kipferl*) made of nuts, and Viennese *Topfentorte* (a light cheesecake), while listing ingredients in English. The recipe for Apricot sponge cake, given its German name ("*Aprikosen bisquit*," actually spelled *biscuit*), came from a Viennese friend and she wrote out "*Aprikosen* marmalade" in awkward English.

Obviously a fan of apricots, she also included an American dish, named "Apricot Delight, (whipped)." The latter included Jell-O, which reached its high point of sales in the 1950s. By that time rapidly acculturating, she, like so many American homemakers, grew to be a fan of gelatin or Jell-O molds, including those with vegetables in them, such as "Beet ring" (with lemon Jell-O) or "Cucumber Supreme Mold."

She served innumerable varieties of glowingly colored fruit or vegetable molds at large family gatherings in the 1950s. Along with this penchant for Jell-O, she tried out other American foods, for example, "Green Bean Casserole," and tuna fish salad (Tuna *Salat*, actually the German should have been *Thun*), completely foreign to her German tastes. She wrote the tuna recipe in German, carefully noting to mix in finely chopped celery.

Some years later, she more easily penned the English instructions for "Yankee Pot Roast," and "Chicken Noodle loaf." She also adopted Thanksgiving, the great American festive meal, with roasted turkey,

BLINTZ DELIGHT

Makes 6 servings

- 2 – packages of 6 Golden Cheese Blintzes (defrosted)
- ¼ lb. (1 stick or ½ cup) Fleischmann's Margarine
- 1 – 8 oz. package Fleischmann's Egg Beaters
- 1½ cup light sour cream
- 1 teaspoon vanilla
- ¼ cup sugar

Place blintzes with fold down in one layer in a 2 quart casserole dish. Melt margarine and blend with all ingredients and pour over blintzes. Bake 45 minutes at 350°.

© 1989 Nabisco Brands, Inc.

FIG. 10-5. Blintz recipe. Personal collection of the author.

cranberry sauce, stuffing, sweet potatoes, corn bread, and gravy, but no ham (often served in American families alongside turkey). German cakes replaced the traditional Thanksgiving apple and pumpkin pies.

Attempting to acquire some American Jewish dishes, she saved recipes from the National Council of Jewish Women, for example, "Gefilte Fish mold" with sour cream and cucumber topping.

She also clipped "Blintz Delight" from *Hadassah Magazine* and included "Blintzes Soufflé" (to be served with defrosted frozen strawberries). An American-Jewish friend's handwritten recipe for "Baked Blintzes" also found its place in the little metal box as did a clipping for "Baked Noodles and Cheese," really a recipe for lokshen kugel, a sweet noodle casserole and staple among Eastern European Jews.

Importantly, she collected a significant number of Passover recipes. Her notes on "*Mazzoh* Rolls," written in English, actually gave the ingredients for what she later referred to as "*mazzoh* balls." Matzoh pancakes,

The cake good enough to deserve Rabbi Levy's blessing.

Passover Orange Sponge Cake made with Domino® Sugar.

⅓ cup matzo cake meal
½ cup potato starch
Pinch of salt
1 cup Domino® Granulated Sugar

10 eggs, separated
Juice of 1 lemon
Grated rind of 1 orange

1. Sift together matzo cake meal, potato starch, and salt, 3 times; set aside.
2. Beat egg yolks until thick. Add ½ cup sugar, lemon juice and orange rind. Continue beating until thick and fluffy. Fold in sifted dry ingredients.
3. In separate bowl, beat egg whites until foamy. Add ½ cup sugar gradually. Beat until stiff peaks form.
4. Fold egg yolk mixture into egg whites.
5. Turn into ungreased 10-inch spring form tube pan. Bake at 350°F for 45 to 50 minutes.
6. Invert pan until cake is cool. Yield: one 10-inch cake.

Domino Sugar is certified "Kosher for Passover" by Rabbi Levy. So it's the perfect ingredient for all your Passover recipes. After all, holiday recipes made with Domino have been a tradition for generations. Domino® America's #1 brand of sugar for over 85 years.

FIG. 10-6. Passover Orange Sponge Cake. Unknown magazine. Personal collection of the author.

spelled in German, and a clipping in English for "Hezekiah Matzo Brei," an egg dish, further enhanced her Passover collection. A "filberts cake," (hazelnuts) made with egg whites, nuts, and sugar, and no flour, would remain a Passover tradition in her household. She seemed very eager to acquire American Jewish Passover recipes, hence the recipes for "Matzo Apple Schalet," "Mocha Sponge Cake," and "Passover Walnut Cake with Chocolate Sauce" that she clipped from Jewish newspapers. Her enthusiasm for these recipes included the sugar ad that she cut out and folded into the box, entitled "The cake good enough to deserve Rabbi Levy's blessing. Passover Orange Sponge Cake made with Domino Sugar."[51]

Her interest in American-Jewish cooking, however, did not mean that she kept a kosher home, something her parents continued to do in the United States. Despite avoiding pork products—with the occasional exception of bacon—at home, her recipe box contained a "shrimp dip," "shrimp marinated," "shrimp-tomato rings," as well as a "shrimp mold" (with the ubiquitous gelatin ingredient). Over about thirty years, while loyal to German meat and potatoes as an everyday staple, she had branched out in both linguistic and culinary terms, adding what she saw as "American" and "American-Jewish" dishes to her expanding cuisine.

Her Passover recipes also underline the importance of family holiday traditions. Tragically, the Nazis destroyed a vast number of German-Jewish families, inalterably changing the postwar dynamic of family gatherings around Jewish foods and customs. Having lost many family members in the Holocaust, holiday gatherings may have taken on extra meaning to postwar Jews: reaffirming the surviving remnants of former families. My mother gathered family from far and wide. For Passover, they came from the local area, from other states in the United States, and frequently from other countries—Canada, Holland, Argentina—to which our family had fled in the Jewish diaspora created by Nazism. She did this because holidays simply meant family to her. Also, she choreographed large numbers of people and abundant food in order both to maintain the religious tradition for her parents and also to pass on to her children a familial-religious-culinary tradition important to her. For this holiday, she sought to acculturate to American Jewish recipes, with the exception of northern German matzoh ball soup (made with matzoh, not matzoh meal). Whereas we can certainly not generalize from one person, this trajectory offers some ideas about the possibilities of food flexibility and food fusion among the newly arrived German Jews.

In sum, then, German Jewish foodways showed adaptability to their surrounding cultures and lands. Jews adjusted with verve to the dessert delights of Central European cultures, willingly called Passover

"Easter," and mixed Sabbath challah with mostly nonkosher meat. They nevertheless retained an aversion to pork and some pork products and maintained family holidays even when they neglected Jewish food rituals. In lands of refuge, they familiarized themselves with newly available foods, from Portuguese fish to Dominican plantains, but retained what they could of the German diet and sought ritual foods for the Jewish holidays. And, finally, in the United States, our *one* sample, my mother, continued, in good German Jewish tradition, to embrace the essence of the German diet (meat, potatoes, and desserts) while reaching out to American and, particularly, American Jewish food cultures.

NOTES

1. Marion Kaplan, "Revealing and Concealing: Memoirs in German-Jewish History," in *Text and Context: Essays in Modern Jewish History and Historiography in Honor of Ismar Schorsch*, ed. Eli Lederhendler and Jack Werthheimer (New York: Jewish Theological Seminary of America, 2005).

2. Ulrich Baumann, *Zerstörte Nachbarschaften: Christen und Juden in badischen Landgemeinden 1862–1940* (Hamburg: Dölling und Galitz, 2000), 113. See also Marion Kaplan, "Unter Uns: Jews Socializing with Other Jews in Imperial Germany," *Leo Baeck Institute Year Book* 48 (2003): 41–65.

3. Early German-Jewish cookbooks appeared in 1815. Between 1815 and 1900 ten titles were published, with each book offering between 300 and 4,000 recipes. Several went through multiple editions. All respected dietary laws, regional variations, and international cuisine. Marion Kaplan, *The Making of the Jewish Middle Class: Women, Family, and Identity in Imperial Germany* (New York: Oxford University Press, 1991), 72.

4. Kaplan, *Making of the Jewish Middle Class*, 73.

5. Heinrich Heine, "Prinzessin Sabbat" [Princess Sabbath]," *Hebräische Melodien* [Hebrew melodies], http://www.textlog.de/heine-gedichte-prinzessin.html. Trans. by the author.

6. Kaplan, *Making of the Jewish Middle Class*, 72.

7. Kaplan, *Making of the Jewish Middle Class*, 72.

8. Toni Ehrlich, "Kindheitserinnerungen," Memoirs, Leo Baeck Institute, New York, 14.

9. Kaplan, *Making of the Jewish Middle Class*, 71.

10. Marion Kaplan, "As Germans and as Jews in Imperial Germany," in *Jewish Daily Life in Germany, 1618–1945*, ed. Marion Kaplan (New York: Oxford University Press, 2005), 246.

11. "Interview with Mrs. Lipton (born 1905)," in *Community of Fate: Memoirs of German Jews in Melbourne*, ed. John Foster (Sydney: Allen and Unwin, 1986), 24.

12. Marie Kauders, *Vollständiges israelitisches Kochbuch: Mit Berücksichtigung der österreichischen, ungarischen, deutschen, französischen und englischen Küche, sowie der Osterküche* (Prag: Jakob B. Brandeis, 1918).

13. Kaplan, *Making of the Jewish Middle Class*, 74.

14. Kaplan, *Making of the Jewish Middle Class*, 74.

15. Kaplan, *Making of the Jewish Middle Class*, 71.

16. Kaplan, "As Germans and Jews," 242.

17. Kaplan, "As Germans and Jews," 279.

18. *Israelitisches Familienblatt* (June 25, 1936).

19. Marion Kaplan, *Between Dignity and Despair: Jewish Life in Nazi Germany* (New York: Oxford University Press, 1998), 17–49.

20. Peter Hanke, *Zur Geschichte der Juden in München zwischen 1933 und 1945* (Munich: Stadtarchiv, 1967), 274.

21. Victor Klemperer, *I Shall Bear Witness: The Diaries of Victor Klemperer, 1933–41*, trans. Martin Chalmers (London: Weidenfeld and Nicolson, 1999), 415.

22. Hermann Pineas, Memoirs, Leo Baeck Institute, New York, 17.

23. Helena Ferro de Gouveia, "Lisbon: From Refuge to Home," DW: *Deutsche Welle* (November 29, 2012), http://www.dw.de/lisbon-from-refuge-to-home/a-16410819.

24. Hermann Kesten, *Dichter im Café* (Wien: Droemer/Knaur, 1959), 12–13.

25. Jan Lustig, *Ein Rosenkranz von Glücksfällen: Protokoll einer Flucht* (Bonn: Weidle, 2001), 93.

26. Howard Wriggins, *Picking up the Pieces from Portugal to Palestine: Quaker Refugee Relief in World War II* (Lanham MD: University Press of America, 2004), 58.

27. "Alix Steel Preece," Re P.III.i, no. 582, 6, Wiener Library.

28. Linda G. Kuzmack, "Oral history interview with Liane Reif-Lehrer," RG50.549 .02*0043, 1999, United States Holocaust Memorial Museum, http://collections .ushmm.org/search/catalog/irn504682.

29. Alfred Döblin, *Destiny's Journey*, ed. Edgar Pässler, trans. Edna McCown (New York: Paragon House, 1992), 215.

30. Lucie W. Weinstein Krebs Holocaust Testimony, HVT-6, Fortunoff Video Archive for Holocaust Testimonies, Yale University Library.

31. George Rony, *This, Too, Shall Pass Away* (New York: Creative Age, 1945), 252–53.

32. Jorge Martins, *Portugal e os Judeus.* Vol. 3: *Judaísmo e anti-semitismo no século XX* (Lisbon: Vega, 2006), 95.

33. Christa Heinrich, ed., *Lissabon 1933-1945: Fluchtstation am Rande Europas: Eine Dokumentationsausstellung des Goethe-Instituts Lissabon* (Berlin: Akademie der Künste amd Haus der Wannsee Konferenz, 1995), 11.

34. Ferro de Gouveia, "Lisbon: From Refuge to Home."

35. Irene Flunser Pimentel, *Judeus em Portugal durante a II Guerra Mundial: Em fuga de Hitler e do Holocausto* (Lisbon: A Esfera dos Livros, 2006), 66.

36. This occurred around 1937. Ferro de Gouveia, "Lisbon: From Refuge to Home."

37. Pimentel, *Judeus em Portugal*, 166.

38. Ferro de Gouveia, "Lisbon: From Refuge to Home."

39. Email from Miriam Sondheimer Gerber to Marion Kaplan, June 14, 2007, in author's possession.

40. "Report of Frederick Perlstein at Board of Directors' Meeting of the Records of the Dominican Republic Settlement Association (DORSA), November 26, 1940," in Reports Sosúa 1940-1945, Records of the Dominican Republic Settlement Association (DORSA), 1939-1977, file #43, American Jewish Joint Distribution Committee, New York Archives.

41. Brookings Institution, *Refugee Settlement in The Dominican Republic: A Survey Conducted under the Auspices of the Brookings Institution* (Washington DC: Brookings Institution, 1942), 89–90, 132, 192.

42. Pierre Bourdieu, *Distinction: A Social Critique of the Judgment of Taste* (Cambridge MA: Harvard University Press, 1984), 72.

43. E. B. Hofeller, "Timetable to Nowhere: A Personal History of the Sosua Settlement," *Leo Baeck Institute Year Book* 45 (2000): 237.

44. Interview with Ernest Weinberg, March 25, 2006.

45. Interview with Ernest Weinberg, March 25, 2006.

46. I. J. Kligler and Helen Kligler, "Report on the Health Survey in Sosua, Dec. 1942," in Reports Sosua 1940-1945, Records of the Dominican Republic Settlement Association (DORSA), 1939-1977, file #43, American Jewish Joint Distribution Committee, New York Archives. Dr. I. J. Kligler was the American head of the Hebrew University's department of hygiene and bacteriology in 1942. These doctors may have been aware that in Palestine, too, settlers resisted giving up meat and fat. Anat Helman, "European Jews in the Levant Heat: Climate and Culture in 1920s and 1930s Tel Aviv," *Journal of Israeli History* 22, no. 1 (2003): 75–81.

47. Kligler and Kligler, "Report on the Health Survey in Sosua, Dec. 1942."
48. Kathleen Doheny, "Craving Carbs: Is It Depression? Many People Crave Carbohydrates when They Feel Low," *WebMD*, http://www.webmd.com/depression/features/craving-carbs#1.
49. Kligler and Kligler, "Report on the Health Survey in Sosua, Dec. 1942."
50. "Report by W. E. Sondheimer on Sosua," (n.d., 1943?), in Reports Sosua 1940–1945, Records of the Dominican Republic Settlement Association (DORSA), 1939–1977, file #43, American Jewish Joint Distribution Committee, New York Archives.
51. *Hadassah Magazine* (n.d.).

11

"To Jewish Daughters"

Recipes for American Jewish Life, 1901–1918

....

ANNIE POLLAND

In February of 1908, "Madame Paley and Madame Amhanitski" announced the opening of their restaurant at 156 East Broadway, the heart of the Lower East Side in New York City. Their advertisements in the Yiddish press highlighted the experience of Amhanitski, who "for years" served "healthy food" to "many friends and acquaintances" at "Amhanitski's restaurant." The ad invited these friends, and ostensibly all the "gentlemen and ladies" who perused the paper, to join them for breakfast, lunch, and dinner at their "strictly kosher" establishment.[1] Paley and Amhanitski certainly were not unique in opening a restaurant to serve the hungry Lower East Side denizens, but most newspaper ads and city directory listings show men as the owners and hosts, even if women served behind scenes.[2] In the case of Paley and Amhanitski's enterprise, however, there were no men. Less than two months earlier, a heart attack had claimed the life of John Paley, the thirty-seven-year-old editor of the *Yidishe Tageblatt*. The Paleys had been living in Borough Park, Brooklyn, a sign of economic mobility, but as Paley's obituaries noted, his death left the "young widow and five beautiful children," all under the age of fifteen, in dire need.[3] Also in the Paley household was John's mother-in-law, Hinde Amhanitski, a widow and retired longtime restaurant entrepreneur. Thus the opening of the East Side restaurant seemed to be in direct response to John Paley's death.[4]

It made sense for Paley to advertise her work with Amhanitski, as the Jewish immigrants undoubtedly remembered the eponymous restaurant right off the centrally located Rutgers Square: as early as 1889 Amhanitski, "widow of Isaac," operated an eating house at 143 East Broadway, and advertisements from the early 1890s referring to S. Amhanitski indicate that Sophia helped run the restaurant before her marriage.[5] Further, in 1901 Hinde published the first Yiddish cookbook in America, *A Manual on How To Cook and Bake*, available in that district's plentiful bookstores and stands, where she noted forty-five years of experience in both European and American kitchens, and in particular highlighted her management of restaurants in New York.[6] By 1905 she had been living with the Paleys in Brooklyn, helping keep house, but Sophia's need to support the family sent Hinde back to the restaurant kitchen. She followed the household to 156 East Broadway, remaining there and, most likely, working until her death in 1910.[7]

While many accounts of the Lower East Side mention the unceasing whir of the sewing machine, and rightly focus on Eastern European Jewish men and teenagers as the drivers of the city's and nation's garment industry, the food business was just as unrelenting, consuming the labor of thousands of tenement women.[8] Though most immigrant Jewish women neither ran restaurants nor published cookbooks, they managed their household economies, collecting the wages of husbands and teenage children and ensuring that the combined wages covered expenses through painstakingly careful shopping and the keeping of boarders. Part and parcel of the economic impulse that brought East European Jews to America in the first place, food enabled many women to be part of the American economy, albeit at its margins. In the semi-autobiographical novel *Bread Givers*, Anzia Yezierska cast into sharp relief this drive to eke out a living through food when a family's economic stress propelled Sara, a child, into the Hester Street pushcart market:

> 'Herring, Herring! A Bargain in the world! Pick them out yourself. Two cents apiece' . . . I cried out my herring with all the burning fire of my ten old years. . . . Nothing was before me but the hunger in our house, and no bread for the next meal if I didn't sell the herring . . . like a houseful of hungry mouths my heart cried, 'Herring, herring, two cents apiece.'[9]

Yezierska did not focus on the herring's taste or its preparation; rather she showed how raw human energy transformed bottom-of-the-barrel fish into the cash desperately needed for the family economy. Notably, an elderly pushcart woman, Muhmenka, guided Sara's Hester Street debut.

Hinde's 1901 cookbook parallels the guidance that Muhmenka offered Sara, and most likely her experience as someone who earned a living through food resonated with tenement women, assuring them that food could be both economical and tasteful. The manual illuminates how the tension between the American market's relative abundance and the persistent need to make a living made business sense essential to the immigrant women's adaptation to American life. Moreover, even as Hinde's 1901 work has a richness in and of itself, its mysterious publication history offers more: somehow, a second edition and third edition appeared after her death. The posthumous "improved and augmented" third edition of Hinde's work in 1918, renamed *The Original Jewish Family Cookbook*, has a slightly altered forward and incongruous additions. In creating the fiction of Hinde's authorship over the entire publication, the editor foisted an entirely new set of homemaking conventions upon the readers.

Looking at the two editions together enables us to examine how the passage of seventeen years during the heyday of immigration changed the perceived outlook and needs of Jewish immigrant women and provides a longer view of their cultural adaptation. Hinde's work is exceptional not just as the first Yiddish cookbook, but for its place among the first Yiddish books authored by a woman in America, and as such is one of the most direct ways to access adaptation from a woman's perspective.[10] An analysis of the first edition, published in 1901, and the third edition, published in 1918, sheds light on the role of food in immigrant women's lives, and underscores the breadth of these women's jobs as mothers, cooks, and businesswomen.

THE 1901 COOKBOOK: HINDE AND HER READERS

The very title of the 1901 edition — *Manual for Cooking and Baking* — dispensed with the notion of cooking as amusement or frivolity. This practical pamphlet guided housewives through the day, week, and holiday seasons. The cover photo of Hinde, modestly dressed and wearing the wig of an observant woman, suggests a homey female relative — a mother, or perhaps an aunt. Indeed, in her introduction she addressed the readers as "dear daughters" and her writing conveys the comfortable, clear tone of a trusted, if stern, relative. Hinde shared no other personal information about herself, other than her forty-five years of kitchen experience and her work as a restaurant entrepreneur.[11] The photo on the manual's cover shows her as a mature woman, one who has indeed acquired almost a half-century of experience. And perhaps the very lack of personal details helped her stand in as a mother or aunt for as many immigrant women as possible.

Some immigrant women might have invested their fifteen cents in the manual not just for the recipes, but for a maternal guidance they often lacked in the new country.[12] The Jewish immigration was relatively young, and many women came to America without their own mothers and entered into marriage and motherhood without their advice.[13] At the same time, they encountered new ideas, styles, fashions, and modes of living that their mothers could never have imagined, not to mention an array of new produce, goods, seasonings, and diets. Hinde's old-fashioned appearance perhaps served as maternal reassurance, even as the guidance reflected a thorough knowledge of the ins and outs of certain American genres of cooking.

Even with this maternal element woven into the presentation, Hinde clearly did not expect tenement housewives to purchase the cookbook solely on the basis of her appearance. She seemed to have sensed that these women needed persuasion and thus presented a cogent, five-pronged justification for the fifteen-cent expenditure. First, she highlighted the recipes themselves, assuring the reader that they were "purely Jewish dishes," culled from "the finest Jewish homes in Russia, Galicia, Hungary, France, England and America." On one level, this might suggest that she traveled and worked in a variety of kitchens, and raised the important background of East European Jews migrating within Europe as well as immigrating to the United States in the late nineteenth and early twentieth century. Even within Eastern Europe, commercial ties brought various Jewish regional cuisines in contact.

From what we can glean from available census records, Hinde was born in Russia in the 1840s and arrived in the United States in the early to mid-1880s. Once on the Lower East Side Hinde joined the burgeoning East European Jewish community, composed of migration streams from Russia, Galicia, and Hungary (some of which stopped in England before coming to the United States) as well as Central European influences from prior waves of immigrant Jews and non-Jews, some of whom continued to live or operate businesses in the neighborhood in the 1890s. Hinde's restaurants right off of Rutgers Square placed her at the neighborhood's epicenter, the headquarters of newspapers, bookstores, and cafes. She cooked for a clientele with a variety of backgrounds, most likely slowly folding new recipes into her repertoire. On another level, noting these various points of origin also ensured that Galician, Russian, and Hungarian housewives would equally feel comfortable purchasing the book.

Whether Galician, Russian, or Hungarian, the Lower East Side housewife would certainly appreciate Hinde's second, most salient point: "Forty five years of experience in cooking, baking, frying and roasting have taught me how to make things very economically; that is, it will cost the cheapest and taste the best, and you can have the benefit of my long years of experience for just a few cents—the price of my book is only 15 cents." Again, here Hinde emphasized her experience, assuring the women that good taste does not have to strain the pocketbook and mentioning the low cost four times in one sentence. Cooking well, she argued in point three, and drawing upon the "tasty" recipes in her book also served another familial purpose, bringing "satisfaction" to the family and protecting the children from "dyspepsia and other maladies." Hinde explained that her "clear" language made the cookbook accessible to women, especially those who would like to "surprise . . . husband and family with the finest, tastiest recipes that refresh the soul and strengthen the body." In closing, Hinde reminded readers that her business experience substantiated all the points: "The best guarantee that my manual will be very useful to every woman and will bring complete satisfaction to every house is the fact that for years I had a restaurant in New York where [we served] the finest people with their capricious tastes and all have been satisfied with my food."[14]

Hinde's introduction lends insight on the perceived concerns of the vast majority of immigrant women who might not have run their own restaurants, but certainly had to negotiate the limitations of their family budgets, not to mention the sometimes divergent tastes of their husbands, children, and boarders. The Lower East Side quickly developed a robust food economy, ranging from the pushcart markets to small groceries and restaurants: an 1899 study of the neighborhood found 631 "food mongers," with groceries, butcher shops, fruit stands, butter and egg stores, candy stores, fish stores, milk stores, sausage stores, and vegetable stores.[15] While census records and city directories list men as storeowners, memoir literature, as well as photographs and postcards of the street markets, show how often these enterprises depended on women's labor. At 97 Orchard Street, for example, Goldie Lustgarten and her children helped her husband, Israel, run their kosher butcher store.[16] The memoir of Jacob Schwartz, whose family ran another butcher store on Orchard, recalled his mother's interest in the store: "Mother perked up her ears and expressed her general satisfaction with the plan because she was aching to become active."[17] While social mores often prevented Jewish married women from working outside the home for wages, nothing prevented them from working in the family store. The tenement structures accommodated this, as often shops had "rooms" in the back for the family; this arrangement lent itself to women balancing both business and household duties.[18]

Whether they ran official businesses, tenement women assumed the responsibility of managing their household accounts. Indeed, almost every tenement mother, wife, or head of household in the tenement served as the family accountant, and in most cases a landlady of sorts. The demographics of the immigrant Jewish family in particular demanded women's economic involvement. Most Jewish immigrants came in family groups, increasing pressure to find jobs immediately upon arrival. At 97 Orchard, for example, fifteen out of twenty households had children living with them in 1900, with an average of 3.6 children per household.[19] As Samuel Joseph explained in 1914, "Jewish immigrants are burdened with a far greater number of dependents than any other immigrant people." Between 1899 and 1910, because of the high proportion of women and children, 45 percent of Jews arriving in the United States listed "no occupation."[20] Jewish immigrants negotiated this strain, in part, by taking in boarders and relying on the wages of their teenage children.

As much as these migration patterns placed inordinate pressure on the young and relatively full households to eke out a living, they also provided opportunities. Jewish families came as part of a chain migration, with husbands and fathers leaving first, securing a job and a place to live, and then sending funds and tickets to bring the rest of the family. As they saved, they often lived as boarders in other homes. Young workers who came without families similarly lived as boarders. This supply of boarders, then, met the economic demand of the households which had reunited but now needed to pay rent and support multiple dependents. Keeping boarders provided crucial income for many Jewish families. In 1910, 43 percent of Jewish homes surveyed in seven U.S. cities had boarders, and in New York City, 56 percent of Jewish homes had boarders.[21] This mutually beneficial situation enabled a boarder to pay several dollars a week and not be bothered with housecleaning or food preparation, while a family earned extra income, often on the shoulders of the women.

Hinde's cookbook might be rationalized as a business expense, as tenement women handled the cash transactions and work involved in maintaining a boarder. Abraham Kokofsky's recollections of boarder management identified his mother as the decision maker. Their Clinton Street apartment accommodated Abraham, his brother, and his father in one room and his mother and sisters in another; a third room housed boarders: "I'm sure that the only reason my mother was willing to give up that bedroom [was] because without that money she couldn't feed the family and pay rent."[22] Keeping boarders was thus closely bound to women's role as chief manager of household funds. It demanded physical strength and keen strategizing. According to Harry Golden, with regard to the household and the renting of apartments, "Mother made all the decisions."[23] Women shopped daily and lugged water for cleaning, cooking, and laundry up and down stairs.

This work also involved constant social networking. Boarders would eventually have to be replaced; the need to pay the landlord, however, remained constant. Establishing a reputation as a good cook aided one in the retention and attraction of boarders. Further, Hinde's point that her clientele had "capricious" tastes probably resonated with immigrant women cooking for their husbands, children, and rotating series of boarders. Given all the time women spent shopping and cooking, having a guide and a storehouse of tried-and-true recipes would be well worth the fifteen-cent investment, roughly the cost of a pound of kosher meat.

Shortly after Hinde published her cookbook, the price of kosher meat skyrocketed, and immigrant Jewish women harnessed their consumer and political power to protest. In the spring of 1902, wholesalers set into motion increases that raised the retail price of a pound of kosher meat from twelve to eighteen cents, prompting demonstrations and a widespread boycott. Historian Paula Hyman's groundbreaking analysis showed how working-class, immigrant women became direct political actors and attracted the city's attention. Journalistic accounts (both the English-language papers and the Yiddish papers) revealed how mothers justified the protests in their responsibility to feed their families as well as their pride in their own household management. "Our husbands work hard . . . they try their best to bring a few cents into the house. We must manage to spend as little as possible." This point—that the husbands hand over the hard-earned wages to their wives—was a common refrain: "My husband brings me eight dollars a week. Should I give it away to the butcher? What would the landlord say?" In protesting the price of meat, they also adamantly defended their role as managers of household funds.[24]

As the strike wound down in mid-June, the *New York Tribune* reported on a consortium of women who had opened a cooperative: "It has been a women's strike throughout, and its efficiency shows what power lies in the hands of the administrator of the family funds. 'Men buy for themselves; women buy for the family,' is the old trade axiom, which has received salient illustration in this boycott." The reporter also noted consortium leader Sarah Cohen's astute business sense, even elevating her as a model for all "American housewives."[25] This coverage shows not only women's management of the household economy, but also the ways in which household business sense could apply to communal and commercial endeavors.

The boycott, of course, shows immigrant women's reliance on kosher meat. Clearly Americanization had not dimmed their allegiance to the laws of kashrut, for if it had, the increase in kosher meat would not have sparked such an uproar. It also underlined Americanization and how its abundance had made meat much more accessible to the Jewish immigrants.[26] Orchard Street alone had thirty stores on a four-block span in 1900.[27] Hinde's recipes likewise demonstrate how embedded meat had become in the weekly diet. Her table of contents features soup recipes that often start with meat, whether called tomato, green pea, sour soup, or bean soup. Meat then takes center stage, with recipes for English pot roast, French cutlets, "French balls," goulash, stuffed spleen, stuffed veal breast, lamb cutlets, hamburger steak, stew, "old style" roast beef, steak, and chopped liver. The index includes recipes for chicken and goose, and just a few for fish.

In the introduction to her manual, Hinde refers to all the recipes as "purely Jewish dishes" and uses this term to encompass both American innovations and traditional holiday dishes. American styles of cooking had begun to influence the tenement kitchen: Hinde added "macaroni" to the chicken soup. Hinde shared recipes for nine pies, the quintessential American dessert. "Cranberry strudel" might have been a nod to Thanksgiving.[28] Hinde kept the Jewish holidays in mind, though she does not highlight them as more Jewish or traditional than the other recipes. A recipe for challah, the traditional braided egg loaves for the Sabbath, follows cookies. Recipes for poppy cake and butter cookies sandwich a cheesecake recipe that might work for the spring holiday of Shavuot and its emphasis on dairy. A citron cake that could be connected to the fall harvest holiday of Sukkot is between sponge cake and corn bread. The fact that these recipes simply appear in the cookbook without great fanfare attests to the notion that they didn't need to be explained and could be taken as a matter of course.

Passover recipes, however, warranted their own section, a testament to the planning, coordination, and labor needed to rid the home of leavened foods and ensure meals throughout the week. Starting in February, all the Yiddish newspapers published advertisements for Passover products: wine, matzo, matzo meal. Sidney Roth, who grew up in the Lower East Side in the early 1900s, recalled both his mother's cleaning of the home and storing of the goods:

Passover preparations started months before the holiday. Beginning about Chanukah, when my mother went shopping for chickens, for "Shabbos," she bought only chickens with a lot of fat, because now was the time to start saving "Schmaltz for Pesach." . . . So mama started collecting chicken fat which she kept in a special stone "Pesachdige" crock, covered with a blanket, in a corner that was already prepared for Pesach.[29]

Selma Katz recalled how her mother, a divorcée with five children who struggled economically and could not afford different sets of dishes for Passover, would simply "go on a pushcart and buy dishes just to use for Passover, buy new dishes. And then she'd use them for a whole year and then the next Passover, buy new dishes."[30] While the children of immigrants recall their mother's preparations, the pushcart market and the small stores similarly attest to how the mothers' preparations for Passover influenced the look and feel of the neighborhood. A *Forward* reporter in 1914 explained that in the United States, "Columbus" weakened Passover, as workers might arrive late to the Seder, the holiday meal, or hasten to the shop on Passover morning. Yet he conceded how the eve of Passover had "not been diminished by even a hair," as demonstrated by the preparations in the home and reflected in the market. "It boils and it hums with matzo, wine, horseradish, onions and greens; pots, furniture, oil cloth, graters, iron handles . . . matzo meal and whatever you'd like" at the markets on Hester, Rivington, and Orchard Streets and in satellite Jewish neighborhoods in Brooklyn and the Bronx.[31]

The reporter also cleverly adapted a Passover Seder refrain on how Passover differed from all other nights, noting that while during the entire year the "housewife" runs to the market for small items, "here a little pepper, there an onion," on Passover she purchases a week's worth of groceries in one fell swoop. Anne Goldman's mother, a widow, ran a butter and egg store on Eighth Street in the 1910s and 1920s, and she recalled how "People would make all their preparations at home. So it wasn't unusual for a family to buy a box of eggs—which consists of 30 dozen eggs—because they make their own cake, they made everything themselves. They didn't buy anything prepared; everything was made at home. So we were very, very busy."[32]

In the midst of the busy season, Hinde's "For Passover" section thus helped transform the market's raw ingredients into baked potato latkes, matzo-meal pudding, matzo balls, blintzes, kugels, and Passover soup noodles; more broadly, Hinde helped immigrant women adapt Jewish customs and traditions to the tenement districts. As all these reports show, women's work—whether standing behind the cart or counter or shopping for the goods—created Passover in these neighborhoods. The tensions of migration and settlement, it has been argued, posed more obstacles to the Jewish male's role than to the Jewish women's role. By virtue of the fact that the Jewish male's work responsibilities often directly conflicted with the traditional male ideal of scholarship and, in many cases, daily and Sabbath prayer, Jewish women, whose chief obligations remained in the home, could maintain their Jewish rituals.[33] That said, these tenement housewives likewise encountered challenges to their rhythms and patterns, and Hinde's inclusion of the Passover section in a cookbook that also featured American pies and new ingredients implicitly assured the reader that one might both adapt to the American market and its abundance, but still maintain Jewish traditions.[34]

Just as Hinde assumed a certain familiarity with the Jewish holidays and traditions, and felt no need to gloss over their meanings, so too did she assume a certain familiarity with the recipes and her readers. Her tone is direct and matter-of-fact; one could imagine her sharing a recipe with a favored restaurant patron. Though the frontispiece promised that the recipes would help "every Jewish woman learn how to cook and to bake," the recipes presumed the readers' understanding of the basics. Rarely did she specify amounts; more often, in place of measurements she instructed readers to pour a "half glass of water" into the bowl without specifying the size of the glass or to simply "take . . . a little flour and some salt," or "take out cooked meat from soup, and chop it very thinly. Cook a bit of fat and pour in a half glass of flour." The recipes stand on their own; occasionally, though, she added a warning, "See to it that it doesn't burn," or a pronouncement, "And this is the best tomato soup."

Even in its minimalism, Hinde's cookbook provided assurance and guidance. As Haym Soloveitchik has written, East European Jewish immigrants found themselves "wrenched . . . from a familiar life and an accustomed environment" and in a "strange country where even stranger manners prevailed." If women could no longer learn Jewish traditions mimetically, from watching their mothers, they could absorb ways of American Jewish life through Hinde's instructions and selections. As one of the first Yiddish books published by a woman in America, the cookbook served as perhaps one of the only guides to American life for Yiddish-speaking housewives who might have been reluctant or simply too busy to visit the settlement houses. In the two decades after Hinde published the manual, advice literature for new immigrants flourished.

HINDE'S COOKBOOK LIVES ON

When Hinde Amhanitski passed away on May 15, 1910, not one news-paper printed a death notice, let alone an obituary; this despite the fact that she ran restaurants in the heart of the newspaper district for at least twenty years. Yet, arguably, the coming decade created more of an audience for her work. Surprisingly, 1916 advertisements in *Varhayt* and in the *Morgen zhurnal* heralded Amhanitski's *Original Jewish Family Cookbook*, available for twenty-five cents at S. Druckerman's bookstore, 50 Canal Street. The ad lifted copy from the 1901 manual's frontispiece, proclaiming this a "book that every Jewish woman needs."[35] More dramatically, in 1918 Druckerman reintroduced this *Original Jewish Family Cookbook* for sixty cents as a new "augmented and improved" edition. Neither notice mentioned Hinde's death. To the contrary, the 1918 volume used Hinde's introduction, with slight adaptations, thereby deliberately creating the impression that Hinde was still alive. The editor appended a wholly new sentence at the end of her introduction: "Therefore, beloved sisters, I hand over the key from my long years of practicing the art of cooking and baking. Use it and enjoy it and remember me well. From your sister, Hinde Amhanitski."[36]

Though Hinde had died, the editor surmised that Jewish women still sought cooking advice from another Jewish woman. Hinde's Yiddish cookbook remained relatively unique almost two decades after its debut. In 1914, the Hebrew Publishing Company issued H. Braun's *The Family Cookbook*, which perhaps prompted Druckerman to reissue Hinde's work and change the name to *Original Jewish Family Cookbook*.[37] We can presume that S. Druckerman hoped that the tenement women remained an important market and audience, and in turn perhaps felt that Hinde's voice was the imprimatur needed to appeal to them and mark the cookbook as different from, and perhaps more authentic than, Braun's.

Immigrant women in 1916–18, in many respects, maintained the same interests as those who had purchased the 1901 edition, but they also had new ones. Many immigrants continued to scrape by, and cooking for families, managing households, and tending to boarders remained top priorities; to this point, in February of 1917 thousands led a boycott protesting the high costs of produce and poultry. Yet by 1918, the population and its concerns had shifted. The Jewish population dispersed well beyond the Lower East Side; at the time of the publication of the first book, roughly half of New York City's Jewish population lived on the Lower East Side, but by the time of the publication of the second, less than a quarter did.[38] Further, World War I had temporarily halted immigration and perhaps the need to keep boarders attenuated slightly. Some of the women who might have purchased Hinde's cookbook in 1901 now found themselves in the outer boroughs, in decidedly less crowded but still very Jewish neighborhoods.

Take, for example, the trajectory of Hinde's daughters. As we know, in 1910 Sophia ran the restaurant on East Broadway; just down the block, at 229 East Broadway, her sister Louisa Lamport and her husband, Samuel, appear to be running a boarding house. By 1920 they no longer resided at their place of business, and all had moved to the more affluent neighborhood of Borough Park, Brooklyn, and held white-collar jobs.[39] Presumably, Hinde's "literary" daughters and sisters also started to encounter middle-class neighborhoods, ideas, and aspirations. Thus, by 1918 even as food and accounting preoccupied new immigrant women, some of the older immigrants settled into more comfortable neighborhoods and ostensibly had additional concerns.

Beyond their class status or residence, the Yiddish publications of the 1910s, whether in the form of advice literature or the newspapers' women's pages, all spoke to expanded ideas about mothers' responsibilities to family, nutrition, health, and child-rearing. Between 1901 and 1918 advice literature and how-to guides for Yiddish-speaking immigrants burgeoned. In 1902, for example, Abraham Cahan, the editor of the *Jewish Daily Forward*, had just begun to experiment with inviting readers' responses to debates and thematic questions; by 1906 he launched the famous "Bintel Brief," enabling readers to turn to the newspaper editors for advice. Soon all the Yiddish newspapers followed suit, and by 1918 many of the Yiddish newspapers, including the *Tog*, the *Tageblatt* and the *Forverts*, featured women's pages. In 1913, the *Froyen velt*, a short-lived Yiddish newspaper for women, published articles on housekeeping; and from 1923 to 1924 the *Froyen zhurnal* published articles on fashion, cooking, Jewish holidays, and Jewish women in history.[40] Yiddish how-to-guides and pamphlets, governing all aspects of daily life, from etiquette to sex, grew in number and style in the 1910s, appealing to immigrant Jews who, as historian Eli Lederhendler has shown, were "undergoing cultural shock" and needed a "'user's guide' in the form of secular Jewish culture."[41]

Hinde's cookbook helps us move away from the tendency to categorize some subjects as religious and others as secular, pinpointing areas undergoing change and priming us to better consider the ultimate role immigrant women, as leaders of their family's Americanization, had in determining the course of their family's practices. Though Lederhendler categorized the new genre of advice literature as "secular," the topics in the advice literature corresponded with issues of daily life that had been under religious purview. Jewish law not only encompasses prayer and study, "but equally food, drink, dress, sexual relations between man and wife, the rhythms of work and the patterns of rest." These guides to daily life, then, even if not written by Jewish scholars, pinpointed the arenas in which Jewish housewives now had to decide whether or not to adapt or dispense with traditional Jewish laws and customs. They also indicated where ignorance might have taken root, requiring education. From another perspective, overtly religious books compiling women's supplications or bar mitzvah speeches might also be considered part of this realm of literature geared to a popular audience, with intent to instruct and inform daily life.[42]

How did Hinde's 1901 manual compare to the 1918 cookbook? As noted, Druckerman not only reprinted, with an amended introduction, the original 1901 version, he also added sections on "1) vegetable and vegetarian dishes; 2) A clean household; 3) How to keep the household economy in order; 4) What to eat and what to drink in the hot summer months; 5) How to keep a strictly kosher kitchen." While most of the introductory copy from the 1901 version remained, the 1918 version replaced Hinde's photo with a new logo and Star of David. Perhaps Druckerman realized that the seventeen-year-old picture of a woman who already had accrued forty-five years of experience might raise questions regarding authenticity, or perhaps he felt the decidedly old-fashioned picture might look a bit too traditional for some potential purchasers. Nevertheless, the justifications for the book remained the same: the recipes reflected the writer's long experience in kitchens, billing the "Jewish dishes" as tasty and healthy, and lauding Hinde's restaurant experience as the best guarantee of the book's usefulness.

As we've seen, Hinde's 1901 cookbook prominently featured meat. The fact that the bulk of the 1918 additions focused on "vegetables and veg-etarian dishes" seemed incongruous, and of course, readers might have wondered how the first, intact section treated meat as a fundamental, and a second section practically eschewed it. Further, the prominent attention to vegetables in 1918 starkly contrasts to the original section, which ignored vegetables other than potatoes and onions, a few recipes for green beans and cabbage notwithstanding. A reader understandably might have wondered how her conversion to the glories of vegetables had not been explained or even alluded to in the introduction.

The tone changed too. The sections had a much more instructive, at times even didactic tone. Consider a section on "how to cook spinach": "Jewish housewives neglect almost entirely such useful greens as *spinat*, or "spinach" as they call it in English. Those who do cook it, throw out the water which contains minerals and also iron. . . . The most important thing about cooking spinach is not how to cook it, but how to wash it."[43] Or this section on "stuffed onions": "Jewish housewives use onions for the most part only to season a recipe of meat or fish. But one can make entirely tasty meals from onions."[44]

The reference to neglectful "Jewish housewives" differs considerably from the matter-of-fact, inclusive tone used for one's daughters or sisters in the original manual. References to minerals and iron, and the incorporation of precise measurements (quarts, teaspoons) and timing directions (soak for twelve hours; fry for ten minutes) further distinguished the second section. Moreover, some of the recipes seem to echo the nutrition that might have been taught at settlement houses, including bran muffins, onions stuffed with peanut butter, and "hygienic" bread. New ideas on vegetarian cooking specifically might have influenced recipes for walnut, bean, and celery "cutlets."[45] While Hinde published recipes for a variety of compotes, from apple to quince, she probably would have been surprised to see one made from "watermelon rinds" in the new edition.[46]

The additional sections also lend the impression that the "Jewish housewife" has more *time* to consider household advice and more household *space* than the 1901 tenement dweller. Whereas Hinde focused solely on the recipes, in the expanded version, chapters teach women "how to freshen up old bread" or "how to freshen up a cake." Tenement kitchens had relatively little space for food storage, rendering this advice more useful to those who had moved to roomier accommodations. The sections also integrate ideas on health and nutrition: in the summer months, avoid too much meat, eat greens and fruit (but not too much). Do not drink beer; do drink seltzer, preferably "plain" without sweet syrups.

The section on a "clean home" blends medical advice with housecleaning. A housewife needs to keep a home clean "not because she should be burdened with lots of work," but rather because her oversight of a clean home keeps the children healthy, "and the mother has the obligation of keeping her children from disease." The section then offers instructions on cleaning in an all-knowing tone—"one can clean a home in a correct or a false way"—that dissuades the housewife from simply moving the dust from one area of the home into another area. Most tellingly, in a section on the best tools for keeping a clean and healthy home, the book advises housewives to use a broom and a soft damp cloth; moreover, they should employ fresh air and the sun and make sure to clean their closets.[47] Given Hinde's understanding of the tenement apartments, notorious for their lack of windows and space, one wonders whether this emphasis on fresh air and sun might be geared more to the women who had moved to the sunnier apartment buildings—replete with windows and closets—in parts of Brooklyn and the Bronx.

The most distinctive difference is the need for a section on keeping a kosher home, with specific subheadings on the laws of salting meat, insects (and how they might relegate water and foods nonkosher), challah, and the holidays.[48] The 1890s advertisements for Hinde's restaurants did not mention kashrut; likewise the 1901 manual emphasized Jewish meals, but did not specifically address kashrut. To a certain extent, kashrut was assumed in this period among the Jewish immigrant community. However, when the restaurant opened in 1908, advertisements mentioned that it was "strictly kosher," implying that other, nonkosher restaurants had opened. By 1918, the fact that Druckerman added a section on how to keep a kosher home to Hinde's cookbook suggests that immigrant women and their daughters might not know how to keep a kosher home.

To this point, a 1908 feature article in the *Tageblatt* detailed how one man had fallen in love with a Jewish girl and, on the verge of proposing, discovered that she knew nothing about "Jewishness: not from the Sabbath and not from kashruth." He loved her dearly, but refused to marry a woman unversed in governing a Jewish home. A solution, however, presented itself when the prospective fiancée agreed to live with the young man's mother in order to receive instructions in the essential laws; a crash course, so to speak, in becoming a "kosher" Jewish daughter. In 1913, a writer in the *Froyen velt* lamented how the early entry of daughters into the factory truncated their learning experiences in the home: "They had no Jewish education but a factory education instead. Because of this mistake we have lost an entire generation."[49] Presumably, the added section on keeping a kosher home functioned as the "mother-in-law's" crash course in Jewishness, attempting to reach the lost generation.

Why, though, combine sections on kashrut, vegetarianism, and cleaning? Was Druckerman trying to espouse a traditional, vegetarian, Orthodox, settlement house ideology of some sort? Or was he just trying to pad the cookbook to make more money? Or both? This kind of cobbled together, posthumous publication was not necessarily out of the ordinary, as booksellers and publishers did not stringently observe copyright laws. Simon Druckerman's store at 50 Canal Street was located around the corner from Hinde's restaurant. Possibly they had met at the restaurant or the bookstore; perhaps she entrusted him with the book and had given him verbal or even written permission to print her cookbook. But this is not necessarily the case. As the historian Eric Goldstein explains, Lower East Side booksellers and publishers did not understand works to be the intellectual property of the author but instead viewed books as merchandise, and the publisher then had the liberty to repackage, reissue, rearrange as he saw fit.[50] If indeed the rival Hebrew Publishing Company's publication of H. Braun's *The Family Cookbook* prompted Druckerman to repackage Hinde's work, he might have felt the need to add more sections so that it could compete with the

Braun's more substantial work. The historian Jacob Rader Marcus, upon reviewing the Druckerman book catalogues, explained that it carried works on socialism and anarchism, but featured works on Orthodoxy and Zionism, specializing in books with a populist religious bent.[51] Thus, adding the section on kashrut at the end would have been right in line with his focus on literature that explained and encouraged religious practice among the masses.

Whereas many of the tenement women in 1901 focused on food as a business, cared for boarders, and navigated the pushcart market, by 1918 Yiddish advice literature lends the impression that they also paid, or needed to pay, more attention to the project of Americanization. In a 1918 book, *Di heym un di froy* (The home and the woman) Hayim Malitz upped the ante with regard to cooking. Serving meals entailed more than putting food on the table; it also encompassed keeping the family together and creating space for parents to guide children. Malitz lamented that the strains of immigration and adaptation made the American Jewish family life one in which children often took the lead, dismissing the parents' advice. Meals provided the opportunity to correct this trend: "It is therefore one of the most important things in family life to put in order once and for all, that in the evening for supper the entire family needs to sit together by the table."[52] Likewise, the strains of immigration on the Jewish family would continue to have reverberations into the next decades. *Mayn Etsah*, a 1931 compilation of 1920s advice letters, similarly acknowledged the prevalence of family stress:

> If you can find in America a single Jewish immigrant family of the first or second generation of immigration, without signs of strain and estrangement among members, then that family is a rare exception. If the strains don't come from economic reasons, they come from religious, social or cultural differences.[53]

By 1918, immigrant women, and also their American-born daughters who grew up in the tenement districts, faced not just the managing of accounts and the placing of food on the table, but the broader project of how to create a strong familial culture. Hinde's 1901 instructions on preparing food still mattered, but new ideas and duties—keeping a family healthy, infusing one's diet not only with Jewish tradition but the most scientific and nutritious ideas, and balancing the broader strains of moving into a more American, middle-class lifestyle—demanded even more guidance.

In May of 1902, as the kosher meat boycott hit its peak, *Forverts* featured a front-page drawing of an immigrant housewife leading the charge against the Meat Trust, with a bold caption: "The power of the women." At the turn of the twentieth century, when Hinde's manual first came out, and as captured by the boycott, the power of women manifested itself chiefly in the marketplace and in the household accounting. By 1918, when Druckerman's edition of Hinde's manual appeared, women's power had in some ways grown to encompass a broader project of Americanization. As various organizations and newspapers vied to spread their ideological messages—whether it was the Sabbath Support Association viewing women as agents of consumer protest and asking them to shop exclusively at Sabbath observant shops or *Forverts* spreading its socialist rhetoric in the women's pages—all seemed to understand the importance of women as arbiters of the home and family culture, and the necessity of reaching them.

As much as we can read these books and articles as a sign that immigrant families needed guidance, we can also read into them the power of the women. In that much of the literature offered a range of advice, and there was no clear, ultimate authority, Druckerman's version of Hinde's cookbook, with its mingling of vegetarian, Orthodox, and settlement house ideologies perfectly demonstrates the broader situation, in which women were privy to a range of advice. At the end of the day, they were the ones reconciling ideas from works like Malitz's *The Home and the Woman* and *Forverts*' women's pages, or even the multitude of ideas packaged in the 1918 cookbook. As some of the sheer economic pressures of the earlier days subsided, they now grappled with the broader project of Americanization and had a decisive role in figuring out what, exactly, that meant in their homes and neighborhoods. The power of the women that came to the fore so strongly in the boycott persisted in the more mundane, but critical cultural and social impact they had on the family and neighborhood.

NOTES

1. *Varhayt*, February 18, 1908; *Varhayt*, February 23, 1908; *Varhayt*, February 24, 1908. See also *Morgen zhurnal*, March 1, 1908.

2. In 1902, *Trow's New York City Directory* restaurant section listed 275 Lower East Side establishments; of these, only 13 listed women's names. *Trow's General Directory of the Boroughs of Manhattan and the Bronx for the Year Ending July 1, 1903* (New York: Trow Directory, Printing, and Bookbinding Company, 1902), 1126–42.

3. *Tageblatt*, December 24, 1907.

4. Another ad in the *Morgen zhurnal* describes the restaurant as "Mrs. Paley's" but noted that it was "under the management of Mrs. Amhanitski." *Morgen zhurnal*, March 1, 1908.

5. *Trow's New York City Directory for the Year Ending May 1, 1890* (New York: Trow, 1889). In 1891, a Louisa Amchanitski (who appears to be another daughter of Hinde, is listed in the NYC directory as running the restaurant at 143 E. Broadway, and the following year, at 138 E. Broadway). Another ad in the *Arbeter Tsaytung* in 1890 announces "S. Amchanitski's" restaurant, with the S. most likely referring to Sophia. The 1905 New York State Census shows "Anna Amhanitski" listed as the mother-in-law of John Paley, husband of Sophia in Brooklyn. New York State Census, Kings, AD 21, ED 24, Block I, June 1, 1905. In 1890s, ads in the *Freie Arberter Shtime* and the *Arbeter Tsaytung* mention S. Amhanitski's restaurant at 143 E. Broadway, with the "best food and most refined people" and says that "the best proof of how good our food is, is that all the most refined people eat here." *Freie Arberter Shtime*, March 14, 1890; *Arbeter Tsaytung*, March 4, 1890.

6. Hinde Amhanitski, *Lehr-bukh vi azoy tsu kuken und baken* (New York: Amhanitski, 1901).

7. Although the *Lehr-bukh* has very little information about Hinde's biography or restaurant career, a strange turn of events a century after her death placed a professional genealogist on the case. In 2010, an East Village resident discovered a lone headstone with Hebrew writing and brought it to the attention of *New York Times* reporter Sam Roberts. In turn, he found Megan Smolenyak Smolenyak, whose research located Hinde's gravesite at the United Hebrew

Cemetery in Staten Island as well as uncovered important—if conflicting—clues to her biography. My research in the Yiddish press, city directories, and censuses led me to the restaurant history. Megan Smolenyak, *Hey America, Your Roots Are Showing* (New York: Citadel Press, 2012); Sam Roberts, "The Curious Mystery of the Sidewalk Tombstone," *New York Times*, July 7, 2010.

8. Alan M. Kraut, "The Butcher, the Baker, the Pushcart Peddler: Jewish Food-ways and Entrepreneurial Opportunity in the East European Community (1880–1940)," *Journal of American Culture* 6, no. 4 (1983): 71–83.

9. Anzia Yezierska, *Bread Givers* (New York: Persea Books, 1975 [1925]), 21–22.

10. More research needs to be done to establish whether Hinde's book could actually be considered the first book in Yiddish by a Jewish woman in America.

11. The historical record is scanty and contradictory. The 1910 census enumerator, for example, recorded her age as forty-nine on April 15, while her death certificate and headstone from May 15, 1910 lists her as eighty-seven years old. Her daughters were born in 1865/1870, therefore she was probably born in the 1840s. If she immigrated at the same time as her daughters, she would have come sometime between 1882 and 1885; by 1889 she is listed as the widow of Isaac.

12. Maxine Schwartz Seller, "World of Our Mothers: The Women's Page of the Jewish Daily Forward," *Journal of Ethnic Studies* 16 (1988): 95–118.

13. Samuel Joseph, *Jewish Immigration to the United States from 1881 to 1910* (New York: Columbia University, 1914), 128; Susan Glenn, *Daughters of the Shtetl* (Ithaca NY: Cornell University Press, 1990), x.

14. Amhanitski, *Lehr-bukh vi azoy tsu kuken und baken.*

15. Moses Rischin, *The Promised City* (Cambridge MA: Harvard University Press, 1962), 56.

16. A family photo, circa 1890, shows the family in front of the store, all clad in aprons. Collection of the Lower East Side Tenement Museum.

17. Jacob Schwartz, Memoir, Collection of the Seward Park Branch of the New York Public Library.

18. Kraut, "The Butcher, the Baker, the Pushcart Peddler," 75.

19. In general, each Jewish wage earner supported 1.8 people, as compared to a non-Jewish immigrant, who supported 1.3 people. Between 1899 and 1914, women constituted 30 percent of all other immigrant groups to the United States, while among Jewish immigrants, women accounted for 44 percent. In the same time period, children under the age of fourteen made up 11 percent of non-Jewish immigrants, and 25 percent of Jewish immigrants.

20. Joseph, *Jewish Immigration to the United States*, 140, 145.

21. Glenn, *Daughters of the Shtetl*, 68–69.

22. Abraham Kokofsky, NS 33–64, Lower East Side Oral History Project, Tamiment Institute, Tamiment Library and Robert F. Wagner Archives, New York University.

23. Harry Golden, "East Side Memoir, 1910s," in *Autobiographies of American Jews*, ed. Harold U. Ribalow (Philadelphia: Jewish Publication Society, 1968), 309.

24. Paula E. Hyman, "Immigrant Women and Consumer Protest: The New York Kosher Meat Boycott of 1902," *American Jewish History* 70, no. 1 (1980): 91–105.

25. "Anti-Trust Women," *New York Tribune*, June 15, 1902, 7.

26. Hasia R. Diner, *Hungering for America: Italian, Irish, and Jewish Foodways in the Age of Migration* (Cambridge MA: Harvard University Press, 2001), 180.

27. Map of kosher butchers on Orchard Street, 1900, Collection of the Lower East Side Tenement Museum.

28. Jane Ziegelman, *97 Orchard: An Edible History of Five Immigrant Families in One New York Tenement* (New York: Harper, 2011): 158–59.

29. Sidney Roth, "Reminiscence of Passover as Celebrated on the Lower East Side of New York," n.d., file 10468, Small Collections, American Jewish Archives, Cincinnati OH.

30. Selma Hirsch Katz, NS 33–36, Lower East Side Oral History Project, Tamiment Institute, Tamiment Library and Robert F. Wagner Archives, New York University.

31. "Es kakht mit erev pesakh in idishin kvartal," *Forward*, April 8, 1914.

32. Anne Goldman, NS 33–58, Lower East Side Oral History Project, Tamiment Institute, Tamiment Library and Robert F. Wagner Archives, New York University.

33. Paula Hyman, *Gender and Assimilation: The Roles and Representation of Women in Modern Jewish History* (Seattle: University of Washington Press, 1995).

34. Paula Hyman, "Gender and the Immigrant Jewish Experience in the United States," in *Jewish Women in Historical Perspective*, ed. Judith R. Baskin (Detroit MI: Wayne State University, 1991), 233–34.

35. *Varhayt*, July 17, 1916, 2; *Morgen zhurnal*, July 11, 1916, 8; *Morgen zhurnal*, July 12, 1916, 2.

36. Hinde Amhanitski, *Der originaler Idisher kokh bukh* (New York: S. Druckerman, n.d. [1918]). Ads in the Yiddish newspapers confirm the 1918 publication though no date is listed in the publication itself. The quote is drawn from the forward, which is not paginated. While the 1918 version is available on microfilm at the Dorot Jewish Division of the New York Public Library, the second, or 1916, version is not in their collection. In this case, too, the date for

the second edition was established through advertisements in the Yiddish newspapers.

37. H. Braun's 1914 *Dos Familien Koch-Bokh* has been translated and republished as *The Yiddish Family Cookbook*, trans. Beverly B. Weingrod, with an introduction by Hasia Diner (New York: Creative Common, 2010). H. Braun's identity and gender has not been established.

38. Deborah Dash Moore, *At Home in America: Second Generation New York Jews* (New York: Columbia University Press, 1981), 8.

39. United States Census, 1910 (Washington DC: National Archives and Records Administration, n.d.); United States Census, 1920 (Washington DC: National Archives and Records Administration, n.d.).

40. Hyman, *Gender and Assimilation*.

41. Eli Lederhendler, "Guides for the Perplexed: Sex, Manners, and Mores for the Yiddish Reader in America," in *Jewish Responses to Modernity: New Voices in America and Eastern Europe* (New York: New York University Press, 1994), 144.

42. See *Shas Tekhine Rav Peninim: Mit Fiele Perushim un Mesholim in Ivri Taytsh* (New York: Hebrew Publishing Company, 1916); *Der Idish Amerikaner Redner* (New York: Hebrew, 1909); *Bar mitzve droshes* (New York, 1908) as examples of religious-oriented literature for a mass audience.

43. Amhanitski, *Der originaler Idisher kokh bukh*, 72.

44. Amhanitski, *Der originaler Idisher kokh bukh*, 73.

45. Amhanitski, *Der originaler Idisher kokh bukh*, 72, 73, 75, 80.

46. Amhanitski, *Der originaler Idisher kokh bukh*, 75. For more on settlement house cooking, see Ziegelman, *97 Orchard Street*.

47. Amhanitski, *Der originaler Idisher kokh bukh*, 82–84.

48. Amhanitski, *Der originaler Idisher kokh bukh*, 85–91.

49. Hyman, *Gender and Assimilation*, 116–17.

50. Email conversation between the author and Eric Goldstein, February 1, 2016.

51. Jacob Rader Marcus, *United States Jewry, 1776–1985*. Vol. 1: *The Sephardic Period* (Detroit MI: Wayne State University Press, 1989), 458, 518.

52. Hayim Malits, *Di heym un di froy* (New York, 1918), 28–31.

53. Dr. Klorman, *Mayn Etsah* (New York: Family Publication, 1931).

12

Dining in the Dixie Diaspora

A Meeting of Region and Religion

························

MARCIE COHEN FERRIS

Since the early eighteenth century, Southern Jews have been tempted by regional foods that are among the most delectable in American cuisine, but are also forbidden by Jewish law. Each generation balanced their Southern and Jewish identities as they considered the plate set before them. When dining with the Deep South Diaspora, we discover both rural and urban Southern worlds and the diverse Jewish populations who came to the region from Europe and the West Indies. They brought a mix of denominational allegiances and shifting personal practices regarding kashrut. In the colonial and antebellum South, Jews interacted with enslaved African Americans, Native Americans, Caribbean peoples, and newly arrived European immigrants. During the nineteenth-century South, Jews adapted their culinary traditions within predominantly white Christian worlds where they adopted the region's contested "traditions" of race, class, and gender. Historian Anton Hieke aptly describes the ambivalent status of Southern Jews during Reconstruction—a cultural memory that has remained in the Southern Jewish psyche—as "integrated outsiders."[1] Never fully Southern, unsure of their acceptance in society, neither firmly Orthodox nor Reform, their "whiteness" was always in constant flux.[2]

Food positions Jewish experience in the American South within a global Jewish history. Throughout their classic narratives of migration and dispersion, Jews have both eaten and rejected foods that are indigenous to the places where they live. Eating patterns reveal how Jews navigated the politics of place as a transnational people and also maintained protective boundaries. Preparing traditional Jewish dishes was often a means to both heal personal and family memories of trauma, displacement, and violence and to celebrate Jewish resilience and heritage. Food thus reflects how Jews both accommodated and resisted acculturation.

As Southern Jewish identity evolved from the eighteenth to the twentieth century, Jewish women were the keepers of family foodways, and they determined the "grammar" of Southern Jewish cuisine in varying ways. While some homemakers separated Southern and Jewish dishes, others mixed the two cuisines, especially in what soul-food scholar Adrian Miller terms "celebration foods."[3] At Friday night Sabbath suppers and holidays, Southern Jews served gefilte fish, matzoh ball soup, potato latkes, noodle kugel, stuffed cabbage, borscht, brisket, and tzimmes. These iconic Jewish foods often featured regional ingredients such as peaches, pecans, and sweet potatoes using recipes that suggest both continuity and evolution of Jewish life in the South. As they gained financial security, middle-class Jews, African Americans, and other immigrant groups shared a culinary pattern of reinterpreting their ethnic celebration foods. Throughout the South, Jewish homemakers substituted Southern specialties such as fried chicken, gumbo, and baked redfish for the traditional roasted chicken entrée typically served for special occasions.

So how can we describe foodways of the Jewish South? We must never forget that Jewish families lived within a deeply race-based society where they defined their religious practice and ideology. Within this world they passed traditional Jewish recipes, memories, and stories from one generation to the next. Their foods were strongly influenced by Southern ingredients, flavors, and cooking methods, as well as a deeply ingrained sense of hospitality. Family and transregional Jewish networks, the influence of skilled African American cooks and caterers, and the culinary impact of an evolving global South also shaped their foods. This complex intersection of cuisine, ethnicity, race, religion, and region in the American South is best understood through historical moments, places, and people in the narrative of the Jewish South.

CHARLESTON AND SAVANNAH

The Southern Jewish experience—and thus, Southern Jewish cuisine—began when Jews joined exploratory expeditions from Europe to the New World in the sixteenth and seventeenth centuries. Sephardic Jews fled Spain to avoid the Inquisition and sought religious tolerance and economic opportunity in the markets of the coastal South. Many settled in Savannah, Georgia, and Charleston, South Carolina, the "northernmost outpost of the Gulf-Caribbean plantation region," where they were joined by Ashkenazic Jews.[4] The subtropical Lowcountry with its beaches, salt marshes, tidal creeks, estuaries, rural rice plantations, and the sophisticated urban townhouses of Savannah and Charleston offered an exotic world to these families. It was a place of vast wealth and terrible poverty, hot summers and cold winters, and a majority population of African American slaves owned by white masters. West Indian influences appeared in the fish and rice dishes enjoyed by Savannah and Charleston Jews. These dishes were prepared by enslaved African American cooks who flavored their foods with hot peppers, tomatoes, spices, and sugar cane.

To fully comprehend the Southern Jewish table in this era, we must recognize the relationship of enslaved people to Africa, to historical trauma, and their central role in food production. Their voice is the most poignant, expressive voice in Southern cuisine, and for generations this voice resonated in Southern Jewish kitchens. African American and Jewish culinary historian Michael Twitty speaks of the "haunted plate" of Southern cuisine, in which lies the rich history, culture, language, and skills of eighteenth- and nineteenth-century African American cooks. A typical West African meal that enslaved cooks would have known in their countries of origin included a starch (rice, millet, or manioc) or a fish dish, served with a vegetable-based sauce or relish.[5] Enslaved Africans brought this core cuisine to the New World, as well as their cooking methods of stewing, boiling, and frying in oil—practices equally common in European Jewish kitchens.[6] Twitty argues that the first "kosher soul cookery" flourished in the coastal colonial South, where a culinary syncretism emerged between black women cooks—enslaved, then free—and Jewish women at the center of mercantile families.

Mercantile trade on the eastern seaboard was central to Jewish life for generations, and buying and selling food was the heart of this economy. In eighteenth- and nineteenth-century Savannah and Charleston, Jews worked as dry goods merchants, grocers, innkeepers, fruit peddlers, bakers, and butchers. They were linked to Jews throughout the Atlantic world by religion, business connections, family ties, marriage, memories of Europe, and most importantly, culinary traditions. During the colonial era, kashrut was a fundamental shared connection within this extended Jewish community, which maintained a healthy coastal trade in kosher meat.[7] Curaçao, Cayenne, Surinam, Jamaica, and other Caribbean communities imported kosher meat, such as smoked sausages and pickled "Jew beef" from Savannah and Charleston.[8] The islands also contributed to the growing Jewish population in the Lowcountry, as Jews left the Caribbean for opportunities on the mainland. Scholar Laura Liebman argues that "almost no one in the American colonies was culinarily independent."[9] This was especially true of Jews because kosher laws required special foods prepared under close Jewish supervision.

In December 1788, John Wereat wrote from Mount Hope Plantation, near Augusta, Georgia, to his old friend Mordecai Sheftall of Savannah. Wereat heard that Sheftall was "coming up this way soon" to conduct business and reminded his Jewish colleague, "Don't forget to bring your sharp knife with you and then you shall not fast here unless 'tis your own fault, as I am putting up some sheep to fatten."[10] Both Sheftall and Wereat were farmers and merchants in eighteenth-century Georgia, and they shared business interests. Sheftall's vast food-related empire included general mercantile stores, cattle, rice plantations, and trade in foodstuffs throughout the Atlantic region.

Wereat's correspondence with Sheftall suggests the complicated negotiation of Jewish life in the Lowcountry and the intimate ties gentile Southerners formed with Jews in business and at the dinner table. Laypeople like Mordecai Sheftall established their own terms for living a religious life because there were no rabbis or "official" functionaries in their nascent Jewish communities.[11] Thus, Sheftall carried a butchering knife with him when he traveled for business so he could adhere to his religious beliefs by slaughtering livestock according to the laws of kashrut. In the newly formed Jewish communities of the South men and women were expected to live Jewish lives, which meant circumcising their sons, observing the Sabbath, and following purity and dietary laws as best they could.

Reverend Samuel Quincy, Anglican chaplain of the Georgia colony, commented on the Jews among the passengers and crew aboard the *William and Sarah* that arrived in Savannah in July of 1733. The thirty-four Sephardic and eight German Jews were sponsored by the Sephardic congregation of London — Bevis Marks — that raised funds to send the "industrious poor" of their community to the Georgia colony.[12] Quincy noted, "We have here two sorts of Jews, Portuguese and German. The first having professed Christianity in Portugal or the Brazils are more lax in their ways . . . the German Jews . . . are a great deal more strict in their way and rigid observers of the law."[13] Reverend Martin Bolzius, a Lutheran pastor, explained what Quincy meant by "the law." "The Spanish and Portuguese Jews are not so strict insofar as eating is concerned as the others are. . . . The German Jews on the other hand would rather starve than eat meat they do not slaughter themselves."[14] It was clear, even to Southern gentiles, that food was central to the religious identity of these newly arrived Jews.

The Jewish community in Charleston grew quickly because the port city offered both economic opportunities and a vital Jewish community.[15] In 1791 Rebecca Samuel wrote her parents in Hamburg, Germany, and told them of her family's plan to move to Charleston from Petersburg, Virginia. "The whole reason why we are leaving this place is because of *Yehudishkeit* [Jewishness]."[16] Samuel feared that if her family stayed in Petersburg, her children would become gentiles. "Here they cannot be brought up otherwise. Jewishness is pushed aside here."[17] She described a shohet who went to market and bought treyfe meat, which he dishonestly advertised as kosher to his Jewish customers. While many Jewish businesses were open on the Sabbath, the Samuel family refused to open theirs. "With us there is some Sabbath. You must believe me that in our house we all live as Jews as much as we can."[18] With its "blessed community of three hundred Jews," Charleston allowed the Samuel family to live, and—most importantly—to feed their family according to Jewish law.[19]

From 1776 to 1820, Charleston's Jewish community exceeded that of New York City and accounted for 5 percent of the white population in the city.[20] Influenced by the Southern ways of white gentile neighbors, they supported slavery, concepts of the Enlightenment, and a lifestyle defined by consumption and a desire for refinement.[21] On September 3, 1749, a group of Jews that included Mordecai Sheftall of Savannah founded Kahal Kadosh Beth Elohim, and built their first synagogue in 1794.[22] Ashkenazic Jews of Charleston adopted the practices of the city's earliest, prestigious Sephardic Orthodox settlers at their dining tables.[23] Ashkenazic women in Charleston refashioned their Jewish lineage by preparing Iberian-inspired dishes, such as lemon stew fish, a chilled poached-fish course served with a lemon-infused sauce.[24]

In 1824, twelve members of Charleston's Congregation Beth Elohim, who represented fifty dissatisfied congregants, petitioned leaders of their synagogue to change the congregation's worship service. The reformers hoped to adapt their religion to the Southern community in which they lived, "to worship God, not as slaves of bigotry and priestcraft, but as

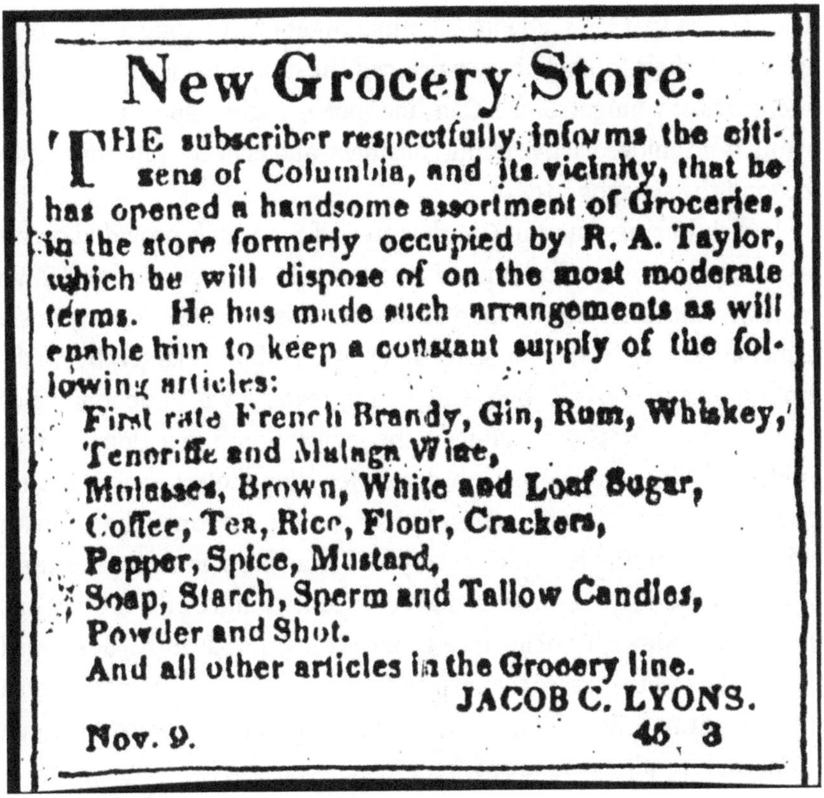

New Grocery Store.

THE subscriber respectfully informs the citizens of Columbia, and its vicinity, that he has opened a handsome assortment of Groceries, in the store formerly occupied by R. A. Taylor, which he will dispose of on the most moderate terms. He has made such arrangements as will enable him to keep a constant supply of the following articles:

First rate French Brandy, Gin, Rum, Whiskey, Tenoriffe and Malaga Wine, Molasses, Brown, White and Loaf Sugar, Coffee, Tea, Rice, Flour, Crackers, Pepper, Spice, Mustard, Soap, Starch, Sperm and Tallow Candles, Powder and Shot. And all other articles in the Grocery line.

JACOB C. LYONS.

Nov. 9.   45 3

FIG. 12-1. Advertisement for the Lyons family's "New Grocery Store," *Columbia Telescope*, November 9, 1827. Operated by Isaac Lyons and his son, Jacob C. Lyons, the business earned its reputation as an oyster saloon catering to students from South Carolina College. Photo courtesy of Special Collections, College of Charleston Libraries, Charleston, South Carolina.

the enlightened descendants of that chosen race."[25] Their demands included shortening the service, incorporating English as well as Hebrew, adding a sermon, and ending monetary "offerings" for the honor to read from the Torah. Their petition ultimately led to a split within the congregation and the creation of the "Reformed Society of Israelites" in 1825—the beginning of Reform Judaism in America. Their call for changes in public worship demonstrate congregants' personal religious practices as Charleston Jews increasingly modified dietary laws. Anton

Hieke notes that Jews "adapted commandments according to their own needs."[26] Their food choices expressed the dual Southern and Jewish identities of younger, South Carolina–born, English-speaking congregants, who enjoyed active family, business, and civic lives in Charleston beyond the synagogue doors.[27]

Jewish businessmen in Charleston and Savannah provided credit to young "drummers" and peddlers who sold their goods from town to town until they could open stores of their own.[28] Historian Hasia Diner argues that the universality of Jewish peddling—largely by single, immigrant men—is among "the paradigmatic Jewish phenomena of the modern world" that connects the Jewish South to a global Jewish history.[29] While on the road, observant Jewish peddlers carried kosher food such as hard-boiled eggs with them and honored the Sabbath whether they returned home or stayed at a farmer's home for the duration of the holiday.[30] By taking in Jewish peddlers and clerks as boarders, middle-class Jewish women in Southern cities like Savannah developed food-related businesses that provided familiar tastes, language, and a religious atmosphere for newly arrived immigrants who were separated from their families in Europe.[31]

Even more than the synagogue, home was the center of religious life for Southern Jewish families. Their "domestic Judaism" closely resembled how Protestant women blended religion and domestic life, and it signaled the growing feminization of religion in the second half of the nineteenth century.[32] In 1836 Miriam Gratz Moses Cohen, the niece of pioneer Jewish educator Rebecca Gratz of Philadelphia, married Solomon Cohen of Georgetown, South Carolina, and in her "commonplace" book she kept recipes.[33] Miriam Cohen's blended heritage is illustrated in her Southern recipes for biscuits, corn bread, sweet potato pudding, and pound cakes—likely prepared by an African American cook—as well as her Jewish recipes for "Pesach Sponge Cake," "koogle," "Haroseth," "Passover soup dumplings, and "biled matzoh."[34] Mealtime revealed both the Cohens' position as a white, slave-owning family and their loyalty to Judaism.

FIG. 12-2. Jake Kalinsky and his mother and sisters, Trestina, Poland, ca. 1912. Jewish Heritage Collection, College of Charleston, courtesy of Special Collections, College of Charleston Libraries, Charleston, South Carolina.

Eastern European Jewish immigrants who settled in Savannah and Charleston opened butcher shops, bakeries, and delicatessens in the early decades of the twentieth century. Here *landsmen* found kosher and traditional foods such as rye bread, borscht, chicken soup, stuffed cabbage, cholent, tzimmes, herring, kreplach, and tongue, all of which they had known in their countries of origin. In Charleston, St. Philip Street, the center of the city's Eastern European Jewish community for two generations, was described as a "southern version of Manhattan's Lower East Side."[35] Robert Zalkin's grandfather owned one of the first kosher butcher shops in the neighborhood and remembered how "when you walked up St. Philip Street . . . you could smell the cooking from the Sabbath dinners."[36] Historian Sol Breibart's parents kept a kosher home upstairs above their store on Charleston's Meeting Street, where his Eastern European mother prepared lokshen (noodle) kugel and gefilte fish for the Sabbath. Downstairs, Ida and Sam Breibart's grocery store was strictly treyfe and sold the collard greens, spare ribs, and pig's feet that their African American customers enjoyed.[37] Black street vendors learned what was kosher and what was not, and from their farms in Mount Pleasant and St. John's Island, they sold fruit, vegetables, and fish door to door in the Jewish neighborhoods of Charleston. Nathan Garfinkle recalled the African American peddlers who sold whiting, a kosher fish, to their Jewish customers and were careful to separate it from their supplies of shellfish, "as they knew the Jews would not eat shrimp."[38]

The Krawchecks kept a kosher home at 3 Colonial Street in Charleston in the 1930s and 1940s that was presided over by Agnes Jenkins, an African American cook who worked for the family for sixty years. Jenkins prepared daily meals for the Krawchecks, oversaw complicated preparations for Passover, and even kashered the family's meat. Saul Krawcheck recalls Jenkins's "old southern recipes," in which she carefully substituted kosher ingredients for treyfe foods—"How about deviled fish in a crab shell? The most delicious dish you ever tasted in your life."[39] Jenkins also prepared Krawcheck's grandmother Bielsky's Old World recipes, easily

FIG. 12-3. Party for Carolee Rosen's first birthday, Asheville, North Carolina, 1931, Collection of Carolee Rosen Fox. Photo courtesy of Special Collections, College of Charleston Libraries, Charleston, South Carolina.

switching between the culinary styles of Southern and Jewish. "One day you'd get a typical southern dinner of fried chicken and rice and okra gumbo and sivvy beans and corn," Krawcheck noted. "And the next day the appetizer would be pickled smoked salmon, and then a bowl of lentil soup, and then potato latkes or potato kugel or tzimmes."[40] Guests at the Krawcheck table witnessed the family's blended attachment to the South, to Judaism, and to their ancestral home in Poland.

Jewish families in Charleston and Savannah mixed Southern and Jewish flavors at their tables with the assistance of African American domestic workers like Agnes Jenkins. For some Jewish families, black cooks prepared a daily "meat n' three" meal of fried chicken, black-eyed peas, stewed tomatoes, and okra, foods commonly served in any Southern home. In the same home a Jewish mother or grandmother prepared traditional foods for Jewish holiday meals. And other families, like the Krawchecks, ate "Southern kosher" one day and "Old World kosher" the next, all prepared by the same African American cook. In some households Jewish women did all the cooking. They preferred to do so out of habit, because of concerns about maintaining kashrut, or because they could not afford the services of a full-time housekeeper and cook.

Although African American women were familiar figures in synagogue and home kitchens throughout the Jewish South, they are rarely mentioned or credited in synagogue and community cookbooks from the early twentieth century to the present.[41] Historian Rebecca Sharpless emphasizes that "white women mishandled African American women's recipes in several ways."[42] They expropriated their cooking knowledge, presented their voices as illiterate, "childlike," and magical, and implied that their culinary skills were innate, rather than based on intelligence and skill.[43] Occasional references to a black cook in a recipe acknowledge only first names, such as "Tillie's stuffed potatoes." A patronizing tribute to "Mammy" in a Jewish cookbook was often the only acknowledgment of a cook who had worked all her life for a white family.[44] In *The Jemima Code*, writer Toni Tipton-Martin argues that African American women have never been credited for their intellectual hand in shaping Southern cuisine.[45] Tipton-Martin cracks this tomb of marginality by foregrounding black woman's voices in America's culinary cultures. Despite the erasure of their history, the influence of African American cooks on Southern Jewish food cultures was profound.[46]

NEW ORLEANS

The Creole world that nineteenth-century Jews encountered in New Orleans and rural Louisiana was as complex as the city's gumbo. Like its rich seafood stew, New Orleans was shaped by the Caribbean and Europe, Choctaw and Natchez Indians, and by enslaved African Americans and free people of color.[47] Large numbers of French Jews arrived in Louisiana after 1830, and their food traditions from Alsace and Lorraine added yet another layer of complexity to the region's distinctive food culture. Creole cuisine embodies the culinary traditions of the South Atlantic rim, which stretches from Brazil to the Gulf Coast of North America.[48] The mix of colonial era French and African food traditions deeply influenced Jewish kitchens in the city. At the heart of the Creole kitchen were African American women who brought the exotic flavors of hot peppers, chilies, and file, yams and eggplants; grains such as rice, grits, and cornmeal; and confections made with cane syrup, coconuts, pecans, sesame seeds, and peanuts.[49] These rich foodstuffs entered Sephardic and Ashkenazic households, where they mixed with recipes from their countries of origin—the West Indies, France, Germany, and Eastern Europe.

Mid-nineteenth-century Jews in Louisiana were a diverse mix of Sephardic and Ashkenazic families, former Charlestonians and Savannahians who moved west with the cotton trade, and recent immigrants from France and Germany. All of these groups embraced a lifestyle that was financially dependent on slavery, strongly connected to place, deeply loyal to family, and passionate about local cuisine. By the 1815 victory of Andrew Jackson at the Battle of New Orleans, the city's reputation for fine food was established.[50] New Orleans and the Louisiana countryside were famous for public displays of culinary expertise, whether at Creole restaurants, such as Antoine's, which was founded in 1840, or at a family *cochon de lait*, or hog roast, in a Cajun village. Jewish peddlers and merchants were drawn to the French-speaking culture of Louisiana and to the area's agricultural economy, which lacked middlemen traders like themselves. With its Creole cuisine, small villages, and a large river that resembled the Rhine, Louisiana tasted and looked like their homes in the Old World. Young Ashkenazic Jews established families, businesses, and charitable organizations bonded by their Jewish heritage.

Judah P. Benjamin was a Jewish ex-patriot from Charleston who arrived in New Orleans in 1828 at age seventeen to pursue his career in law. Benjamin later became the Confederacy's secretary of war and secretary of state. Benjamin bought Belle Chasse, a three-hundred-acre plantation downriver from New Orleans. Benjamin's kitchen was run by enslaved African American cooks, whose food suggested the influence of his Catholic wife, Natalie St. Martin, rather than his Sephardic Jewish heritage.

As the South approached secession in the fall of 1860 and the nation prepared for war, well-established Louisiana Jewish families and recent Jewish immigrants both embraced the Confederate cause and affirmed solidarity with their white gentile neighbors.[51] From June 1861 to July 1862, sixteen-year-old Clara Solomon kept a diary that detailed her experiences as a teenager, a daughter, a sister, a Sephardic Jew, a member of a slave-owning family, and a loyal Confederate in New Orleans. On the one-year anniversary of the firing on Fort Sumter, Solomon wrote, "What true Southerner can ever fail to remember that on the 12th of April 1861, the first collision of the Confederate and Federal forces took place."[52] In her descriptions of daily life during the war, Solomon recalled favorite foods—shrimp, blackberries, and "mush-melon"—as well as her family's diminishing supplies of butter, flour, coffee, and meat.[53] During Passover in the spring of 1862, Solomon noted the matzoh shortage in New Orleans, "Our motzoes are so miserably sour that I don't think I have eaten a whole one."[54] After the Civil War, Jewish peddlers and merchants returned to their trades and filled an important niche in the cash-poor South during Reconstruction.[55]

Eastern European Jews had established a modest presence in New Orleans by the 1850s. Rampart and Dryades Streets became the commercial business center for African Americans and Eastern European Jews, where kosher butchers, bakers, shohets, and delicatessen owners were located. In an 1881 issue of the regional newspaper, the *Jewish South*, Mrs. E. Block, "dealer in Family and Fancy Groceries," advertised foods that appealed to both Eastern European Jews and those of German descent: "a fresh supply of kosher smoked and pickled beef, sausages and tongues," goose grease, New York salt pickles, "Basler and Berliener Lebkuchen," herring, and "cakes, chocolate and potatoe flour for Pessack. [Pesach or Passover]."[56] Non-Jewish food businesses like J. O. Zatarain's declared, "The Best Jewish People buy their wines of us."[57]

In the January 1895 issue of the *Jewish Ledger*, B. Moses advertised his "Southern Matzos Bakery," including "Yomtofick Cakes" (*yom tov*, the Hebrew phrase for "holiday").[58] Mr. Moses assured both urban and rural customers that their orders would be "promptly attended to."[59]

Unlike Northeast urban areas, which experienced growth in their immigrant populations at the end of the nineteenth century, New Orleans's foreign-born population gradually declined in the 1880s.[60] Yellow fever epidemics deterred new industry and immigration in the city, as did the combination of nativist politics, rising racial terrorism, and Jim Crow segregation, all of which focused on African Americans and newly arrived immigrants throughout the South. Despite the small size of its Jewish population, antisemitism permeated the region. By the turn of the century, prominent Jewish New Orleanians were no longer allowed in exclusive clubs associated with Mardi Gras, such as the Boston Club.[61] Fearing that the presence of unassimilated, Eastern European Jewish immigrants would only make things worse, the Jewish aristocracy of New Orleans disassociated itself from the new arrivals, and their food choices symbolized this distancing. A blatantly treyfe menu for an 1886 fundraising banquet hosted by a local B'nai B'rith for the Jewish Widows and Orphans Home featured turtle soup, oysters, soft shell crabs, and French wines.[62] The evening was designed to showcase the Reform Jewish community and their New Orleans–style taste because they were acculturated, had embraced modernity, and disregarded religious dietary laws that they considered outdated, "archaic" practices.

ATLANTA

During the first decades of the twentieth century, Atlanta Jews considered themselves citizens of the New South. With new railroads, hotels, factories, office buildings, and warehouses, their Atlanta became the capital of this newly envisioned region.[63] Businessmen from established German Jewish families—immortalized in Alfred Uhry's Pulitzer Prize–winning play *Driving Miss Daisy*—about his Atlanta Jewish family—as well as Jews more recently arrived from Eastern Europe, became important

FIG. 12-4. Max Feldman's grocery store, 131 Chapel Street, Atlanta, Georgia, ca. 1925. William Breman Jewish Heritage Museum, Atlanta, Georgia.

voices for white Southern boosterism. Concurrently, the horrific 1915 lynching of Leo Frank, a young Jewish industrialist and member of Atlanta's elite Jewish society, was a defining moment in an era of growing racial radicalism, as Southern whites determined who could be counted among their ranks.[64] The virulent antisemitism associated with Frank's case impelled Jews to firmly position themselves on the white side of the color line through their civic and economic lives. Daily vigilance in one's behavior, appearance, activities, and even the food one ate, affirmed racial and ethnic solidarity with whites.

The New South was "an anxious place" because the old rules that had governed white and black racial conduct no longer existed.[65] Those with and those without power both felt the insecurity of these changing times. White Southerners so longed for the Old South they virtually reinvented it.[66] During the first half of the century, the region was caught

FIG. 12-5. Thirty-fifth anniversary dinner in honor of Mr. and Mrs. Emil Dittler, Standard Club, Atlanta, Georgia, February 14, 1935. Photo courtesy of the Ida Pearle and Joseph Cuba Archives of the William Breman Jewish Heritage Museum, Atlanta, Georgia.

in a freeze-frame fantasy of the plantation era. This mythic world was used to market "Dixie's finest" food products with stereotyped black "mammies" and "uncles," and in sentimental Southern songs written by Jewish songwriters in New York's Tin Pan Alley, such as Irving Caesar's "Is It True What They Say about Dixie?" (1936), made famous by singer Al Jolson.[67] Although many of their ancestors had immigrated to Atlanta *after* the Civil War, Jewish families in the city romanticized the Old South as did their gentile neighbors.

The mythic South influenced a National Council for Jewish Women (NCJW) luncheon held in honor of the organization's national president, Mrs. Maurice Goldman. Three hundred and fifty Jewish women attended the October 1939 event at the Standard Club, Atlanta's elite Jewish social organization. Excluded from the city's gentile society, German Jewish families formed their own groups like the Standard

Club and then promptly excluded Eastern European and Sephardic Jews who in turn organized their own clubs. Inspired by the highly publicized film premier of *Gone With the Wind*, the council chose "Dixie" as their theme.[68] An Old South tableau on each table featured "Pick-a-ninnies" and a miniature clothesline hung with miniature wash. A "washboard band of darkies" provided musical entertainment.[69]

The Atlanta chapter of the NCJW sponsored charity work throughout the city and as New South boosters they encouraged their members to be "civically useful."[70] They looked after their "own," with activities such as Southern cooking classes for "foreign mothers" offered throughout the 1920s. Mrs. Max Gholstin, oversaw the council's "Americanization" activities and argued that cooking classes made foreigners more like "native born," and children preferred their mothers to "do the same as the neighbor."[71] By learning to cook Southern food, immigrant women would "thereby increase their love for the country."[72] The Dixie luncheon is a compelling racial symbol of middle- and upper-class Jewish worlds in Atlanta, but the event reveals only one sector of the city's Jewish worlds.

Atlanta's German Jewish society with their impressive Hebrew Benevolent Congregation—known locally as "the Temple"— their Standard Club, downtown department stores, and decorous benevolent organizations were a foreign world to the Eastern European Jews who began arriving in Atlanta in the late nineteenth century, including Orthodox, socialists, and labor Zionists.[73] Eastern European merchants who settled in Atlanta refused to abandon the tastes of their homelands. Excluded from both white gentile and German Jewish clubs in the city, they formed a tightly knit community that was grounded in the small grocery stores, delicatessens, and cafés of Atlanta's South Side.[74] They served Jewish and African American customers and catered to the tastes of both. Eastern Europeans Jews formed Orthodox synagogues, such as Atlanta's Ahavath Achim and Shearith Israel. They hired African American cooks and caterers, who mastered the rules of kashrut and recipes from the Old Country. Barbecue meant beef brisket, and turnip greens were flavored with schmaltz. Delicatessens supplied basic Jewish-style foods such

FIG. 12-6. Bar mitzvah celebration of Charles Borochoff at the home of Tobias Borochoff, Atlanta, Georgia, 1934. Charles Borochoff is seated first on left. Photo courtesy of the Ida Pearle and Joseph Cuba Archives of the William Breman Jewish Heritage Museum, Atlanta, Georgia.

as corned beef, kishka, knish, salami, smoked and cured fish—tastes savored at Sunday suppers and shul gatherings.

In the early 1930s, Rabbi Tobias Geffen of Shearith Israel received inquiries from Orthodox rabbis across the nation about the kosher status of Atlanta-based Coca-Cola.[75] After conferring with the Coca-Cola chemists, Geffen confirmed that the soft drink could be made with sugar cane instead of corn syrup at Passover. Coca-Cola manufacturers agreed to use cottonseed oil in their recipe instead of a tallow-based product. In 1935, Geffen published a *teshuva*—a Jewish legal response. "With the help of God, I have been able to uncover a pragmatic solution according to which there would be no question or any doubt concerning the ingredients of Coca-Cola."[76] In 1935, the Atlanta bottling company

FIG. 12-7. David Hazan's fruit stand, Atlanta, Georgia, ca. 1920. Photo courtesy of the Ida Pearle and Joseph Cuba Archives of the William Breman Jewish Heritage Museum, Atlanta, Georgia.

produced a bottle cap with the first ever Coca-Cola kosher certification in Hebrew.[77] A spring 1936 issue of the *Southern Israelite* advertised, "Coca-Cola in bottles now kosher for Passover."

No group in Atlanta's diverse Jewish community preserved their Old World culture through food more strongly than the Sephardic Jews who arrived in Georgia and Alabama from Greece, Turkey, and other regions of the Mediterranean during the first decade of the 1900s. Fear surrounding the Leo Frank case colored their early years in Georgia. Regina Rousso Tourial's father-in-law warned his wife "not to dare go out of the house" during the Frank trial. The desire to stay among "their own kind" strengthened the retention of Sephardic cooking methods and recipes. Regina Tourial explains, "We weren't roast and brisket

FIG. 12-8. The Economy Deli located on Auburn Avenue in Atlanta, Georgia, was a Jewish-owned business serving only black customers. Left to right: holding on to chair, owners Nace Galanti, Ralph Galanti, and Abraham Romano. Photo courtesy of the Ida Pearle and Joseph Cuba Archives of the William Breman Jewish Heritage Museum, Atlanta, Georgia.

eaters. That came much later in our lives."[78] Sephardic pastries like *boyos*, a popular savory turnover, as well as an assortment of olives and feta cheese were mandatory at social gatherings. Today a sense of community is reaffirmed each year at a Chanukah-time Sephardic food bazaar, an important fundraising event for Congregation Or VeShalom begun in the 1950s. Sephardic-descended women in Atlanta continue to prepare dishes passed down by their Jewish mothers and grandmothers. "This food holds us together," said Jeanette Arogeti. "It's in our blood."[79]

By the 1950s Atlanta's Reform Jews appeared and acted as Southern as their Christian neighbors. The Magnolia Room café menu at Rich's Department Store belied its Jewish ownership with dishes preferred by gentile Junior League members such as Chicken à la King, congealed

FIG. 12-9. Fleischer store, Shaw, Mississippi, April 26, 1991. Following her husband's death, the family of Goldie Fleischer (center) gathered to close the family dry goods store, the last Jewish landmark on a street once lined with Jewish-owned businesses in this Mississippi Delta town. Photo by Bill Aron, courtesy of the Institute of Southern Jewish Life, Jackson, Mississippi.

salads with homemade mayonnaise, and dainty hot biscuits.[80] The New South dream of Jewish acceptance exploded with the bombing of "the Temple" in the fall of 1958 by white supremacists. What the Reform congregation had strived so hard to achieve—affluence and acceptance in elite, white society—exposed them to persecution because of their visibility within the community. The bombing was aimed at Rabbi Jacob "Jack" Rothschild, Hebrew Benevolent's spiritual leader who bravely voiced his progressive views and criticism of racial segregation from the pulpit.

During that same era, a Jewish-owned business in Atlanta became the focus of the civil rights struggle when Charlie Lebedin refused to integrate his popular restaurant, Leb's.[81] Although Lebedin served barbecue to his customers, pork was not the problem. The Atlanta Jewish community was embarrassed that "one of theirs" was a holdout segregationist. The restaurant was a frequent site of student protests and sit-ins, including a volatile gathering in January 1964.[82] After the passage of the Civil Rights Act that July, and under mounting pressure from the Jewish community, Lebedin finally integrated his restaurant. He printed a statement in the Atlanta newspapers, "Henceforth, my restaurants will be open to all citizens who come to eat and who conduct themselves as ladies and gentlemen. I have been told that my business may suffer."[83] Like businessman and politician Lester Maddox, whose Pickrick restaurant in Atlanta became a battleground in the fight to desegregate restaurants, Lebedin employed many blacks in his business. Maddox and Lebedin believed "their negroes" were satisfied with their situation. Historian Jason Sokol describes the "revolution in consciousness" that rumbled across the South, as conservative white Southerners like Maddox and Lebedin encountered activist blacks who shattered these stereotypes.[84]

THE DELTA

The Mississippi and Arkansas Delta—a fertile alluvial plain formed by the Mississippi River and its tributaries—is far removed from the urban worlds of Atlanta. Jews have built businesses and organized congregations here since the late nineteenth century. In his Delta memoir, *Lanterns on the Levee*, William Alexander Percy described how Jewish peddlers became merchants, bankers, and plantation owners, sent their children to universities, and became involved in the arts and politics, "Every American community has its leaven of Jews. Ours arrived shortly after the Civil War with packs on their backs, peddlers from Russia, Poland, Germany, and a few from Alsace."[85] A compelling source of Delta Jewish identity is associated with food served at the dinner table, in the synagogue kitchen, and in Jewish-owned grocery stores and dry goods stores.

Obtaining "Jewish" foods in the Delta was the biggest challenge of living far from a center of Jewish population. Jewish women in the Delta traveled with an ice cooler in the trunks of their cars to keep their foods fresh, and no one visited Jackson, Memphis, St. Louis, and especially New York without bringing home bagels, lox, corned beef, and dark loaves of pumpernickel. Cecile Gudelsky's grandfather brought these foods on the train when he returned from St. Louis to Paragould, Arkansas. He sat with friends on the way to St. Louis and on the return trip he sat alone because the smell of salami and pastrami was too strong for his companions.[86] Kosher and kosher-style delicatessens like the Old Tyme Delicatessen in Jackson and Rosen's, Segal's, and Halpern's in Memphis were known in the Delta through advertisements in Jewish newspapers like the *Hebrew Watchman* and the *Jewish Spectator*. They guaranteed "prompt attention given out-of-town orders" as foods were delivered to Delta Jews by bus and by train.[87] In Chatham, Mississippi, Rabbi Fred Davidow recalled his Lithuanian great-grandmother, Sarah Stein, and her oldest child, Fannie Stein Schwartz, his maternal grandmother, as an "island of kashrut" in the Delta in the early 1900s.[88] They *adjusted* the rules of kashrut, allowing no pork or shellfish in their homes, keeping kosher during the week of Passover, and overlooking treyfe foods eaten outside the home.

Because of their small numbers and the lengthy drives between home and synagogue, Jews in the Delta often gathered together at holiday time for community seders, Rosh Hashanah dinners, Yom Kippur break-the-fasts, and Hanukkah latke parties. Depending on the number of participants, these events were held in private homes, at the synagogue, in a Jewish social club like Vicksburg's B. B. (B'nai B'rith) Club, the Olympia Club in Greenville, or at a local restaurant. The annual sisterhood-sponsored deli lunch in Greenville, Mississippi, raised money for the synagogue and also "demystified" the Jewish community for hundreds of gentiles who came to purchase corned beef sandwiches.[89] Leanne Lipnick Silverblatt of Indianola remembers the Young People's Jewish League, or the YPJL as her parents called it, which sponsored a monthly supper club. "They met every month or so to eat—Jewish couples from all over the Delta belonged," said Silverblatt.[90] During the civil rights movement in the 1960s, such hospitality was seldom extended to Jewish "freedom riders" from the Midwest and Northeast who threatened the Jewish community's tenuous position in the racially charged state of Mississippi.

After World War II few Jewish youth returned to the Delta after they completed college and served in the military. The region's overall population declined due to the arrival of the boll weevil in the early 1900s, the mechanization of cotton picking in the 1940s, and the Great Migration — the exodus of African Americans from the South to industrial cities like Chicago and Detroit. Downtown business districts withered as the growth of regional discount stores forced third- and fourth-generation Jews out of their small mercantile businesses in the Delta and into professions located in cities. Historian Jennifer Stollman cautions that the "end of the story of small-town Jewish life in the Delta has not been written."[91] Like all Jewish history, the history of Delta Jews is a story of perseverance and migration.[92] "Their numbers may be small," Stollman explains, "but they celebrate as if they have hundreds of members."[93]

Southern Jews have negotiated ethnic and religious worlds through food cultures that vary from the Lowcountry to the Mississippi River, and their history enriches and expands our understanding of the American Jewish experience. An older generation of Jewish Southerners preserves flavors that remind them of family, ancestral places, and historic memories, while their children and grandchildren create spicier, healthy versions of old-style Jewish recipes. Today religiously observant Southern Jews keep kosher, as a growing number of young Jewish Southerners embrace ideological and political beliefs that resonate with conscious eating and sustainable practices. Contemporary Jewish Southerners, including a new diaspora of active Jewish retirees, also support the local food movement and are loyal customers at farmers' markets, farm-to-table restaurants, as well as newly imagined delis, bagel shops, and the first-ever knish bakeries. (The North Carolina Piedmont is home to the award-winning Neal's Deli—try the pastrami biscuit—"The Bagel Bar," and Knish-a-licious, including their savory sweet potato knish. (A new "Jewish-style" delicatessen is soon to open in Raleigh.)

Jewish youth in the region more likely identify Greek, Lebanese, and Middle Eastern specialties as "Jewish cuisine"—rather than Ashkenazi classics—given the popularity of food entrepreneurs like Jamil Kadoura, whose beloved Mediterranean Deli in Chapel Hill is a favorite catering choice for local bar and bat mitzvahs, Jewish brit/brit bat, weddings, and funerals. Chefs like New Orleans's Alon Shaya, winner of the 2015 James Beard Award for "Best Chef: South," integrate seasonal and regional ingredients into traditional Jewish recipes. Shaya recently opened an Israeli restaurant in New Orleans that features Middle Eastern tastes in dishes such as shakshouka, hummus, slow-cooked lamb, and handmade pita baked in their own wood-burning oven. His menu also honors the city's Jewish immigrant history with roasted beets, matzoh ball soup, and chicken paprikash. In the spring of 2017, Shaya joined a vibrant gathering of chefs, food entrepreneurs, scholars, journalists, and one Jewish barbecue pit master at a University of North Carolina–sponsored symposium to explore Jewish food in and of the Global South. Conversations examined the innovation and activism within contemporary Jewish culinary traditions that perpetuate specific tastes and customs, and that expand an understanding of how Jewish culinary traditions influence—and are influenced by—the cultures in which they are embedded.[94]

In the twenty-first century, Southern Jewish life is centered in cities such as Atlanta, Charlotte, and Memphis, where an upswing in observance is seen in Jewish day schools and impressive kosher sections of local supermarkets. New and established Jewish studies programs at the College of Charleston, Duke University, Emory University, Tulane University, the University of North Carolina, the University of Virginia, the University of Texas, and Vanderbilt University represent the region's commitment to Jewish education and the growing canon of Southern Jewish studies. Food in the Jewish South highlights the transformative voices of Jewish Southerners now and throughout the region's history. It is a culinary narrative of reinvention and revitalization as each generation grapples with their Southern and Jewish identities, ultimately bringing old and new flavors to yet another home in the arc of the global Jewish experience.

NOTES

Parts of this chapter are reprinted from *Matzoh Ball Gumbo: Culinary Tales of the Jewish South*, Copyright © 2005, and *The Edible South: The Power of Food and the Making of an American Region*, Copyright © 2014 by Marcie Cohen Ferris. Used by permission of the University of North Carolina Press, www.uncpress .unc.edu. Parts also used from Ferris's essay "Dixie Diaspora," which appears in *Jewish Roots in Southern Soil: A New History*, edited by Marcie C. Ferris and Mark I. Greenberg, Copyright © 2006. Used by permission of the University Press of New England, Lebanon, New Hampshire.

1. Anton Hieke, *Jewish Identity in the Reconstruction South: Ambivalence and Adaptation* (Berlin: Walter de Gruyter, 2013), 2; Leonard Rogoff, "Is the Jew White? The Racial Place of the Southern Jews," *American Jewish History* 85, no. 3 (1997): 195.

2. Hieke, *Jewish Identity in the Reconstruction South*.

3. Adrian Miller, *Soul Food: The Surprising Story of an American Cuisine, One Plate at a Time* (Chapel Hill: University of North Carolina Press, 2013), 265.

4. "First Families," in *A Portion of the People: Three Hundred Years of Southern Jewish Life*, ed. Theodore Rosengarten and Dale Rosengarten(Columbia: University of South Carolina Press, 2002),61.

5. Jessica B. Harris, *High on the Hog: A Culinary Journey from Africa to America* (New York: Bloomsbury, 2011), 11; Frederick Douglass Opie, *Hog and Hominy: Soul Food from Africa to America* (New York: Columbia University Press, 2008), 1–15; Miller, *Soul Food*, 11–28.

6. See Michael Twitty's website and blog, http://afroculinaria.com; and his book, *The Cooking Gene: A Journey Through African-American Culinary History in the Old South* (New York: HarperCollins, 2017). In 2016, the *Forward* recognized Twitty in their annual list of influential Jewish leaders who have impacted American life, "Michael Twitty: The Jewish Afroculinarian," *Forward*, 2016, http://forward.com/series/forward-50/2016/michael-twitty/.

7. Eli Faber, *A Time for Planting: The First Migration, 1654–1820* (Baltimore MD: Johns Hopkins University Press, 1992), 50.

8. Jacob Rader Marcus, *The Colonial American Jews, 1492–1776*. Vol. 2 (Detroit MI: Wayne State University Press, 1970), 193, 345; see also Jonathan D. Sarna, *American Judaism: A History* (New Haven: Yale University Press, 2004), 7.

9. Laura Arnold Liebman, *Messianism, Secrecy, and Mysticism: A New Interpretation of Early American Jewish Life* (Portland OR: Vallentine Mitchell, 2013), 182–83.

10. John Wereat, "Letter to Mordecai Sheftall, December 1788," Small Collections, file 11344, American Jewish Archives, Cincinnati OH; B. H. Levy, *Mordecai Sheftall: Jewish Revolutionary Patriot* (Savannah: Georgia Historical Society, 1999), 40.

11. Hasia R. Diner, *A Time for Gathering: The Second Migration, 1820–1980* (Baltimore MD: Johns Hopkins University Press, 1992). 141.

12. Mordecai Sheftall, "The Jews in Savannah," *The Occident* 1, no. 8 (1843).

13. Saul Jacob Rubin, *Third to None: The Saga of Savannah Jewry, 1733–1983* (Savannah GA: S. J. Rubin, 1983),6.

14. Rubin, *Third to None*, 6.

15. Sarna, *American Judaism*, 19.

16. Rebecca Samuel, "Letter to her parents, 1791, Petersburg, Virginia," Small Collections, file 14104, American Jewish Archives, Cincinnati OH; Hasia R. Diner and Beryl Lieff Benderly, *Her Works Praise Her: A History of Jewish Women in America from Colonial Times to the Present* (New York: Basic Books, 2002), 15–23; Rosengarten and Rosengarten, *Portion of the People*, 45–46.

17. Samuel, "Letter to her parents."

18. Samuel, "Letter to her parents."

19. Samuel, "Letter to her parents."

20. Deborah Dash Moore, "Freedom's Fruit: The Americanization of an Old-Time Religion," in *A Portion of the People*, ed. Rosengarten and Rosengarten, 11.

21. James William Hagy, *This Happy Land: The Jews of Colonial and Antebellum Charleston* (Tuscaloosa: University of Alabama Press, 1993), 1.

22. "250th Commemorative Program for Kahal Kadosh Beth Elohim," Kahal Kadosh Beth Elohim, Charleston, South Carolina, 1993, 3.

23. Rosengarten and Rosengarten, *Portion of the People*, 88.

24. Joan Nathan, *An American Folklife Cookbook* (New York: Schocken Books, 1984), 271.

25. "The Petition of Forty-Seven Members of Beth Elohim Asking for Changes in the Ritual, 1824," cit. in Hieke, *Jewish Identity in the Reconstruction South*, 257.

26. Hieke, *Jewish Identity in the Reconstruction South*, 309.

27. Hieke, *Jewish Identity in the Reconstruction South*, 258.

28. Rosengarten and Rosengarten, *Portion of the People*, 112–13.

29. Hasia R. Diner, "Entering the Mainstream of Modern Jewish History: Peddlers and the American Jewish South," in *Jewish Roots in Southern Soil: A New History*, ed. Marcie Cohen Ferris and Mark I. Greenberg (Hanover NH: University Press of New England, 2006), 86–87.

30. Isaac Jacobs interview, oral history interview by Dale Rosengarten, Charleston, South Carolina, February 1, 1995, Jewish Heritage Collection, College of Charleston, Charleston SC.

31. Mark I. Greenberg, "Savannah's Jewish Women and the Shaping of Ethnic and Southern Identity, 1830–1900," *Georgia Historical Quarterly* 82 (1998): 758.

32. Paula E. Hyman, *Gender and Assimilation in Modern Jewish History: The Roles and Representations of Women* (Seattle: University of Washington Press, 1995), 25–26.

33. Greenberg, "Savannah's Jewish Women," 760. See also Rosengarten and Rosengarten, *Portion of the People*, 107; Diane Ashton, "Shifting Veils: Religion, Politics, and Womanhood in the Civil War Writings of American Jewish Women," in *Women and American Judaism: Historical Perspectives*, ed. Pamela S. Nadell and Jonathan D. Sarna (Hanover NH: University Press of New England for Brandeis University, 2001), 93–101. Miriam Gratz Moses' "Commonplace and Recipe Book" is dated 1828 on its cover and is located in the Miriam Gratz Moses Cohen Papers, file 2639, Southern Historical Collection, Wilson Library, University of North Carolina at Chapel Hill.

34. Miriam Gratz Moses Cohen, "Commonplace and Recipe Book."

35. Rosengarten and Rosengarten, *Portion of the People*, 154.

36. Robert M. Zalkin, Oral history interview by Dale Rosengarten, January 6, 1999, Jewish Heritage Collection, College of Charleston, Charleston SC.

37. Sol Breibart, interview with author, September 22, 2001, Charleston SC.

38. Nathan and Frances Garfinkle, oral history interview by Dale Rosengarten, June 4, 1996, Jewish Heritage Collection, College of Charleston, Charleston SC.

39. Saul Krawcheck, oral history interview by Dale Rosengarten, July 6, 1995, Jewish Heritage Collection, College of Charleston, Charleston SC.

40. Krawcheck, oral history interview by Dale Rosengarten.

41. Rebecca Sharpless, *Cooking in Other Women's Kitchens: Domestic Workers in the South, 1865–1960* (Chapel Hill: University of North Carolina Press, 2010), xx–xxvi, 1–2.

42. Sharpless, *Cooking in Other Women's Kitchens*, xxi–xxv.

43. Sharpless, *Cooking in Other Women's Kitchens*, xxi–xxv.

44. Sharpless, *Cooking in Other Women's Kitchens*, xxiv–xxvi.

45. Toni Tipton-Martin, *The Jemima Code: Two Centuries of African American Cookbooks* (Austin: University of Texas Press, 2015).

46. For more information about the historic influence of African American women on southern Jewish foodways, and the complex racial and domestic dynamics between African American and Jewish women, see Robin Amer's "The Last Jews of Natchez," *Gravy* 14, May 21, 2015, https://www.southernfoodways.org/gravy /the-last-jews-of-natchez-gravy-ep-14/, and "Dee Dee's Kitchen," May 28, 2015, https://www.southernfoodways.org/dee-dees-kitchen/ produced by Tina Antolini for the Southern Foodways Alliance, University of Mississippi, Oxford MS.

47. John Egerton, *Southern Food: At Home, on the Road, in History* (New York: Knopf, 1987), 110–11, 278. See also Bill Neal, *Southern Cooking* (Chapel Hill: University of North Carolina Press, 1985), 15–16.

48. Jessica B. Harris, *Beyond Gumbo: Creole Fusion Food from the Atlantic Rim* (New York: Simon and Schuster, 2003), 1.

49. Harris, *Beyond Gumbo*, 1–17.

50. Egerton, *Southern Food*, 111.

51. Robert N. Rosen, *Jewish Confederates* (Columbia: University of South Carolina Press, 2000),xi.

52. Elliot Ashkenazi, *The Civil War Diary of Clara Solomon: Growing Up in New Orleans, 1861–1862* (Baton Rouge: Louisiana State University Press, 1995), 326.

53. Ashkenazi, *Civil War Diary of Clara Solomon*, 29, 46, 67, 233, 325, 353, 363, 383.

54. Ashkenazi, *Civil War Diary of Clara Solomon*, 334.

55. Michael Wayne, *The Reshaping of Plantation Society: The Natchez District, 1860–80* (Urbana: University of Illinois Press, 1983), 151.

56. Mrs. E. Block, advertisement, *Jewish South*, August 5, 1881.

57. J. O. Zatarain, advertisement, *Jewish Ledger*, March 13, 1896.

58. B. Moses, advertisement for "Southern Matzohs Bakery," *Jewish Ledger* (January 18, 1895).

59. B. Moses, advertisement.

60. Bobbie Malone, *Rabbi Max Heller: Reformer, Zionist, Southerner, 1860–1929* (Tuscaloosa: University of Alabama Press, 1997), 45.

61. Malone, *Rabbi Max Heller*, 37–38.

62. "Menu for banquet given by the District Grand Lodge No. 7, IOBB, West End Hotel, May 11, 1886, New Orleans, Louisiana," Jewish Children's Regional Service.

63. George Tindall, *The Emergence of the New South, 1913–1945* (Baton Rouge: Louisiana State University Press, 1979), 99.

64. Grace Elizabeth Hale, *Making Whiteness: The Culture of Segregation in the South, 1890–1940* (New York: Pantheon, 1998), 237; Eric L. Goldstein, "Now is the Time to Show Your True Colors: Southern Jews, Whiteness, and the Rise of Jim Crow," in *Jewish Roots in Southern Soil*, ed. Cohen Ferris and Greenberg, 134–36.

65. Edward L. Ayers, *The Promise of the New South: Life after Reconstruction* (New York: Oxford University Press, 1992), viii; C. Vann Woodward, *Origins of the New South, 1877–1913* (Baton Rouge: Louisiana State University Press, 1951/1971), 155.

66. Ayers, *Promise of the New South*, 143.

67. Stephen J. Whitfield, "Is It True What They Sing about Dixie," *Southern Cultures* 8, no. 2 (2002): 11, 19.

68. "Local Women Guests of Atlanta Council Jewish Women," *West Point News*, West Point GA, October 1939, William Breman Jewish Heritage Museum, Atlanta GA.

69. "Local Women Guests of Atlanta Council Jewish Women."

70. Beth Wenger, "Jewish Women of the Club: The Changing Pubic Role Of Atlanta's Jewish Women (1870–1930)," *American Jewish History* 76 (1987): 322.

71. Mark Bauman, "Centripetal and Centrifugal Forces Facing the People of Many Communities: Atlanta Jewry from the Frank Case to the Great Depression," *Atlanta Historical Journal* 23, no. 3 (1979): 37.

72. Bauman, "Centripetal and Centrifugal Forces Facing the People of Many Communities," 37.

73. Josh Parshall, "In Southern States: Historical Texts from the Arbeter Ring's Southern District," *Southern Jewish History* 17 (2014): 149–80; and Josh Parshall, "Yiddish Politics in Southern States: The Southern District of the Arbeter Ring, 1908–1949," PhD diss., University of North Carolina at Chapel Hill, 2017.

74. Steven Hertzberg, *Strangers within the Gate City: The Jews of Atlanta, 1845–1915* (Philadelphia: Jewish Publication Society of America, 1978), 98–138.

75. Rabbi David Geffen, interview by author, January 9, 2002, Scranton PA.

76. Joel Ziff, *Lev Tuvia: On the Life and Work of Rabbi Tobias Geffen* (Newton MA: Rabbi Tobias Geffen Memorial Fund, 1988), 120.

77. Rabbi David Geffen, interview by author.

78. Regina Rousso Tourial, interview by Patty Maziar, May–July, 1989, Jewish Oral History Project of Atlanta, William Breman Jewish Heritage Museum, Atlanta GA.

79. Jeanette Arogeti, interview by author, August 21, 2001, Atlanta GA.

80. Melissa Fay Greene, *The Temple Bombing* (New York: Addison-Wesley, 1996), 28, 115, 118–19.

81. Jack Nelson, "Ready to Sell, Says a 'Disgusted' Leb," *Atlanta Constitution*, February 14, 1964, William Breman Heritage Museum, Atlanta GA.

82. Kevin M. Kruse, *White Flight: Atlanta and the Making of Modern Conservatism* (Princeton NJ: Princeton University Press, 2005), 216.

83. Charlie Lebletter, 1964, Atlanta, Georgia, Charlie Leb Collection, William Breman Heritage Museum, Atlanta GA.

84. Jason Sokol, *There Goes My Everything: White Southerners in the Age of Civil Rights, 1945–1975* (New York: Vintage Books, 2006), 62.

85. William Alexander Percy, *Lanterns on the Levee: Recollections of a Planter's Son* (Baton Rouge: Louisiana State University Press, 1948), 17.

86. Cecile Gudelsky, email to author, July 17, 2001.

87. Segal's Kosher Delicatessen advertisement, *Hebrew Watchman* (Memphis TN), March 30, 1928; Halpern's Kosher Snack Shop advertisement, *Hebrew Watchman*, (Memphis TN), December 12, 1946; Rosen's Kosher Delicatessen advertisements for Dalsheimer's Brothers, Albert Seessel and Son, *Jewish Spectator* (Memphis TN), 1908.

88. Rabbi Fred Victor Davidow, "Greenville, Mississippi," in *Jews in Small Towns: Legends and Legacies*, ed. by Howard V. Epstein (Santa Rosa CA: Vision Books International, 1997), 244.

89. Jennifer Stollman, "We're Still Here: Delta Jewish Women in the Twentieth Century," Lecture, Southern Jewish Historical Society Annual Conference, Memphis TN, November 1, 2003.See Philip Graitcer's "Corned Beef Sandwiches in the Delta," GRAVY, April 6, 2017, https://www.southernfoodways.org/gravy/corned-beef-sandwiches-in-the-delta/; for the Southern Foodways Alliance, University of Mississippi, Oxford MS.

90. Leanne Lipnick Silverblatt, Southern Jewish Food Survey, Marcie C. Ferris, Indianola MS, November 1998.

91. Stollman, "We're Still Here."

92. Stollman, "We're Still Here."

93. Stollman, "We're Still Here."

94. See Jewish Food in the Global South: A Symposium, March 4–5, 2017, University of North Carolina at Chapel Hill, http://jewishstudies.unc.edu/events/jewish-food-in-the-global-south-a-symposium/.

CONTRIBUTORS

Ari Ariel teaches at the University of Iowa. He is the author of *Jewish-Muslim Relations and Migration from Yemen to Palestine in the Late Nineteenth and Twentieth Centuries* (Brill, 2014) and the editor of NYFoodstory: *The Journal of the Culinary Historians of New York*. He has a doctorate in Middle Eastern Studies from Columbia University and a diploma in Classical Culinary Arts from the French Culinary Institute (now the International Culinary Center). His interests include migration, ethnic and national identity, and culinary history and foodways.

Joëlle Bahloul is Professor Emerita of Anthropology and Jewish Studies at Indiana University at Bloomington. She has conducted the ethnography of migrant Jewish groups in France and in the United States for several decades, with a focus on Sephardic Jewries. Her research is a social anthropological exploration of collective memory, kinship, and gender in postcolonial Jewish migration, the anthropology of food practices, and urban ethnography. Her books include *The Architecture of Memory* (Cambridge University Press, 1996) and *Le culte de la Table Dressée* (A. M. Métailié, 1983).

Nancy E. Berg chairs the Department of Jewish, Islamic, and Near Eastern Languages and Cultures (JIN) at Washington University in St. Louis where she is Professor of Hebrew and Comparative Literatures. Her research includes a trilogy on the modern heirs of Babylonian Jewry: *Exile from Exile: Israeli Jewish Writers from Iraq* (State University of New York Press, 1996); *More and More Equal: The Literary Works of Sami Michael* (Lexington, 2005); and *We Remember Babylon: Iraqi Jewish Memories of Home* (forthcoming). The recent past president of the NAPH, an international association for professors of Hebrew, Berg is currently coediting a volume of essays by American Hebraists.

Adriana Brodsky, Associate Professor of Latin American History at St. Mary's College of Maryland, obtained her doctorate from Duke University in 2004. Her book *Sephardi, Jewish, Argentine: Creating Community and National Identity, 1880–1960* was recently published with Indiana University Press. She has coedited with Raanan Rein (Tel Aviv University) a book titled *The New Jewish Argentina* (Brill, 2012), and most recently, with Beatrice Gurwitz and Rachel Kranson, a special issue of the *Journal of Jewish Identities* on Jewish Youth in the Global 1960s. She has also published on Sephardic schools in Argentina, and on Jewish beauty contests. Her new project explores the experiences of Argentine Sephardic youth in Zionist movements from the 1940s to the 1970s.

Flora Cassen is Associate Professor and Johan Martinus Arnold and Sonya Van der Horst Fellow in Jewish History and Culture at University of North Carolina at Chapel Hill. She specializes in the history of the Jews in early modern Italy and Spain. Her book *Marking the Jews in Renaissance Italy: Politics, Religion, and the Power of Symbols* is forthcoming with Cambridge University Press.

Simone Cinotto is Associate Professor of History at the Università Scienze Gastronomiche, Pollenzo, Italy, where he is the director of the master's program Master of Gastronomy: Food Cultures and Mobility. He has been Visiting Professor at the Department of Italian Studies at New York University, the School of Oriental and African Studies at University of London, and the Italian Academy for Advanced Studies in America at Columbia University. Cinotto is the author of *The Italian American Table: Food, Family, and Community in New York City* (University of Illinois Press, 2013) and *Soft Soil Black Grapes: The Birth of Italian Winemaking in California* (New York University Press, 2012), and the editor of *Making Italian America: Consumer Culture and the Production of Ethnic Identities* (Fordham University Press, 2014), which won the 2015 John G. Cawelti Award for the Best Textbook/Primer of the Popular Culture Association/American Culture Association.

Hasia R. Diner is the Paul and Sylvia Steinberg Professor of American Jewish History at New York University and the director of the Goldstein Goren Center for American Jewish History. Diner is the author of numerous books, including *In the Almost Promised Land: American Jews and Blacks, 1915-1935* (1977, reissued 1995); *Erin's Daughters in American: Irish Immigrant Women in the Nineteenth Century* (1984); *A Time for Gathering: The Second Migration, 1820-1880* (1992); *Lower East Side Memories: The*

Jewish Place in America (2000); and *Hungering for America: Italian, Irish, and Jewish Foodways in the Age of Migration* (2001), which was a finalist for the James Beard Award. More recently, she published the history of American Jewish women, *Her Works Praise Her* (with Beryl Leif Benderly) (2002); *The Jews of the United States: 1654–2000* (2004); *We Remember with Reverence and Love: American Jews and the Myth of Silence* (2010), which won both the National Jewish Book Award and the Saul Veiner Prize of the American Jewish History; and *Roads Taken: The Great Jewish Migration to the New World and the Peddlers to Led the Way* (2015).

Gennady Estraikh is Clinical Professor at the Skirball Department of Hebrew and Judaic Studies, New York University. From 1988 to 1991, he was the managing editor of the Moscow Yiddish literary monthly *Sovetish Heymland*. In 1991, he moved to Oxford, England, where he defended his doctoral dissertation and worked at the Oxford Institute of Yiddish Studies. His publications include *Soviet Yiddish: Language Planning and Linguistic Development* (1996); *In Harness: Yiddish Writers' Romance with Communism* (2005); *Yiddish in the Cold War* (2008); *Yiddish Literary Life in Moscow* (2015, in Russian); *Yiddish Culture in Ukraine* (2016, in Ukrainian); the coedited volumes *1929: Mapping the Jewish World* (2013, winner of the National Jewish Book Award); *Soviet Jews in World War II: Fighting, Witnessing, Remembering* (2014); and *Children and Yiddish Literature: From Early Modernity to Post-Modernity* (2016).

Marcie Cohen Ferris is a Professor in the Department of American Studies at the University of North Carolina at Chapel Hill, where she serves as an editor for *Southern Cultures*, a quarterly journal of the history and cultures of the U.S. South. From 2006 to 2008, Ferris served as president of the board of directors of the Southern Foodways Alliance. Ferris is the author of *The Edible South: The Power of Food and the Making of an American Region* (University of North Carolina Press, 2014); *Matzoh Ball Gumbo: Culinary Tales of the Jewish South* (University of North Carolina Press, 2005); and coauthor of *Jewish Roots in Southern Soil: A New History* (Brandeis University Press, 2006). Her current work, "Carolina Cooks, Carolina Eats: Foodways of North Carolina," explores the history, culture, and contemporary politics of food in the Tar Heel State. Ferris is co-chair of University of North Carolina at Chapel Hill's academic theme, "Food for All: Local and Global Perspectives," 2015–2017.

Marion Kaplan is the Skirball Professor of Modern Jewish History at New York University. She is a three-time National Jewish Book Award winner for *The Making of the Jewish Middle Class: Women, Family and Identity in Imperial Germany* (1991); *Between Dignity and Despair: Jewish Life in Nazi Germany* (1998); and *Gender and Jewish History* (with Deborah Dash Moore, 2011); as well as a finalist for *Dominican Haven: The Jewish Refugee Settlement in Sosúa* (2008). Her other publications include: *The Jewish Feminist Movement in Germany, Jewish Daily Life in Germany, 1618–1945* (ed.); and *Jüdische Welten: Juden in Deutschland vom 18. Jahrhundertbis in die Gegenwart* (with Beate Meyer) (2005). She has edited books and taught courses on German Jewish history, European women's history, German women's history, German and European history, as well as European Jewish history, and Jewish women's history. See: http://hebrewjudaic.as.nyu.edu/object/marion.kaplan.

Carlo Petrini is the founder and the president of the Slow Food international association, which promotes a sustainable and fair global food system. A gastronome, an activist, and a writer, he is the author of many books, including *Slow Food: The Case for Taste* (Columbia University Press, 2003); *Slow Food Revolution: A New Culture for Dining and Living* (Rizzoli, 2006); and *Slow Food Nation: Why Our Food Should Be Good, Clean, and Fair* (Rizzoli, 2007). Petrini was elevated to the Order of Grand Officer of Merit of the Italian Republic in 2004 and named FAO Special Ambassador Zero Hunger for Europe in 2016.

Annie Polland is the Senior Vice President for Programs and Education at the Lower East Side Tenement Museum, where she oversees exhibits and interpretation. Her book with Daniel Soyer, *The Emerging Metropolis: New York Jews in the Age of Immigration, 1840–1920* (New York University Press, 2012),is volume two of the three-volume *City of Promises: A History of the Jews of New York*, which won the National Jewish Book Award for Jewish Book of the Year. She received her doctorate in History from Columbia University, and also served as Vice President of Education at the Museum at Eldridge Street, where she wrote *Landmark of the Spirit* (Yale University Press, 2008).

Yael Raviv is the director of the Umami Food and Art Festival and Director of Business Development at Splacer Inc. She is the author of *Falafel Nation: Cuisine and the Making of National Identity in Israel* (University of Nebraska Press, 2015). Yael received her doctorate from New York University's Performance Studies Department and her research and writing focus on food and national identity and food and art.

Rakefet Zalashik is a research fellow at the University of Edinburgh in the department of Anthropology. She has been a post-doctorate fellow at Skirball Department for the Hebrew and Judaic Studies at New York University and at the Department of Jewish Studies at Beer Sheva University of the Negev and a visiting scholar at University of Virginia and Vanderbilt University. Zalashik is the author of *Das Unselige Erbe: Psyhciatrie in Palestina und Israel* (Campus Verlag, 2012) and *Ad Nafesh: Newcomers, Immigrants, Refuges and the Israeli Psychiatric Establishment* (Hakibbutz Hameuchad, 2008). She is the coeditor of *Jews Best Friend? Jews and Dogs Through History* (Sussex University Press, 2013) and *Trauma's Omen: Israeli Studies in Identity, Memory and Representation* (Bar-Ilan University Press, Hakibbutz Hameuchad, 2016). She has been the inaugural Ben-Gurion Chair for Israel Studies at Heidelberg University and the inaugural Mirowksi Israeli Studies scholar at Temple University.

INDEX

Abboud, Jumana, 218–19
Abu Shakra, Walid, 219
Aciman, Andre, 73
Acrich, Esther, 186
Adamovsky, Ezequiel, 187
amba, 77, 103
American Jewish Joint Distribution
  Committee, 125–26, 254
American Relief Administration,
  125–26
Amhanitski, Hinde, 266–67, 270, 278
Amhanitski, Sophia, 267, 279
Amiti, Sarah, 104
Appadurai, Arjun, 109
Arad, Boaz, 232
Argentina: Buenos Aires, 185–86, 188;
  Córdoba, 186. *See also* Argentine
  Sephardim
Argentine Jewish cookbooks, 181–82;
  Cocina sefaradí, 200–201; *Cocinando
  al estilo sefaradí*, 199–200; *El Libro
  de Doña Petrona*, 186–87, 189; *Espe-
  cialidades de la cocina judía*, 190–92,
  195; *La cocina judía: tradición y vari-
  aciones*, 195, 198–99; *La cocina judía
  moderna: de acuerdo a las normas*

tradicionales, 192–94; *Sabores y misterios de la cocina sefaradí*, 201–2
Argentine Sephardi foodways:
  embrace of Argentine cuisine, 194–
  95; preservation of, 199; time and
  health concerns, 194–95
Argentine Sephardim, 182–84; and
  Ashkenazim, 183, 198; class and
  taste, 187–89; and cultural nostalgia, 199, 200; organizations and
  clubs, 183
Arons, Ruth, 253
Aronson, Grigori, 129
Ashery, Oreet, 231

Bahloul, Joëlle, 194
Bardenstein, Carol, 210
Bemporad, Elissa, 116
Ben-Gurion, David, 92–93
Benjamin, Judah P., 303–4
Berliner Klinischer Wochenschrift (jour-
  nal), 168
Bevis Marks Synagogue, 295
Bhabha, Homi, 211
Bilbul, Yaacub, 75
Bill'-Belotserkovskii, Vladimir, 126–27
blanquette de veau, 149

AVAILABLE IN BISON BOOKS EDITIONS

To order or obtain more information on these or other University
of Nebraska Press titles, visit nebraskapress.unl.edu.

CPSIA information can be obtained
at www.ICGtesting.com
Printed in the USA
LVHW01*1544220418
574400LV00004BA/47/P